The Pedagogy of Resurrection

The Christian Formation of the Handicapped

Henri Bissionnier

Translated by
Sister Carolyn Frederick, O.S.F.

PAULIST PRESS
New York/Ramsey

© 1959 Editions Fleurus

Translation © 1979 by
The Missionary Society
of St. Paul the Apostle
in the State of New York

Library of Congress
Catalog Card Number: 79-52104

ISBN: 0-8091-2214-6

Published by Paulist Press
Editorial Office: 1865 Broadway, N.Y., N.Y. 10023
Business Office: 545 Island Road, Ramsey, N.J. 07446

Printed and bound in the
United States of America

Contents

Acknowledgement

We wish to thank all of those who have cooperated, directly or indirectly, in this work—
—in the first place the handicapped people themselves from whom we have learned so much,
—and in the second place, the parents and other relatives of the handicapped, the physicians, psychologists and psychiatrists, the occupational therapists and physical therapists, the nurses and social workers, the directors of various agencies and organizations, our confreres, the catechists, and our colleagues the special educators, and finally, and in particular, our students and former students for whom several chapters of this book were thought out and with whom they were often written or corrected.

I know that my Redeemer lives and that on the last day I will be raised up from the earth and once again I shall be clothed in my skin; and in my flesh, I will see my God; it is him that I myself will see and not another.

JOB 19:25-26.

Foreword

"Handicapped" is a word that arouses many reactions. In all probability it will already have raised a few. While it may seem surprising, we ourselves do not really like the word. Then why use it? Simply because we have no other that can be used to identify the group of people we are going to discuss. Consequently, we accept it.

The chronically ill or infirm, the disabled, the deficient, the abnormal, the disturbed, the maladjusted—all of these are possibilities, but none seems entirely appropriate. Above all, none actually encompasses all of the group about whom we are going to speak: those people who because of physical, psychical or social deficiencies find themselves in special living situations or in need of special education. All of these people—the handicapped—are, whether we like it or not, set apart from everyday life.[1]

Inadapte is the word now commonly used in France. Initially it was reserved for young delinquents, then extended to children in "moral" danger: the abandoned, the rootless. Then it was used to describe the handicapped of a social order; it encompassed the psychically deficient, the emotionally disturbed, the slow learner. Next, it was broadened to include those affected by various types of retardation: the unstable, the dyslexic, the dysgraphic, the dyslalic. Finally, the definition came to include the physically disabled, the chronically sick or infirm, and those with visual and auditory difficulties.

In English, the word closest to this definition of *inadapte* is "handicapped," for it is applied to those with all forms of physical disability and various types of maladjustment: intellectual, emotional, social, etc. And "handicapped" is applied in practice to all

1

those whose difficulties are sufficiently severe to set them apart from the normal or ordinary ways of living, learning and doing things.

Let us also note here that another translation problem arose with the French word *éducateur*. In the broadest and etymological sense, the word in French means all those involved in the formation of persons, not only their teachers but also other professionals and staff employed in caring for them; parents, volunteers and leaders of youth organizations; and last but not least, in this book, catechists, priests, etc. Such a definition comes from the Latin *e-ducere* (to lead out, to help go further, to develop, to improve). However, in the United States, while education has the broader meaning, "educator" has more often been restricted either to one skilled in the theories and methods of teaching or to one engaged in the more pretentious processes of teaching, especially at the university level. Teacher is the generic word used to describe anyone who causes another to know, and not necessarily in the classroom. And while special educator is the term for one trained in the process of instructing the handicapped, this person when actually working with the handicapped in a classroom setting is usually called the teacher.

(Therefore, in many places in this book and especially in the second half where concrete suggestions are given, "teacher" is used. But it must be understood that the word refers not only to professional teachers, including those trained through special education, but also to medical staff, parents, volunteers, catechists, youth leaders, priests—all those who help a handicapped person to know and to experience.)

Thus, we believe that handicapped (*inadapte*) is the word least liable to cause confusion, even though we recognize its inadequacy and we deplore its official use. Some people maintain this classification is unfair. It is society, they declare, that is not adjusted to the handicapped; it is not they who are maladjusted. And in fact, we believe this remark is well-founded, at least in part. The handicapped are certainly victims and not blamable. It is evident in more than one case that it is society that has left no place for them. Moreover, it is society that very often has created the maladjustment through mishandling or lack of resources. Objectively, however, these people are handicapped. (And we ourselves personally experienced this some forty years ago. We became "handicapped," physically at least, before our time.) But undoubtedly, perhaps all people are a bit handicapped. Are we not all "maladjusted" in a certain way? And cannot one claim in a certain sense that it is desirable to be so?

If we were all well-adjusted, the world would not know it. And wouldn't humanity become dangerously satisfied with itself and even stronger in mediocrity without stimulus to change? Maladjustment, then, is an evil regarded as a good. We will return to this idea later in the book.[2]

Finally, some people claim—and they are right—that the term handicapped arises from society's view of it. This is precisely the mistake. Such an expression reveals the common tendency—and still more common today—to see people only in terms of adaptive behavior and as destined for social life, like a spoke in the wheel of community. Adjustment is set up as an idol to which the person is sacrificed so completely that when he/she does not want to adjust he/she is rejected. We shall also speak of this again throughout these pages. God knows if such a concept of man is outlandish or even odious. But by utilizing the term handicapped, we state the fact objectively and with the purpose of transcending the fact and seeking its causes. It is being used especially for the purpose of approaching man/woman in his/her own uniqueness, of serving him/her for his/her own value and of helping him/her to exceed his/her own limitations. This is why our work is pedagogical and religious.

This is not a treatise on medicine or psychology or sociology. It borrows something from each of these sciences, however. It is not a treatise on theology, but it is inspired by Christian revelation. As we have said, it is religious because its purpose is to help the handicapped person excel in his/her own development, in his/her journey toward the One who alone can assure his/her total development. It is religious, especially, because it professes to be dependent upon God who has lovingly created man/woman for his praise and for an eternal reward. At the same time this leaves man/woman loved eternally by God, called by him, and able to find happiness only in his love and in going to him.

Finally, this book is pedagogical, even remedially pedagogical[3] since it concerns the handicapped. One has to admit that it is a question more especially of youth and even more of children, but the word pedagogical[4] now refers to adults as well. That is why we shall speak very often of the education of adults.

We shall also speak often of the handicapped without specifying whether some principles are equally for all men and women, who are never perfect in reality, but always need education especially when it is a question of their religious lives.

Moreover, we shall not separate this religious life from everyday life. For this reason we shall speak of Christian education in the full sense of the word inasmuch as religious education is the way of helping a person to live his/her whole life in Christ.[5] The one is really inseparable from the other: a religious formation in the strict sense, in the most "classic" sense of catechesis aiming at a total Christian life and Christian education finding its base—or its summit—in a religious formation that is boldly demanding and solid.[6]

*   *   *

Hopefully, this book will help all those who approach the handicapped, those who already love them, and those who do not know them and are still a little afraid of them.

This book seems important for priests, especially those whose ministry includes the handicapped. In fact, we would like it to be an introduction to a specialized ministry for them, a special catechetical pedagogy, so-called, provided this word does not frighten the uninitiated. We think that these pages will answer their needs in a delicate task for which they are so often inadequately prepared. We hope also that they will assist in the formation of catechists and in animating the personnel of the institutions in which they minister.

When we wrote this work we also had in mind the parents of the handicapped whom God has severely tried and who are often so distressed in the presence of this cross. We understand them and wish to help them, if only to reveal the grandeur of the task to be accomplished for their children and the value of giving themselves to it.

We have thought principally of special educators, those professionally trained to teach the handicapped. Many years of almost daily contact with them makes us esteem them highly. We know the difficulty, even the asceticism of their work, their "mission." We would like once again to show them the full extent of their mission and have them discover the joy of it. We would be happy if on reading this, they find that the love which animates them increases for all whom God has placed in their hands.

And so to doctors, nurses, social workers, psychotherapists, occupational therapists, psychologists, friends of the sick and the handicapped, organized or not, in institutes or in societies, and to all whom we have so often met in our studies and in our work, we dedicate this book.

Finally, we hope that it will be read not only by these specialists. In the world there are millions of handicapped people. There are in France at least four or five million.[7] Everyone, if he opens his eyes and his heart, sees some of them each day without even wishing to meet them. This book then is written for all men and women of "good will," priests of parishes, all who have the responsibility for the sick and the handicapped, chaplains of institutions, teachers of normal classes, all called to meet handicapped or retarded children as well as specialized educators; for parents of normal children, for friends, neighbors of parents of handicapped children, or the sick. Who, then if he/she is Christian, or simply human could remain uninterested in such a problem?

We will pose problems in the first half of the book and in the second half respond to them. To the general principles of religious formation, thought out in this context, we will add the perspective of the total situation of the handicapped in the world and in the Church today, and lastly, in the plan of God himself. Given these diverse themes, we shall then try to sketch out a Christian educational therapy and a catechesis of the handicapped. To this, we will add experiences, which are not intended, however, to be set up as a model. We will conclude by stating some principles for action hoping that others, with us or following after us, will also make contributions to this work.

We think the above clarifies the sub-title of this work and perhaps justifies it. The reader will decide after sharing some of it. An explanation of the title, *The Pedagogy of Resurrection*, remains.

I
The Current Problem

1
I Have Faith
in the Resurrection

If there is one dogma that ought to animate those who work with the sick, the infirm, the handicapped or the retarded, it is certainly the dogma of the resurrection of Christ. One is convinced of this in reading the Acts of the Apostles where this dogma, the center of primitive catechesis, is retold. Moreover, isn't this tenet of faith at the base of all authentic Christianity? Does it not, together with the passion of Christ, form the central mystery of our faith? How many of our contemporaries, however, have stopped at the foot of the cross on Good Friday without considering the following day?

This false, always dangerous attitude of not passing beyond the mystery of the suffering and death of the Savior, this real contradiction, is capable of many deviations. They are often criticized, certainly deserving of criticism, and particularly annoying when considering children of adolescents who are suffering or handicapped. Real faith in the resurrection of Christ, on the other hand, gives a true spirit and meaning to the mission of the special educator, as well as to that of doctors, nurses, occupational therapists, physical therapists, or other members of the para-medical or medico-social professions. It does the same for priests who approach the social outcasts and the physically or mentally handicapped, as well as their parents.

"Death will not have the last word." That is the certitude that Christian faith brings us. It has already triumphed in Christ who by his death has conquered death. The glory of Christ is also our glory.

We have faith then in the victory of life.

The longing, the hope for survival in love and by love, is not an empty dream. It is not only the theme of beautiful legends, which from Tristan to "the evening visitor," have enchanted our youth. It is really true that love is a conqueror.

Indeed, true love, the love gift, has once and forever triumphed over death, over the basic evil which is egoism, hate or pride. This love has triumphed in God and by God who, as St. John says, is love itself. From now on we have the assurance of finding in him and by him the victory over death.

There is a pedagogy that the Swiss French language calls "curative." For this the English language has borrowed the word "orthopedagogy" from the Greek. In German there is a wonderful but untranslatable word "heilpadagogik": the pedagogy of healing, of salvation. And yet, isn't all "divine pedagogy" from Abraham to the apostles and to our day a "healing pedagogy," a saving pedagogy whose cornerstone is the resurrection of Jesus Christ, conqueror over every ill and every death by his love?

This reminds us of a meeting a certain philanthropic association organized one evening for the benefit of the mentally handicapped. Someone had the idea of showing Cocteau's lovely film, *Beauty and the Beast*. Handed over and subjected to horrible treatment by this Beast whom no one was able to love and for whom the lack of love was his worst torment, Beauty experienced a strange paradox: she began to love him with a foolish and incomprehensible love. And nothing more than this love was needed to change the Beast into his human form and the original beauty he had lost through evil and sin.

That is powerful love which transfigures the disfigured—as the incomprehensible love of the Word, the Incarnate God, has cured man and made him lovable. Would that many people that evening had understood the lesson of the film and of the legend and regained their faith in love and its power.

Faith is part of the triumph of life; it is part of the value of love. Faith is the right of the person, every person, to be loved. Even the filthy beast has a right to receive our love. What can one say of a human being who, we believe, has infinite value. We Christians know that man/woman is not merely body but soul as well. We know that each human being is unique and irreplaceable. We know that each human being has been loved by God with an eternal and limitless love!

This sickly child, that mentally retarded child, the insane person who jeers at us and drools, and even the sociopath is infinitely worthy of love. If I am not profoundly moved by this realization, am I a real Christian? Still more, can I pretend to serve the child as a loving and effective educator?

Faith is a belief in a God who is love and who is one in three persons: the Trinity. The mystery of the Trinity was often presented to us as a lesson in plane geometry. Yet, isn't the mystery of the Trinity the mystery of the gift of total and infinite love of person for the persons in God? And is it not to this life of love that Christ calls us in his prayer at the Last Supper? "Father that they may be one as you and I . . . abide in unity. . . . " And is it not for this that Christ sent us the Spirit of Love, his own Spirit from the Father? The paschal mystery is completed in this way by Pentecost, as we pray: "*Spiritum nobis, Domine, tua caritatis infunde; ut, quos sacramentis paschalibus satiasti, tua facias pietate concordes. Per Dominim nostrum Jesum Christum Filium tuum. . . .* " "Fill us, O Lord, with the Spirit of your love so as to unite all the hearts of those nourished by your paschal sacraments in tenderness, through Jesus Christ our Lord your Son. . . ." From the morning of the resurrection, isn't this one of the most perfect prayers of petition?

Let us say, moreover, that this prayer is a model for all prayer. How truly it conforms to the prayer of Jesus Christ himself! Indeed, does not every prayer return basically to ask the Father for the Spirit of Love through Jesus Christ, our Lord? Here, then, is what seems to be the foundation of all special pedagogy or healing as it is for all worthwhile education and certainly for a totally authentic Christian life.

To avoid misunderstanding let us point out certain deviations here: We have already pointed out those which stopped short at the mystery of physical and moral evil, even at the mystery of suffering. Some look with disdain at attitudes falsely dubbed Christian—self-punishment, sadism and masochism. Indeed, we perceive a risk corrupting the Christian sense of suffering by such more or less psychopathological attitudes. We believe that it is certainly fostered by the mind-set which consists in stopping at the cross of Christ instead of going up to his glorious Resurrection. And we miss the consequences which for us as for him flow from it.

Without giving undue attention to it, we might mention another deviation—a kind of self pity, a "victim" attitude, a "what's the use" feeling, a "refuge" in illness or even in death which, as a psychologist has noted, finds it pseudo-justification in this kind of concentration on Christ's sufferings. Such morbid behavior sometimes arouses the admiration of pious people, receiving their encouragement and nourishing hagiography or funeral orations.

And yet, what could be more opposed to the attitude of Christ who wept before the tomb of Lazarus, who shows at the least his distaste for suffering: "Father, save me from this hour" (Jn. 12:17); "Take this cup from me" (Mt. 14:36)? He accepts it only to fulfill the will of the Father, to give him a proof of his love (a love that will triumph in his glorious Resurrection) and to give it to us for ourselves. In no part of the Gospel does Christ suggest that we love, much less seek out, suffering for its own sake. When he meets the sick and infirm he gives them health and brings them back into the community. Christ brings with him and radiates health and life, not morbidity and death. "A power went forth from him and healed them all" (Lk. 6:19), says the Gospel text. He is the "resurrection and the life" (Jn. 11:25). There are the dead whom he brings back to life and to their families before rising himself so as to raise us with him in his glory.

Love for the sick and infirm, for the physically and psychically handicapped, urges us primarily to cure them, to rehabilitate them and to give them back to society and the Church. Even the prayers of the Sacrament of the Sick (unfortunately, until recently, called Extreme Unction) are proof that such is the tradition even of the Church.[8]

But is love always well understood? Here again how many deviations and how many false interpretations are possible!

We shall not delay over negative attitudes which approach the physically or psychically handicapped from motives of overprotection, sentimental infantalism, a failure complex, or sadistic masochism. Nor shall we speak of the tendency to regard them as little dolls, teddy bears, or mascots. We wish only to acknowledge a kind of self-seeking which slips easily into a sort of "paternalism." Also, we think of the sort of condescension which creeps into the attitude of the educator who expends himself/herself according to his/her own testimony, bending over backward for the sick and abandoned.

The love that these children need is of an entirely different quality. Here is how we describe it:

1. True love is esteem for the person one loves.
2. Love is characterized by seeking the good of the one loved.
3. True love does not exclude but demands competence.
4. Love is synonomous with the gift of self to the "other."
5. Love constitutes a real way of knowing.

We will make just a few comments here.

The child, the person we call deficient, retarded, infirm or slow-to-learn, has a need to be valued. This is true of everyone but still more so for this child. He/she needs to be esteemed and loved not only because of a handicap (a tendency found frequently) but in spite of his/her handicap. In other words, he/she wants to be loved and esteemed not only with the love of mercy and pity ("a dirty pity" as someone said)[9] for what is negative, harmful or degrading in him/her, but also and especially with a love of consideration, even of admiration, for what he/she has of positive value, unblemished, even superior at least on certain points and aspects.

But who can love this simple and deformed little mongoloid with a love of esteem and admiration? It is possible, at least for a Christian educator.

Is this mentally or physically deficient child going to rate the title "holy innocent" or "special" privileged which so often pious persons call him/her? That would betray, it seems to us, a lack of strength and truth, of mature and informed Christianity. To treat as "innocent" a mentally retarded person is to play dangerously on these words. To consider sickness and infirmity in itself as a "privilege" is a very serious contradiction. Again, what is good in this handicapped child is found elsewhere in all that remains unblemished in him/her and in the positive gifts God has given to him/her. The real Christian will understand this better than anyone else. He/she not only sees in each created being the image of God, but he/she knows the incomparable splendor of a soul, of a baptized body, raised by God to his own life. This child is then lovable and infinitely worthy of my esteem. My esteem and my love are preliminary conditions for all true effective action.[10]

To love is to be willing to seek out the good of the one loved. Let us recall the *Symphonie Pastorale* of Gide and the day when the pastor realizes that he has only forgotten to seek sight for this young blind girl whom he thought he loved. Only then does he grasp the wretched quality of his love which will soon show itself degraded to the rank of the most selfish passion. But do we not sometimes, more of less unconsciously, sustain persons whom we profess to love in a state of weakness or infirmity so as to be able to gratify our own acknowledged need to hover over them condescendingly?[11]

And this is why we repeat that genuine love calls for true understanding. Like many other perennial questions, this problem of devotion and understanding seems to us to have been poorly treated. Indeed, can one imagine genuine love that does not put forth every effort to insure real effectiveness? A doctor or a nurse who would profess to love his/her sick patients and who would not initiate every effort to insure continual implementation of their scientific knowledge and of improved skills to aid a patient would be in strong opposition to their professed purpose. It would be the same for an educator who consciously neglects the indispensable means for using his or her skills and who does not continuously seek to improve them. It is indeed clear that without real love appropriate educational skills will remain almost fruitless. Strictly speaking, one can give an injection without love. But one cannot teach without love, still less rehabilitate a human being without it.

God preserve us from heartless psychologists for whom the child or the adult is only an interesting experience. Preserve us as well from human stock breeders or geneticists preoccupied above all with the efficiency of society and the betterment of the human race.

Love indeed is synonomous with the gift of self to the "other." And it is here that the important distinction between a closed and open society is to be found as noted by Bergson.[12]

A strong tendency in the modern world supports an ideology that pleads for education and rehabilitation of a person for his/her "social adjustment" and for his/her usefulness in the service of the community. Community in itself would be considered the ideal justifying all kinds of individual sacrifices. True, from this perspective the handicapped person often finds himself/herself receiving help, but it is for the purpose of his/her being "salvaged" by society. Woe to those who are not deemed worthy of "salvage." This tendency is clearly evident in the work *L'Eugénique et L'Euthénique*[13] which advocates spending money to rehabilitate the physically handicapped, but is indignant at the amounts given to the psychically incurable, "hopeless cases." Sooner or later the door is closed and one faces the same selfishness, less odious or fearful because it is collective.

For that matter, what has become of service to the person, the disinterested search for his/her welfare? In a word, what has become of genuine love? Does it go unheeded? Who would free humanity from its closed cycle? Love, the gift of self, is something other than passionate love, although in a sense it flows from it and in passing beyond it, makes itself whole and prolongs itself.

It matters little if these persons are idiots or aged infirm who can or cannot be "retrieved," as long as it is their welfare and their happiness that I seek and as long as I am ready for the total gift of life desiring to insure and to increase a little the happiness of these "others." However foolish it may seem, they value this sacrifice and in making it, I love them a little though it is hardly like that of God who loves them and knows how to love them.

Of course, those who truly love these people would be willing to give them every chance to be useful, and to give and to be given, for there is no greater happiness for a human being. But it is for them, first of all, that I will do this, not for myself or for society, since this would only be self-aggrandizement.

Finally, this selfless love will establish the most perfect manner of knowing. Knowledge which does not turn to love is a barren knowledge.[14] In turn, genuine love supposes and perfects understanding. Isn't love the only form of contact with a person deprived of the means of expression, as in the case of the sensory[15] impaired? (Think of Helen Keller when her instructor taught her.)[8] Isn't it strange that one who is the object of such love practically never mistakes it? The direct access to our true feelings, even unconscious feelings, is one of the privileges of the handicapped.

Love then is not easy. It is something difficult even if it is simple. Certainly, to speak so much of it at the beginning of this book is not useless. But as indispensable as these warnings are, they may not be enough. The love that a Christian wants to give, with which God has loved him/her, and which God wishes him/her to give in return, that very love of God is the Spirit sent by Christ from the throne of the Father who has spread love and diffused it into our hearts according to the word of the Gospel (Rom. 5:5).

In the Gospel the grace of healing the possessed is obtained only through prayer and fasting. Is this not, moreover, the *grace par excellence* since grace is etymologically love? At the same time the one who is himself love and grace, is he not God himself? "God is Love."

As educators of sick or retarded persons, we celebrate with the Church the triumph of the risen Christ. May all those who approach the physically, socially, or psychically handicapped ceaselessly repeat this prayer: O Lord, pour into us the Spirit of your love. . . .

2
Some Principles of
Religious Formation

Practical procedures which comprise the second half of this book will seem incomprehensible or inadmissible to anyone who is not convinced of the value of the basic principles that we will be stating below. These principles of education are not solely for education of children who are know to be handicapped or maladjusted. It seems to us that they constitute fundamental considerations of a total religious formation for every Christian. In the same way the principles that we enunciate in the following chapter are fundamental to all education.

*   *   *

"The proper and immediate end of Christian education is to cooperate with the action of divine grace in the formation of the true and perfect Christian, that is, in the formation of Christ himself in man regenerated by baptism." Such is the impressive definition that Pius XI gives in his encyclical on the *Christian Education of Youth* which remains a living reality for the Christian educator. Moreover, such principles are immutable, unchanging.

As we see it, the perspective that this definition reveals goes beyond the simple didactic teaching of certain revealed truths. In no way does it exclude them. But it is more a question of a transmission of life that goes beyond the mere presentation of truths. In fact, it surpasses such a procedure but includes it.

Is what is involved here just a concern for "transmission of life" in the proper sense of the word, or rather is it a humble (and at the same time great) "cooperation" in the task of living according to the pontifical formula? It is indeed God who transmits this life, and the educator has for his/her function to assist the one being educated to place himself/herself in the most favorable disposition to welcome such a life, to respond to its demands, to live in it and to give witness to it.

Father Foulquié's controversial commentary on the above-mentioned encyclical has an excellent note on this precise point.[16] "The formation of the supernatural man/woman, being the work of grace, is above the power of the educator who can only be a collaborator. His/her collaboration consists of assisting the child to place himself/herself in the necessary disposition to receive grace and to create a favorable environment in him/her. The Christian educator must take into account the words of St. Paul (I Cor. 3,6): 'I have planted, Apollo has watered, but it is God who gives the increase.' "

We see immediately the breadth of such a statement and the importance of such a perspective in that which concerns religious education, especially that of the mentally handicapped. To reduce instruction to didactic teaching would be to commit oneself, at least in part, to an impasse and to expose oneself to bitter deceptions. To see religious formation at one and the same time in all its dimensions as total education, as being in touch with persons and as a modest cooperation in a work of which God is the author, and at the same time to see the subject of that education as the one primarily responsible for and the first to cooperate in it—such an understanding opens to us infinite possibilities and helps to prevent all discouragement.

Nevertheless, didactic instruction must have its place in the pedagogical plan. It may be, even with the severely retarded, that the Christian educator or re-educator could never see himself/herself deliberately omitting didactic techniques completely. Yet this type of didactic instruction, to be truly "didactic," must construct its content logically, whatever be the point of departure and the articulation of the system. Again it must itself be oriented toward life from the start, remain faithful to it and flourish in it. It must know how to go first to the essential and to return to it ceaselessly to rediscover the lines of strength.

Stating immediately that we understand very well other attempts at synthesis allows us to propose a plan for this vital and essential system of Christianity.

Here is what we have arrived at after twenty years of catechetical experience: Jesus has taught us that we have the same Father who loves us and who is the all-good, all-powerful God. This Father has given us all, and above all he has given us his Son, Jesus, who is also all-good and all-powerful, who loves us and who has asked us to love our brothers and sisters as we love ourselves. So that we could do this, Jesus has sent us the Spirit of Love from the Father whom we must ask for in our prayer with him. He aids us always to be united to God and among ourselves. He is stronger than evil (estrangement from God, division among us, selfishness). This Spirit of Love, Jesus gives us in baptism, confirmation, and the eucharist, and we rediscover it in penance if we have been turned aside by our sins. All these sacraments unite us indeed to Jesus, conqueror of evil and death, who lives forever in heaven as on earth in his Church.

This Church is the great family of God, our Father—the sheepfold of the good shepherd (pope, bishops) in which we live unceasingly united by the Spirit of love in Jesus with all Christians of all times and especially with Mary, our Mother.

This development permits one to follow the liturgical cycle in the general plan of its essentials. So Advent is centered on the revelation of God, our Father, through all his good deeds of which the greatest is the gift that he has made to us of his Son, Jesus.

Then comes the witness of the love of Christ Jesus which culminates in his passion and resurrection and his commandment of love. The Spirit of Love is awaited, allowing us to realize the will of our Father manifested by Jesus and at the same time to experience the unfolding of the Paschal perspective. (Cf. Post-communion of the Mass for Easter.) Let us not forget that it is also in this Paschal perspective, the true center of life and of Christian catechesis, that the sacraments of Christian initation and even the mystery of the Church are presented.

As we see it, our concern is to draw close to the teaching of God in the story of his people, of Christ in his Gospel ministry, and finally of the Church in its primitive catechesis. In other words, instruction starts with the notion of God the Father, preaches above all filial and fraternal love in continual contact with this love in the Spirit that Jesus announces to us and sends to the Father. Finally, it centers on the mystery of the risen Christ, who is the conqueror over death, eternally living and present in the sacraments of his church.[17]

As for the liturgical cycle, this instruction is concentric in explanation: each year brings back its essential lines, but each year allows us to live it more deeply and to advance further in the "explanation," or better in the gradual revelation, similar to a development in the explanation of dogma, and consequently, consistent with the action of God himself and of his Church.

Of course, methods of presentation vary and are facilitated by the individualization of instruction to which we will refer later. For some children, inevitable uncertainties remain more or less for a long time. The annual review is going to recapitulate at the same time that it brings a chance to discover something new for those who already possess sufficiently sound foundations to support this knowledge. If only all Christians already knew where the essential elements of their Christianity lies!

It is not only a question of teaching these fundamental aspects of Christian life but of living them. It is here that education goes far beyond teaching and greatly surpasses it, if it implies continuous instruction.[18] For this reason it seems to us, that several principles should be recalled among others here. We will state them as follows:

—the importance of climate
—the proper sense of the mission of the Church
—active participation on the part of those being educated
—knowledge of the student and of environment
—the bond between catechetical instruction and life:
   "the entire Gospel in every life and a life-long study of
   Christian doctrine."

First, the importance of climate. Let us speak of the atmosphere in which the student learns. It is here that we insist on the importance of a Christian setting for education (more than a setting of Christian education).

A Christian, especially a child, ought to live, at certain hours at least, in an authentic Christian atmosphere. The ideal would be that the culture provide the child with the image of and the milieu of a Christian atmosphere. He or she should find this climate at least in his/her home or in that which is the extension of home or the substitute for it.[19]

And what appears to us as fundamental about such a "climate" seems at least to be summed up in what we could call a *sense of prayer* (at least the sense of the sacred) and that of *fraternal charity*. Stated in another way: the love of God the Father and the fraternal love of neighbor, according to the recommendation of Jesus himself, the second love having its foundation in the first (love of God), working only with the first, and the first being only a lie without the second, as St. John says.

Let us repeat: The effort to create such a "atmosphere" of sense of God and love of neighbor must include the kind of instruction explained above, but this instruction will not have the slightest value unless it is the illustration and application of a "lived example" and "climate of life" that are as real and complete as possible.

Thus it must be realized that if the Christian educator is in contact with children and adolescents only one or two hours a week, that hour, that brief span of time, must be lived by the child in an atmosphere of love and prayer. It must furnish him/her with myriad opportunities to experience the love of God and of neighbor. He or she ought to receive there the revelation, of a great love, the very great love of an infinite God who welcomes him/her, and by whose love he/she is surrounded. He ought to feel himself/herself surrounded also by brothers and sisters who are to be loved and who love him/her. It is obvious to say that a catechism which consisted only in hearing theoretical explanations or in reciting a lesson, whatever it might be worth for good marks, could offer very few opportunities to foster love of God and of neighbor. An active and authentic Christian education, on the other hand, always provides a favorable atmosphere for such an "experience": permitting freedom of expression, work in cooperation, time for communal prayer—liturgical or para-liturgical—every opportunity for living as a Christian even if only for short periods of time. What can one say when it is a question of a life-long contact in the framework of the family or of an established institution?

But we see also that all depends in the end on the personality of the educator and on the sense he/she has or does not have of his/her mission, of the greatness of this mission, and its immediate consequences.

"He began to work and teach" is written of the Lord. He began by action, then by teaching. That is also true of the educator. Christian educator, they will hear you perhaps, but first they will watch how you live your life as a Christian.

Who would understand the profound preparation and asceticism that this life of a Christian supposes? And how can one conceive of a true Christian educator who would not have an interior life, to a great degree exacted by his/her mission, nourished and enlightened by his/her indispensable theological knowledge? Children watch us closely, and they see through the least of our gestures, from a slight smile to a hasty genuflection.

But seeking to furnish a Christian climate and to witness and teach in a Christian climate is not sufficient; all this is scarcely possible if the child is kept in a passive attitude. The child must be made active, or better yet, an alert attitude on his/her part must be nourished, so that he/she, has the distinct opportunity to participate in the establishment of this climate by reflecting on this evidence and being a witness in his/her turn, by assimilating this teaching in a practical way and then beginning to live it. From us God awaits an active approach. This search will be a sign to him that the discovery has already begun. "You would not look for me if you had not already found me."[20] Here again an active pedagogy is indispensable.

Some people, scarcely understanding what this active pedagogy, "especially the discovery method" is, are indignant that one introduces such a process or, to state it in a better way, recommends such as an approach in religious education. Is not the gift of faith "revealed"? How can one presume that people will discover what God has already uncovered; or are we to act in the manner of a Pascal reinventing the theorems of Euclid's discovery?

This is not simply a question of catechetical method. For that matter, in today's active academic situations students are no longer limited like Pascal's to a blackboard and a piece of chalk. They are free to dig for treasures; rich learning situations are at their disposal. They have an environment in which it is possible to learn for themselves and to find out how to do it, making their own syntheses.

But it is not in themselves alone that they make this discovery, this particular synthesis.

On the evidence, active participation is therefore a superior method, although on a different plane, in the domain of religious education. This area is, or in any case ought to be, a spiritually rich milieu from which the child can draw strength if the means are put within his/her reach. Enlightened by the supernatural riches of light and love that he/she carries within himself/herself, at the same time aided by the Christian educator, and with the Spirit of God acting in him/her and around him/her, he/she will take inventory of the supernatural riches around him; he/she will discover the plan of God's love for him/her and for the world.

What do we understand by a spiritually rich milieu? We shall have an opportunity to return to this point, but in answer to this question, it suffices to ask oneself where the revelation of God is expressed and where it is manifested. We find it in Holy Scripture in the first place, tradition in all its forms, the life of the Church in its witness of liturgical or private piety, charity whatever be the manner in which it is displayed. The marks of the Church, recognizable in so many concrete ways, are a roadmap to be opened to the student and its resources put at his/her disposal. At the same time his/her efforts must also be nourished; he/she must place his/her confidence in the action of the Holy Spirit in recalling that "faith also has eyes."[21] Let us not forget that too often we are "men of little faith."

We do not see enough of this interior action of the Holy Spirit in those intrusted to us. That is very obvious. But do we know them even on a natural level, personal or social? We will speak of this again in considering the principles of general education. The indispensable foundation for setting up an authentic pedagogy is to know the student and his/her milieu in order to begin where the student is and with his/her sociological condition. Let us underline this. It is on these terms and on these terms alone that Christian education will be capable of influencing a child in the totality and in the detail of his/her existence. Catechetical instruction that is not aware from the very beginning of the concrete problems of the child's existence as well as of his/her youthful mentality—any religious instruction that does not concern itself with meeting this life, with bringing some concrete elements of solution to these everyday problems and with responding to the real needs of this resolute child mentality—risks remaining a dead letter in a large measure. It is understood that cooperation requires attention from various persons and agencies that correspond to the various areas of a child's life especially the cooperation between parents and catechists. But this opening into everyday life constitutes one of the essential aspects of a Christian education different, in reality, from pious prattling.

This daily real life lived as a Christian in every detail (we have seen it) is what must be achieved from the beginning in this Christianized environment, whether it be that of a family or a brief weekly hour of catechetical instruction or of mechanical tasks. It is even more important for activities of the various church-sponsored youth movements. That is why we should not be surprised to see young people engaged in such activities, even in religious education strictly speaking, that are very near to basic educational activity and seem to be—one might be tempted to say—utterly "secular." To wash paintbrushes, to lend a helping hand in sorting clay or setting up chairs, to copy a song that is not necessarily a hymn, to discuss freely a film that is not a part of the catechism, to play and to appreciate a record that is not Gregorian chant—all these are activities of daily life capable of being lived in a Christian manner, as it is necessary that everyone's existence be lived in each small detail.

This is one of the reasons why the student should be invited to enter entirely into "the game" of this totally Christian education. His/her body as well as his/her spirit, all his/her senses and all his/her faculties will be solicited in this alliance to a life of prayer and fraternal charity. We have seen that this life of charity constitutes the basis itself of our religious initiation. From this initiation arises the call to all the techniques of expression: design, painting, modeling, song and the most diverse modes of bodily expression such as sacred dance which we like to see considered in a religious sense as an exceptionally rich expression of prayer. Of course, as the comments of the French bishops have stated, these diverse activities must not distract attention from or replace the actual instruction. On the contrary they will, if they are well handled, focus attention on the instruction, reinforcing it and insuring its effectiveness. Do we not have to bring about a return to God through all his creation, beginning with all that with which he has endowed each human being? Do we not have to put ourselves entirely at the service of our brothers/sisters?

We have to involve ourselves totally in the life of charity as well as in the life of prayer. Here again we perceive the complete meaning of the dogma of resurrection: that our body, the totality of our human personality today, is prepared to enter into glory. Grace, which penetrated us at baptism and the eucharist, which places in us the germ of immortality, destines us from today on to integrate ourselves ceaselessly in the act of filial love that God looks for from us and in the exercise of fraternal love that our brother/sister calls forth from us. In this way we see what a religious education worthy of its name involves. It is a very demanding task.

Despite this fact, however, let us say it again—religious instruction is accessible even to the most handicapped human beings whom infirmity or deficiency strikes. We shall return to this but one will notice without difficulty from now on, for example, how a synthesis of the didactic program will allow giving to each one what he or she can absorb without risk of omitting "essentials." We do see the advantage of an instruction that is first of all global and non-analytical, responding to the laws of psychological evolution which for a child, and even in the understanding of an adult, goes from the global to the analysis, then to the synthesis. We do see the advantage of a gradual concentric sequenced course of instruction for children which guards against any gaps when there has been a lack of continuity. Establishing the proper climate takes on even greater importance here where the actual imparting of information is particulary laborious and difficult. Who has not realized that a handicapped child is a most astute witness of our virtues if they exist, or of our faults, small as they may appear? Who cannot recall some incident where an "idiot" has "simply" (and do not forget what this idiot was trying to say) revealed to us—frankly but without scorn or bitterness—some pettiness he/she had observed in our actions?

Let us recall finally that active pedagogy has had its birth, or rather has found its truest and most Christian tradition, in service of the retarded and of the handicapped in general. Let us think only of the works of Sequin, the Brothers of Charity of Gand or the Montessori and Decroly school. In the domain of religious education, as much as and even more than elsewhere, active, authentic teaching constitutes the only approach and the sole threshold for these of children who are also called to the God who is love, and consequently to initiative and to liberty. Only this initiative and this liberty permit, in effect, a response to God and a going forth to him with all of our being, all of our life. It is this that he awaits. It is he who saves us, and he really has no need of us to accomplish that. But in his wisdom he did not wish to do this without our agreement and the cooperation of our love.

3
Some Basic Principles
of Education

A review of fundamental principles for all education would be fitting here. There is a type of education that has mistakenly been called "new education" but it brings together in fact the most traditional precepts of pedagogy—what we call "active" or "participative" education. Moreover, participative education is in itself a redundant expression for there is no other true education, especially for a Christian, than that which is "active." Methods spoken of as being passive are only pedagogical caricature and a lazy imitation of education. Still, it is necessary to understand on exactly what such labels are put. It will suffice to treat here briefly what is detailed in various educational reviews.

The first and fundamental principle of education is that it must start with the student. This means that one must examine her/his own pedagogical attitude toward his/her knowledge of the student, his/her mentality, his/her profound needs, his/her psycho-physical and psychosocial conditioning. But starting at this point does not mean staying there. Quite the contrary! Let us state exactly and at once that "to begin" with the student does not mean in any way that one fails to take into account at the same time the ideal to be proposed to this human being and the means to help him/her reach it according to his/her own aptitudes. The student, the goal, the method—these are the three dimensions that any entirely traditional pedagogy requires. But let us remember that to know the student is just the primary goal upon which an educator must insist.

I remember the surprise of the director of an educational institution when we asked her to tell us the age of each of her pupils. She had to admit that she did not know and that the teachers responsible for these children did not know either. Anyone who has at least an elementary idea of developmental psychology knows, however, what changes a student can undergo from one year to the next. Doubtless, this educator at the institution that I am referring to, thought that "religion is the same for everyone." The objective was indeed identical but how can one formulate a method without at least elementary knowledge of the student's development? After that incident, it was not surprising to see orphans of twelve years of age obliged to recite daily the Office of the Blessed Virgin with the religious of the house or even very young children led to long vespers or to the recitation of the rosary during October.

Moreover, let us recall that it is a question not only of taking into account the age of the child but also the characteristics of such a child, be he/she gifted or retarded. He/she may be endowed with particular personality traits and may already be somewhat molded by living in a particular social and geographic milieu. In order to teach English to someone—let us call him John—it is important to know John. We have to know whether he is gifted with specific abilities or the victim of particular deficiencies. It is no less true that in order to teach English to John, the teacher has to know English and how to teach it.

We begin with the student, as we have stated above, but we cannot remain there. We disagree with the opinions of certain psychologists who see themselves, automatically, as educators because they are psychologists. Unfortunately, there are actual psychologists who, while well-trained in child psychology, are often ignorant of the science of teaching. Seeing thousands of psychologists produced each year in the framework of institutes and universities can be somewhat disturbing. These young men and women may launch out into practices immediately. Now we will entrust our children to them not only for observation and testing but also for teaching and for this they have not been prepared. Even those who will become psychological counselors cause some apprehension. We are thinking of a diploma known as psycho-pedagogy which includes proficiency only in psychology for its program provided only a few lessons in theoretical pedagogy. Too many schools, even those officially dedicated by their course content to the formation of educators, have neglected to oversee the pedagogical formation. Psychology, they think, is sufficient.

To educate means to start with the student, that is, to begin with him/her and to help him/her to come out of himself/herself, to surpass himself/herself, to "ex-ducere," to draw out of him/her what he/she is capable of surpassing, the power of life. The Christian educator must be the first one to be convinced of this. He/she knows what a divine spark God has placed in this human being, what infinite powers he/she has received and only asks to have increased, to blossom, and to bear fruit. To begin with the student is therefore, for the Christian educator, to start from God in him, from Christ with whose growth it is a question of cooperating, according to the words already cited by Pius XI.[22] To start from the student, from his/her nature, is displeasing to those who see nature as synonymous with sin. But that is what God himself does. Pope Pius XI gives us explicit assurance of this; consequently, the participative pedagogy of which he gives a marvelous definition will be commented on later. He states that participative pedagogy conforms not only to Christian traditional education in the Church, but in the manner of God who calls each of his creatures, "according to his proper nature to cooperative activity. . . . "

Naturalism! Would these pedagogists, would the pope, would God then be "naturalists" in the sense that the pope has forbidden it? Let us be willing to reread that condemnation of naturalism in the sense in which it was forbidden: "All pedagogical naturalism is false that, in whatever manner it appears, excludes or tends to lessen the supernatural activity of Christianity in the formation of youth. Every method of education is erroneous which is based in whole or in part, on the negation or the forgetfulness of original sin or of the role of grace, supporting itself only on the strength of human nature." In no way does the pope condemn a pedagogy which starts with the child and what that child is. The pontiff cannot accept an education that is satisfied only to consider the strengths and aptitudes of human nature to the exclusion of the richness of grace and the recognition of sin.

Moreover, the Holy Father insists on the supernatural values, showing that he prefers to stress the positive. Consequently, would he not have to deplore the fact that an incomplete and sketchy theological formation too often places the Christian educator in a pessimistic form of reference, falsely attributed to St. Augustine and in every sense far distant from the traditional doctrine of the Church? Far too numerous are those Christians and their adversaries who think that Catholic theology presents man/woman as basically evil in nature, corrupted, objects of mistrust and punishment since birth. Too many Christians forget the words of St. Paul who teaches us that "there where sin abounded grace does more abound" and under the New Law they remain in the spirit of the old, daughters and sons in bondage. At a time when Christians must be educators of the free children of God according to the law of love, they remain submitted, and submit others, to the law of fear and to antiquated pedagogy. Read the epistles of St. Paul, St. Peter, and St. John or very simply the Gospels. We also advise the reading of Verriele's small book entitled, *The Supernatural in Us and Original Sin*,[23] unfortunately now out of print, and the *Christian Understanding of Man*,[24] by Mouroux, but there are many other works available from the most traditional to the most recent that can supply us with fuller theological knowledge and we recommend their reading.

The principle of all pedagogy, as we have repeated, is to begin with the student. We should not be afraid to support this principle and to affirm it. But the first sign of the method itself appears in a child's pedagogical development. To begin with the student is indeed to leave the "start," the beginning, the *initium*, to the student, although this is not his/her right exclusively.

"Initiative," or more simply the reality it implies, seems the key. At the same time, initiative is the criterion, the touchstone, of authentic participative education. Many times while visiting schools we have heard our guide say, "Of course, here we practice participative methods." And we asked, "What do you mean by that?" And they answered, "See such and such activities have been carried out by the students themselves." "That is fine," we answered, "they have done it themselves . . . but have they really done it by themselves?" That is the real question. To put it another way: Has the initiative come from the teacher or from the student? There is authentic participative instruction where a child can, on his/her own initiative, pick ten daisies from a field and place them in a vase to decorate the common table. Is this not preferable to a situation where, under the direction of the teacher, twenty-five boys decorated the walls of a recreation room or a dining room?

Some will argue that such initiative will lead to anarchy if each one does what is in his or her own mind. But one should understand that initiative does not preclude control and coordination of activities, a role which must revert to the instructor and must always, in the final analysis, revert to him or her. In this way, initiative does not exclude the exercise of obedience by the student nor the exercise of authority by the instructor. On the contrary, authority prudently exercised and obedience intelligently practiced are the best encouragement of initiative. Passivity begets only sluggishness in the student and dictatorial authoritarianism in the instructor.

It is true that initiative can only develop when given a certain climate of liberty. That simple word, however, is enough to frighten more than one instructor, especially in certain religious settings. This is truly very strange but at the same time it is very understandable.

It is odd that certain Christian educators fear any idea of freedom in their understanding of pedagogy. Does not Christian morality teach us that there are no human acts in the true sense of the term that are meritorious acts unless they are free and deliberate? Despite this certain educators seem to fear this freedom and are content to forge "automatons," as Mauriac said.

Consider the plan of God for the world and the total story of the realization of this plan. Is it not a plan of dialogue, of dramatic encounters with the benevolence of God and his loving care for us and the freedom of response of the people of God or of each soul in particular?

Even more paradoxical is the fact that Christian philosophy is made the defender of liberty. It bases its claim on the spirituality of the human soul. On the other hand, materialists are determinists and negators of liberty. Here one sees a contradiction which finds Christian educators reacting against a pedagogy of liberty while at the same time participative pedagogy is extolled by materialists. Could it be that these Christian educators are materialists and do not know it and that these materialists do not dare to admit that they have spiritualistic philosphies in their orientation? Indeed, do materialists call liberty a simple non-intervention on the part of the teacher who lets the child find himself, governed as he is on the one hand by instincts and on the other by his environment, both regarded as given and good? Does the Christian know the price of true liberty but at the same time does he also know how to evaluate its dangers? Or, again, would authoritative education be simpler and easier for everyone?

It is the Christian educator who finds himself everywhere, and not without reason, the defender of all liberty. He must be at all times an educator according to the spirit, that is, according to liberty.

Of course, let us not forget to say that an education for liberty is not to be left to chance. The capacity for self-determination should be a gradual self-realization. Here, again, the terms of the encyclical on education are clear and precise and of unusual perfection when the pope specifies an "active cooperation and gradually always more awareness in the work of his own education" (the student's), and when he presents this as the traditional pedagogy of the Church and God's own manner of acting in the realization of his plan.

If it is not then a question of allowing full liberty from day to day, a solution as idle as it is imprudent and unfitting, it is a question of knowing how gradually to allow a little more liberty and more initiative to the student. But let us repeat that this style of education, because it is truly education, is no shiftless or simplistic formula.

Finally, some will say there are risks in this. But he/she who risks nothing gains nothing, as the proverb says. And the proverb is of value in education. Not to take risks in this is to risk everything. Has not God himself taken risks in creating man endowed with the valuable gift of free will? Without it there certainly would not have been sin, but neither would there have been love or merit.

It would not suffice to begin with a person and gradually to allow him/her freedom if the environment in which he/she lives does not offer rewarding activity by which he/she can feel stimulated and see himself/herself in a state of displaying this initial ability. We will repeat here what we have said in the preceding chapter, and we will also recall some laws of developmental psychology for this proposal.

This law teaches us that all human beings act to satisfy a deep-seated attraction that is entirely different from fantasy or whim. This attraction itself is a projection of a need. The basic need of a living being is to continue in being (therefore, to sustain himself/herself in equilibrium in his/her surrounding environment) and to become better, to go beyond himself/herself in being, which for a child means to be developed, and for an adult to go as far as the gift of self in which he/she sees himself/herself continued.

This development of persons comes about through a certain number of stages that succeed each other in a consistent order. Each one of these stages corresponds exactly to needs, then to deep interests which lead a person to act. Action, in its turn, fosters development. It is true that the exercise of a faculty is the condition for its development and the blossoming forth of other hidden faculties.[25] But such needs will only be evident, such an action only effective, such interest only awakened and, consequently, such development only produced under a double condition: namely that the student have the freedom for initiative and that he live in an environment rich enough to meet his needs, arouse his interests and permit his capacity for action to be exercised in developing corresponding faculties.

A rich environment does not mean a luxurious and expensive environment but one that offers a student stimulants for research and opportunities for his/her own activity. It is for the educator to provide this environment where it does not naturally exist. Whoever has visited authentic activity classes or schools knows what ample but scarcely expensive riches are put at the disposal of students— something as simple as clay or flowers in a garden can provide teacher and students with a thousand new discoveries in daily life. Such riches have little relationship to those scholarly museums that are forever relegated to dust behind their imposing show windows.

This reminds me of an instructor at my primary school in Biarritz when I was eleven years old. We had an active educator at a time when the new pedagogy constituted a real novelty. His class was a world of flowers, of animals, of many colored stones. The walls were a perpetual tapestry of student work and discoveries. One day a young lad, the son of a fisherman, on his own accord brought to class a large sea urchin. Another teacher might have cried out in disgust and rebuked the boy. But our teacher thanked him, welcomed the animal joyously and placed it in a large tin box. What was our surprise the next day to see our sea urchin consideraby reduced in size and to discover that he had only cast out the sea water which had inflated him. I still remember that incident when many other lessons from textbooks have been forgotten. How many similar incidents remain deeply engraved in our memory and have been better assimilated than those from a class limited to a blackboard and students.

Creating a rich environment does not mean staying there. That leads us to another fundamental principle of participative education: to begin with the concrete in order to go to the abstract means precisely that we start with the concrete but do not stay there. Indeed, on the contrary, Scholastic philosophy, whose principles the pedagogy of Herbart has caused us to forget, states precisely that nothing will be in the intellect unless it is first in the senses. In other words, we can only reach the intellect through the use of the senses and the concrete. We are not angels. Here, again, nature takes its own revenge.

The promoters of active pedagogy have had recourse to the paradox of children, bound hand and foot, condemned to hear if not to listen to theoretical explanations by their teacher.[26] Should it be surprising to learn that too often they become intellectuals without feeling and bodies that react as without souls since from the most tender age they have been accustomed to rid themselves of their bodies and become pledged to passivity in the face of the abstract? What serious harm has been done to them when their religious instruction has been imparted to them in this manner!

To go to the intellect by way of the senses, to the abstract by the route of the concrete, is an elementary principle of psychopedagogy found in tradition but unfortunately still seen as revolutionary. Here again there is a difficult task to accomplish, namely to lead a child to pass progressively from action to thought, from the particular to the general, from the concrete to the abstract. No doubt this is repugnant to the overburdened or not too industrious educator. Such educators wrongly believe that they save time while overlooking the route marked out by providence.

But it is also very simplistic and annoying to remain ensconced in the particular and the concrete or to continue in activity. Here also the way is one of ascent which leads from the clay to the metaphysical or better to contemplation. This happens provided that all the time the instructors are confident and competent, they know the point of departure and destination, and that they never forget the real purpose of the journey.

To begin with the student means, finally, to know in what this student is involved and to know it in a personal way. Education must be communal as well as personal. [27] Moreover, how would Christians be able to understand instruction otherwise? Is not the Trinity of God the most absolute one of communities in the infinite diversity of persons? Has not this God created us in his own image, raised us to his own likeness, made us participants in his nature, invited us to live his life eternally? Humanity then is fashioned according to his plan of love, invited, destined to realize among its members and in this trinitarian God, who animates it, a personal community in the image of this trinitarian community and in communion with it.

Indeed, as has often been said, unity and diversity are not in any way contradictory concepts. On the contrary, they are reciprocal and complementary. They are contradictory only for the simplistic soul who confuses unity and uniformity, diversity and multiplicity or division. But he/she who has grasped what true unity and real diversity are understands that unity and diversity may appear, on the contrary, correlatively completed as one progressively ascends the ladder of being. What magnificent arrangement when, from the first, God in his infinite perfection is at one and the same time all-perfect unity and diversity. And that since woman/man are called to participate in his life, he also has to live this double law of unity and diversity in humanity and first of all in the Church. Now in this communal personalism the individual blossoms so much the more as he/she is united to the community, and the community itself is so much the more united as it is more diverse and developed by the individuals who comprise it. This communal personalism ought to be realized at all levels, from the family circle to the United Nations and passing through all the intermediate communities. The Church, the mystical vine, with its diverse branches in the unity of the same stock, the mystical body with its diverse members in the unity of the same organism, an edifice with rich materials held together with brick and mortar: the Church, insofar as it is perfect, offers us the model on earth of such a communal personalism. The Church, insofar as it is temporal, human, imperfect and uncompleted, invites us to work according to God's law in order to become this ageless and spotless spouse waiting for Christ, the eternal bridegroom.

Christian education then should prepare men and women from their infancy to be members of this community. Such education, sensitive to persons, should envision giving each one the opportunity for full development. From this stems the interest here again for education in initiative, the progress in human liberty of which we have spoken earlier. Should we not only let each human being be himself/herself as God planned for him/her, wanted for him/her, loved him/her and now loves him/her, but also should we not also aid him/her in becoming himself/herself? And how do we do that? Certainly understanding character traits and types will be useful to the educator, provided he/she makes prudent use of them, but especially useful will be real participative pedagogy. In particular, it will be necessary to allow, favor, and encourage true liberty of choice. Let us lead the individual in all possible ways to choose, for example, his/her own clothes, his/her leisure pastimes, his/her work for today and tomorrow, his/her friends, his/her spirituality, his/her life. . . . Let us avoid the misuse of uniformity, of rank, of large collective games on overcrowded recreation courts, of standardized work, of forced friendships, of "directing" consciences and lives. Indeed, these choices cannot be oriented without control. To lead one to choose, to aid in choosing, to teach how to choose is still very different from caprice and anarchy. And that in no way excludes obedience or even discipline.

It is here that personalism rejoins the community and that personalized education becomes more communal. Indeed, to hold in esteem, to love each person and to wish his/her full development are to teach him/her with the same stroke the meaning of values and the respect of the person of others. And community is made first of all from that. Community starts with the keen sense of the inestimable worth of the human person, of every person, the physical person but also the ethical person. And by this fact persons build the bridge of real love between each other. In the same way, as between the Father and the Son, the Spirit of Love makes a bond in the Holy Trinity just as in the human community. Thus with good reason it is animated with the love of God himself; it spreads from person to person with a generous love, fashioned out of esteem and respect, capable of leading to the most generous deeds and sacrifices. Responsible for himself/herself before God, each member feels himself/herself, through God, responsible for others.

What then is one to think of a principal who visited the class taught by a young Christian instructor in which a system of Christian cooperation had been established? The principal sharply reprimanded the instructor before her/his pupils saying to them, "Children, here each one is for himself/herself and God for all." Is it not surprising that often student cooperation,[28] the sharing of responsibilities entrusted to students and called in an equivocal fashion "self-government,"[29] is too often instituted by non-Catholics! Are such practices not in the most authentic Christian tradition and more than any other system of education capable of permitting the child to practice the fundamental precept of love today and tomorrow? And if some abuses are introduced into such a system of communal[30] education, has one not the right to speak of Christian ideas becoming "foolish" because the Christians themselves have neglected to make the most of them?

Then how is a student to act, given his/her freedom, adaptability and unique personhood? How is one to respond when faced with the concrete realities of this world in which God has placed him/her? What is the educator going to teach him/her to do; what is he/she going to help him/her to accomplish? It is a question of first knowing this world, some will say, of interpreting its nature. We would be strongly tempted to answer: No, it is first a question of contemplating this world.

It is characteristic of our modern world—but without doubt an evil—that man, put in the presence of nature, seeks directly to discover what he can make of it, how he can transform it, how he can utilize it. This leads us to rechanneling a large part of our mountain streams, without doubt, for useful purposes. That leads us to criss-crossing our mountain peaks with railroads which travel over glaciers to make it possible for tourists, greedy for experiences, to see the countryside that has been disfigured just for their convenience. Perhaps some day we will see all our mountains changed into arenas for building cities and all our streams channeled into waterways to make them more navigable. But let us stop here or we will be considered anti-modern and reactionary, which would be far removed from our intention. Let man/woman transform the earth; that is acceptable. We would even go so far as to say that it appears to be in God's plan. Can man/woman spiritualize the material world in such a way that while humanizing it, he/she is putting it to his service? And in spiritualizing creation ever more, does he/she not draw closer to the Creator who is the Spirit? As long as he/she at least lives in an order desired by the Creator, can he/she not cooperate in such a way in the divine work Christ accomplished by his redemptive incarnation?

But this wish to transform the world must not hinder man/woman from contemplating it. To harness creation, moreover, should not end in its destruction or even in the misusing of it. On the contrary, there should be a development that takes for granted that the true value has been discovered, recognized, appreciated and admired.[31] But what do we do to develop this "virtue of admiration" in children and young people?

This virtue, this capacity, exists, and we scarcely have need to prove it. The teacher has so much experience with the wonderment of the very young, with their ability to be caught up before the marvels of the universe. Later with an older child, with young people and with adults, he experiences the satisfaction of admiring at length the beauties of nature or of a work of art, but he does not neglect to point out the strength and the good quality of machine-made products. Then does the teacher let the child take the time for contemplation? Does he help the young with it, or is he too impatient, too mechanically minded so that he allows only practical activities?

At this point we would like to say a few words on educating the aesthetic sense and the importance of beauty in education. Antiquity made the arts the base even for the formation of the young. Modern society relegates them to the background when it does not neglect them entirely. Certain religious educators consider them as all but a dangerous frivolity, hardly tolerable. Few instructors would dare encourage a child or an adolescent to devote himself/herself to painting, to sculpture, to music, still less to poetry or dance. Apart from the exceptions of the candidates at the conservatory or some young genius, contemporary youth generally look upon aesthetics as the least of their concerns and certainly the last preoccupation of their instructors.

In fairness one has to note the laudable efforts of certain schools and some educational centers but, in our opinion, one has to deplore strongly a general shirking of responsibilities. And what can one say about the environment in which a large part of our children and young people live? We made a surprising discovery recently in finding a parlor of a boarding school run by religious with its walls decorated with good reproductions of Van Gogh, Sisley and Seurat. Let one recall in contrast the decoration of a great number of our chapels, our oratories, our youth hostels! We are scandalized by the excesses of modern art but why don't we condemn the bad taste of the art labeled Saint Sulpice?

It would be necessary, first of all, to begin by educating the educators on this point. . . . It would be worth the trouble. Indeed, we think that the development of the aesthetic sense and life in the framework of authentic beauty is a fundamental preparation for any true gift of self, and consequently, for true love. In a certain measure, we think that this natural contemplation can prepare for contemplation in the true sense of the word. We even believe that the sense of the sacred can be promoted in its awakening and its development by this beauty and the respect it inspires, the uplifting of feeling it allows, and the appreciation of value it provides. All these establish firm foundations for an authentic religious education or strengthen those already in place.

Yet some will protest that all this takes time and money. That is in part not accurate. Beauty is no more costly than ugliness. (Religious congregations of teachers and nurses sometimes overspend buying showy decorations instead of simple and beautiful ornaments for their chapels.) But even if it were true, the fundamental problem remains: that of preparing the young for a diploma, a bachelor's degree, or for life. The education of the aesthetic sense merits a place in the budget of an institution or of a family.

Another way of arousing the aesthetic sense is the appeal to the means of expression. But "the expression" that we mean here is also a fundamental need of man/woman.

Each year we who receive almost two hundred students at the beginning of their studies at the university or teachers' colleges, are shocked by the number of these young men and women, representing for the most part the elite of society, whose use of the English language is so meager and unpolished. Few of them are capable of expressing themselves clearly; few know how to write correctly. As for those who have creative or artistic talents, or can play an instrument or sing, their number is very small in France. Let us not speak of fine arts or dance for aside from the very rare exceptions of students in special schools, such skills are seldom found in any child, adolescent or youth at the present time.

Sometimes one of our small corps of specialists for various artistic activities intervenes and introduces a sudden freedom. This does not create a real impact because regrettedly it is too slow in coming and will be too short-lived. Then a timid lad begins to speak in modeling clay or painting a picture; a silent girl, withdrawn and fearful but now uninhibited and sure of herself, speaks with amazement through her gestures or her expressive dance. And one guesses what such an outlet would have allowed, what it would have avoided, had it been employed ten years sooner at an age when doors could have been opened or closed.

But let us add a well-known fact that we often have stated—that such liberation, when given sufficient time, brings with it other benefits. A young man, having succeeded in playing the reed pipe, reaches the level of his class in a few months. Able to speak body language, a young girl, timid to the point of silence, becomes responsible for her own promotion. A paralyzed adolescent, a stammerer and at fifteen years old unable to go out without his mother, finds reassurance by painting in bold outlines; he can now travel alone and is succeeding in mathematics. Man/woman has need for self-expression and accomplishment as much as for bread and clothing. But modern education does not usually assure them of either.

Are we surprised then when our contemporaries seem so far away from the highest form of contemplation, the celebration of the liturgy? And why be surprised at the current movement which so many of our contemporaries clumsily pursue toward a return to the official prayer of the Church, so contemplative and at the same time so expressive?

This liturgical renewal is indeed a comfort and a happy sign of the times. But lest it be only a straw fire, we must give renewal a firm foundation. It will be absolutely necessary, in this connection, to introduce into all education a regular, methodical initiation into expression in all its best forms. From well-controlled bodily movement to the gestures of prayer, from good diction in class to the proclamation of the word of God in assembly, there is a continuity that one cannot ignore without real harm. Observe the manner in which almost all the faithful attend Mass and you will know why.

We arrive at the summit of all education in the act of *consecration*. Here is the goal which, as we have said, the educator should ceaselessly set for himself. Search, contemplation, development, expression, then consecration, such is the normal way willed by God for all so-called human action. Man/woman begins with the discovery of the world. When he/she finds created being he/she contemplates it and sometimes transforms it. In either case he/she assimilates it and then expresses what he/she has taken into his/her possession. And this expression, the primary form of gift, is achieved through the consecrated offering returned to God from his own creation. This is the priestly ministry of each Christian.

Ultimately, for us Christians, this gift is the action of the community united to Christ, the mediator and the "perfect-religious of God." That is why all liturgy is celebrated through the Church.

It is then true sons of the Church, that is sons of God, whom we wish to form, or better help form themselves. Our task involves cooperation not only with other educators and with the student but also with the author of all education, God present and acting on the spirit of the person being educated and his teacher. This is why our task is that of the Church, that is, ecclesial.

At the same time, as the encyclical already quoted underlines, this son or daughter of God is a son or daughter of mankind and this Christian is an active member of his city. The temptation to withdraw from earthly tasks or become uninterested[32] in them is foreign to this Christian if he/she has understood his/her vocation. Hopefully he/she sees farther and beyond, and places his/her action ceaselessly on the altar of God, the holy altar of the Mass. At this level the structure of a closed society is passed by. Man/woman makes way for the priest. And all the everyday work of man/woman opens up to admit a perspective of eternity. All true human value, far from being abolished, is not only maintained but also infinitely exalted. Glory is given to the Father in the risen Christ and in his Church by all creatures. And should not this goodness of God coincide with that of the human family and the happiness of each person in it?

Can the handicapped people with whom this book is particularly concerned be recipients of such humane and Christian education? That is what we do not hesitate to affirm. And that is the point we must now examine, but first we must write this prologue. We shall then proceed to consider the place of the handicapped in the world and in the Church today.

Next, we shall do our utmost to discern who they are in reality, to see them as God sees them, to want them as he wants them. Finally, we shall go on from these principles to develop a pedagogy concerning Christian education and religious formation for those the world calls handicapped.

4
The Handicapped
in the World Today

There is nothing more indicative of man's/woman's perception of his/her understanding of the world and life, of his/her sensitivity and his/her real capacity to love, and of his/her faith than the way in which he/she respects and deals with the sick and infirm. One could say as much for society, civilization and countries. . . . "Tell me what you think of someone with very little physical and mental ability and I will tell you what you are."

We have already pointed out that wherever in our modern world physical effectiveness and productivity are supreme, there is the tendency to look down on the handicapped person to the degree that this handicap makes him/her less useful. "What do you expect? This is business!" retorts the employer. Tell him/her he/she is wrong and he/she will cite statistics, however inaccurate, derived from psychological studies. These statistics are enough to prove his/her point: education of the slow learner is of no use in the modern world.

As a logical conclusion to such reasoning: an excellent school of special education is closed; the children are sent back to their families. Then, the institution is reopened as a center for the most infirm, those judged to be hopeless cases, irretrievable. From then on, for these "hopeless cases" no kind of education is provided.

We were at one time on an educational mission in a distant, underdeveloped country[33] where an official who received us remarked, "Retarded children? But, my dear sir, we don't even have

the means of taking care of normal children. Fortunately many of
the others die." And another chided us, "You busy yourselves with
retarded children but at the present time very much is being done for
these children, perhaps too much. If they would only do as much for
respectable people as they do for these retarded." Such comments
come from important people who are circumspect, esteemed, influen-
tial, sincere.

Because the handicapped do not constitute a useful commodity,
a sure investment, because one should "first" be concerned with
others—the useful ones—certain members of modern society do not
consider handicapped persons worthy of such education. (How does
this attitude differ from former pagan societies or the neopagan of
today?) Some recoil before the horror of sending them, as did Hitler,
to a crematory but they relegate them to a life in institutions with the
minimal care required to appease the conscience of "respectable
people" and allow them a good night's sleep.

For others, it is true, distinctions are made. Examiners fortified
with testing materials, properly selected for testing ability, evaluate—that is a "sacred term"—the handicapped student. They test
his/her intelligence, then his/her practical aptitudes, even his/her
character, to see if he/she will be able to surmount his/her "difficulties." In the examiner's judgment the goats are separated from the
sheep. The sheep only have the right to an education. The others
return to their homes or a shelter.

This is why at the present time many directors of institutions
tell us, "We do not take the weak. . . . Certainly there are some who
are less debilitated who can be salvaged but not the profoundly
debilitated—those, our place is not made for them." "But where do
they go?" "Oh, that is the problem." And so it is always and
everywhere the "problem," a problem for which we leave the responsibility for solution to others. There are the epileptics whom we
systematically reject in the same manner and also the cerebral
palsied. In an institution for deaf mutes, directors refuse the retarded, the multi-handicapped as they are called. In an establishment
for spastics, they admit only those with a normal IQ. The others can
benefit if some room is left, but certainly none will be left.

And many young teachers with special education also make the
same remark. "I cannot busy myself with the retarded. That would

not be worth the trouble. Nor with epileptics; I am afraid of them. Nor with the cerebral palsied; they drool at the mouth. Nor with the physically disabled; their scars are repugnant to me. . . . " So they are asked to reeducate some with minor reading and speech problems or slight changes in character, by preference as day students for they are sorely in need of a few special lessons. Delinquents have more chance for assistance especially if they are willing to talk about some of their really exciting experiences. That is why psychotherapy holds such a strong interest and is so popular with some young professionals—especially those who disdainfully say, "As for me defectives are distasteful." Again, a young psychologist reported, "I have left shelter X. There were only outcasts there."

In his turn, a chaplain speaking of an institution for mentally retarded under his jurisdiction said, "These children, these young people, are not interesting." In another small parish community, generally regarded as up-to-date, they speak of the slightly retarded at a boarding school as "the crazies." Therefore, this community has abandoned interest in such a group. Again, two medical students discussing the retarded while riding the subway said, "We should give these children [meaning those seriously afflicted] an injection." "They are better off dead," another doctor declared when we informed him of our trip to the Far East and what we had seen there of childhood misery.[34]

Of course, one must not generalize and I do not intend to. Nothing could be more misleading and false than to declare: "Here is what directors, professionals, special educators, psychotherapists, psychologists, priests and doctors think. . . ." We hope rather to prove the contrary. But the reflections cited here betray a mentality so much in the spirit of our world and in a sense so much the normal outlook of human beings that we must not be greatly surprised to find them on the lips of others, much less to find ourselves sometimes approving them or at least excusing them and understanding them.

It is undoubtedly true that physically-handicapped human beings, and still more the mentally-deficient, remain persons of limited ability. The least infirmity is always an obstacle for everybody. From there it is only a short step to considering such a "limited" person as not only inferior but even a dead weight, to treating him/her like a parasite and "another mouth" to feed. It is very evident also that the modern world, governed by efficiency and production, does not value the slow worker. "Too bad for the slow," as leading officials of the Labor Ministry told us. Unless the unusual perfection of their product compensates for their slow speed, they are not accepted. And yet, "perfection is not of this world," one could say making a play on words and turning the expression aside from its usual meaning. In today's world one more often looks for quantity at a small cost than for exceptional quality.

· From the point of view of production, certain classes of the handicapped receive less support. The mentally backward and multi-handicapped, as we have stated before, are in this category.

In general on the basis of our psychiatric consultations,[35] the mentally retarded are the "poor relatives." Too many doctors are uninterested in them. They dismiss them summarily and with finality. "Madam, you can see that your son/daughter is an idiot," one leading doctor is accustomed to say in consultation. "You can never expect much from him/her," declares another as soon as anyone brings in a child of less than normal IQ. "But rest assured he is happy," he adds to console the family in a small way.[36] This same doctor is extremely attentive to the next patient, a talented young lad who could be described perhaps as "neurotic."

In dealing with the handicapped, men/women have always not only sensed instinctively that they were dealing with a person of lesser ability but also that they themselves were experiencing feelings of repulsion and fear. Such a reaction is justified, and in certain circumstances, normal and sound. The opposite attitude could even be qualified as morbid. Is it not good that evil repels us, and that human beings guard cautiously against it to the degree that they feel threatened by it? Yet to judge strictly, this first reaction seems to us not only rigid but unjust and illusory. It is excellent to avoid evil inasmuch as it is evil, but in the same way it is unjust and cruel to turn away from the sick and infirm.

Only love for the afflicted will help to overcome feelings of repugnance regarding their affliction. More specifically these two emotions are closely bound to each other. The unstinted love of our fellow man/woman will provoke in us the desire to help the sick person to struggle against his/her misfortune. Here may we remind you of the resurrection spirit that is inspiring this book? We have already said a little about this in our introduction.

A certain more or less unconscious paternalism might also be mentioned here. That, thank God, is diminishing somewhat in the modern world. Some people, saddened by this, confuse paternalism with true compassion or deplore the replacement of the Samaritan's charity by anonymous administrative procedures, which, it is true, are sometimes terribly slow, even inefficient. Admittedly welfare assistance, which disperses public funds out of tax monies in the name of strict justice, does not know how to substitute for the love of charity. Such love will always be needed. Anonymous giving may respect the poor man/woman but ignore his/her dignity as Monsieur Vincent recognized in the days when he served, "our masters, the poor." Yet it seems to us that both forms of action can be employed or indeed combined. Better still, we believe in the absolute necessity of the one and the other.

We now speak of the most offensive attitude of all in this largely negative picture, in order to acknowledge that it exists. This attitude consists in being interested in the handicapped in order to exploit them.

Unfortunately, even in our times such an attitude is not unusual. We remember a delegate from the Red Cross in another developing country to whom we spoke of the blind, who said, "Impossible to do something for them. Even if we would open institutions for them, they would not come because their families keep them at home to beg in the streets." Is that true? We dare say it is, but even if it is true, is it not unfortunate to cooperate with such a state of affairs?

And what about the great number of the mentally handicapped and the infirm employed at lower salaries! When it is a question of young girls, one can easily guess how often they are abused and bodily exploited even for gain. Then, what can we say of the type of government assistance that places these young people, referred to as the multi-handicapped—the blind, mentally deficient, or retarded— in foster homes which are not properly selected or do not provide adequate care? Yes, all this goes on in the twentieth century in countries called civilized. But let us stop this sad account. . . .

If we admit it is true that the world today is harsh to the

physically and mentally handicapped, we must also acknowledge the progress of science and of civilization—or at least the efforts achieved—to better the lot of these people and to give them a humane place in modern society.

First, in the scientific field, it appears unquestionable that the most recent progress in the area of research has not only provided better methods of seeking out clients, of diagnosis and treatment, but in addition there is now a better understanding of the individual as a physical and psychical whole.

As a consequence of new insights relating to heredity, we now understand how closely the sick person is tied to his ancestry. The most basic studies in this field have also provided evidence that is vitally necessary if we are to avoid the type of overly rigorous conclusions which in the past led to measures practiced in the name of "eugenics," such as sterilization. More recent developments have clearly demonstrated the almost total uselessness of such methods.

The influence of the milieu—or environment in the widest sense of the word—is also being studied scientifically, and these results have in turn modified and rounded out the laws laid down by the geneticists. A distinction is being made between the congenital and the hereditary (distinction, however, which is still far from being clearly expressed in practice). The science of the environment is coming to the aid of the science of heredity. Sick people and their problems are thus seen as linked not only to their parents and ancestors but also to their contemporaries and this at social, geographical and historical levels. The sick are seen as being linked to both, not only for the causes but also for the cure of their ills.

The ways in which the environment exerts its influences are also being explained more precisely. The thought is that the "terrain" or ground—those aspects of one's life that are present at birth and are to some degree fixed—can, nonetheless, be modified by "external" and "acquired" factors which are themselves influenced by the toxic or traumatic aggressor agents whose importance was recognized at the close of the last century with the invention of the microscope.

But man does not appear out of harmony with his environment only, bound to this earth at the physical level alone. He is also being viewed, more and more, as dependent on the social, psychial and spiritual influences of that environment and capable of entering into the complex system which sociology has brought to light. As a service to the sick, as well as to the so-called normal person, a whole psychosocial science has developed, off-spring of an earlier sociology but freed from its excesses. Although derived also from current analytical psychology and the full range of dynamic psychology, this science has, however, not hesitated to adopt a new though very traditional orientation toward Hippocratic medicine. That orientation we call psychosomatic medicine.

This new science has benefitted from the discoveries of dynamic psychology, which better explain the role of the emotions (already underscored by Thomistic philosophy) and especially the influence of the subconscious on a person's conduct and the importance of the conflict and shocks experienced in early childhood upon his attitudes. Other benefits have come from the progress in physiology which emphasizes the importance for behavior of the inner recess of the brain, notably the hypothalmic area; the role of the alimentary process and its connections with the central nervous system; the role of the endocrine glands in harmony with each other and with the nervous system, especially at the point where the pituitary stimuli arise; the effects of metabolic controls at this same level; and finally, the relationship between enzymes, hormones and genes which are underlining the extraordinary unity of the human being in itself and in relationship to the environment.

On course, the temptation was strong—and some people have succumbed to it—to try to reduce the human being as much as possible to a complex mechanism, to make of him/her simply a network of conditioned reflexes registering emotions, like a robot receiving messages and in return exercising more or less controlled actions at various levels of consciousness. The purpose of all this was seen as furnishing the individual with the best possible adjustment to a world in continuous evolution. Fortunately, some trends of philosophic and medical thought, as for example the theory of the organodynamic in psychiatry, have provoked the realization that no single mathematical equation could ever be entirely adequate to solve the problems of men/women and take into account their behavior, his/her malady and his/her cure. We are indebted also to existentialism for the benefits derived from a new emphasis upon man/woman in the first person, the "I—", as someone who should not be seen merely as a behavior or even as a problem but rather as a mystery.[37]

Granted that there may be some questionable and tentative discoveries, trends and theories able to serve as scientific hypotheses, this new awareness of two factors—the unity of man/woman in herself/himself and in relation to his/her environment, and on the other hand, the extreme complexity of his/her relationships with his/her milieu—is bringing about an evolution to a more humane attitude toward the sick and the infirm. Here, as in other areas, it appears that civilization is making progress.

Let us see what this perspective of psychosomatic medicine represents when it is well understood and efficiently administered by specialists, possessing at once the qualities of common sense and sensitivity and also the necessary specialized training and background. The casework methods, which originated in America and are spreading across France and Europe, have brought some good things and some not so good, since unfortunately they did not bring with them sufficient precautions. This taking into consideration of the total make-up of the sick person, including not only the economic but also the psychological and social factors which play such an important part in the breakdown of physical and mental well-being, and the efforts being made to bring about the person's full recovery and re-entry into family, professional, social and religious life, is certainly worthy of our sympathy. Are we not right to see here if not a present, as least an eventual, humanizing of this new modern institution, social service? And this is similar to the humanizing taking place in medicine and its related fields.

Now this medical-social—or rather medical-pedagogical and psychosocial sphere—comprises an ever-growing number of specialists. This is also a sign of the times. Those people who always fear a multiplication of specialists deplore this development. Sometimes, however, their reserve is not always quided by the best motives, but rather for example by a fear of competition in their own well-established specialty. We, on the contrary, find in this phenomenon a reason for added hope.

Among these specialties, there are some which are not new but are rather a continuation of previous efforts to understand the handicapped person and effect his rehabilitation, that is, his return to function and active life.

We shall point out just a few of the newest or less-known specialties—those of the psychologist, the physical therapist, the vocational counselor, the psychotherapist and the special educator about whom we shall explain more later. In order to be complete, it is also necessary to add here the changes, significant in our opinion, that are taking place in the more traditional professions which are opening themselves up to the new techniques and disciplines. These activities have value in the measure that they do not represent an effort to learn in order to control the new disciplines, but rather to learn about them in order to promote better cooperation in interdisciplinary projects. For example, it is pleasant to see doctors, social workers and hospital chaplains becoming open to psychology without seeking themselves to supplant the psychologist. It is also necessary to salute the desire of nurses and therapists to acquire the basics in pedagogy without pretending to take over the functions of the special educator or the trained instructor. It is especially encouraging to see teamwork among the various personnel who actually work as a group on a common task.

This cooperation of a medical-pedagogical and psychosocial team, to the extent that it does not pretend to remain an empty formula, is something not as easily accomplished as one might think. In order to start at the beginning, we will say a few words about some of these new professions.

We will begin with the psychologist; his or her work enjoys considerable prestige. As we have said, thousands of students enroll each new university year to begin preparation for a degree in psychology. They decide whether to follow the courses and work in an institute of psychology or school of practical psychologists, or in both. Competition is such that each person tries to gain as many degrees as possible. But where does this invasion of young psychologists leave us when they spread themselves among diverse applications of their science? It would be premature to predict the results. For the moment in France, at least, psychologists have still to penetrate the hospitals and medical consultation. In America, actual teams of psychologists already function in the most diverse branches of medicine and not only in psychiatry. Of course, some people fear the presence of the psychologists. Some joke about them; they criticize him/her while at the same time they point to his/her professional claims, phobias, and indiscretions. Doctors are not always encouraging to say the least. Some seem to take a malicious pleasure in contradicting the psychotherapist, in humiliating him/her publicly or in practically negating his/her conclusions laboriously researched after long, tedious examinations and analyses. . . . One can only look at such an attitude as regrettable and fruitless. Fortunately, some of the best doctors demand, esteem and utilize the work of the psychologist. Freed from the ancient and infantile image of the all-knowing and infallible doctor, sure enough of themselves and their own science, they have nothing to fear from psychology. So they accept the dialogue and even the contradiction and eventually they complete and revise their diagnosis with the aid of reputable psychological examination. They are now in a position to appreciate the value and to interpret the conclusions of such an examination.

On the other hand, the "self-complacency" of some psychologists (not the best) also seems to us deplorable. It is, it seems, a question of immaturity if not adolescence; perhaps it is also an overreaction to a certain feeling of inferiority that will disappear little by little as members of a team are able to consider themselves of value and with competence analogous if not equal to the scientist's. Some psychologists are criticized as being hard-hearted. These criticisms are without doubt more apparent than real due to the method of nonintervention which the examination often requires. Such immaturtre attitudes are not found, we must repeat, in "real" psychologists. On the contrary, their understanding of people and respect for the intrinsic worth of each individual command our admiration, as does their gentleness and deep awareness of their own limitations. We are grateful for much of what psychology has taught us and will yet teach us about the mentality not only of psychially-ill persons but also about the chronically sick and disabled, their reactions to their handicaps and the living conditions imposed upon them, and even about the causes of their illness or disability. Projective tests have been invaluable here; so have tests of mental ability, so useful sometimes in setting up therapy, to say nothing of other approaches that have been developed through psychology, of which vocational training is especially important.

In France, it is usually the psychologist who sets up such

vocation programs. In America the psychologist works with another specialist, the vocational counselor whose role goes beyond what is usually thought of in France as a *"orienteur professionnel"*—a career counselor. The counselor, for example, serves as an intermediary between his/her clients and employer. He/she refers to employers disabled persons who are ready to resume work and in some cases have been retrained in a special education program or at a rehabilitation center. The counselor then follows his/her client for a period of time, observes his/her work and where necessary helps to arrange a change of duties, of living quarters or even of employment. Such a change of work can prove advisable if the disabled person is unable conveniently to do the assigned tasks or if he/she shows himself/herself ready to assume more advanced duties. Here again, knowledge of people and understanding of particular circumstances are indispensable for anyone undertaking such counseling. The very fact that someone "thought" of such a profession is a credit to modern civilization!

The vocational rehabilitation we just mentioned is one of the purposes of occupational therapy, but not its only or even its primary purpose. Such therapy is primarily intended to give the physically or psychically ill person an opportunity for satisfying creativity, something he/she is able to do by himself/herself which in the process of doing confers therapeutic benefits. As paradoxical as it may seem, such therapy has in the first place a psychological, or better, a psychosomatic value. For this reason, the therapist is required to have a thorough formation in psychology.

Occupational therapy, however, also aids the restoration of the motor-impaired person (the paralyzed, arthritics, accident victims, etc.). In this, it is related without much overlapping to the work of the physiotherapist. It allows various forms of expression—painting, clay modeling, weaving—all equally useful. Such therapy completes the action of the psychotherapist without in the least competing with it. This occupational therapy, which had just begun to appear in France in 1954,[38] is now widespread in many countries, especially the Nordic and Anglo-Saxon countries, and contributes to all branches of rehabilitative medicine. It is truly a specialized profession which requires lengthy and serious theoretical, technical and practical formation (two or three years of university study in the United States which actually employs tens of thousands of such therapists in the various departments of therapy beginning with psychiatry which has openings for many times their number).

It is good to remember that psychotherapy means not therapeutics of psychical illnesses but instead "the therapeutics by psychical methods" which extends the field of that science considerably. No one should be surprised to hear that this is in itself also a happy sign of contemporary understanding of the cause and treatment of disease. Psychotherapy even more than the previously mentioned specialization is a delicate profession; it calls for a serious, solid and prolonged training which can only be obtained through strictly controlled training.

Unfortunately, it is necessary to admit that at the present time in France, but also in almost all countries of the world, indecision reigns as to the preparation, regulation, and conditions for the practice of this profession. This seems to us to be very serious. The preparation? Some advocate a medical formation . . . but one sees doctors under the pretext that they are psychiatrists or simply pediatricians who are rushing into psychotherapy of adults and children. Psychotherapeutic doctors do not consider medical preparation even with training in psychiatry enough. Others advocate training as a psychologist . . . but that too is dangerous, if not more so, when one sees psychologists becoming psychotherapists with only a classroom preparation in psychology or even in psychopathology. Personal psychoanalysis, the practical experience of psychotherapy under control, in the view of many experts, is needed to complete the medical or psychological training. We will not take part in the controversery that has arisen around the question of knowing if these last conditions are desirable or necessary. In any event, we do not know if they assure in themselves a sufficient preparation. What to do? It seems to us urgent that the problem should be resolved. As for the regulation of psychotherapy and conditions for the practice of this profession, everyone knows that in France as elsewhere at the moment, the situation appears very far from having any satisfactory, clear solution. We will then limit ourselves to regretting the condition while we avoid participating in the controversy. Perhaps the solution could be clarified to some degree if those involved would examine seriously a different question, but one related to it, that is asked by educators specializing in childhood handicaps. It is to this that we turn our attention now.

*   *   *

What is a special educator? The definition adopted by the international meeting of experts that the Medico-Pedagogical and Psycho-Social Commission of the International Catholic Children's Bureau held in Rome in January 1953,[39] states: "He is a professional educator who possesses the special training required by his country to qualify him for the education of handicapped children outside of the standard classroom, or workshop or care situation. Such children are those deprived of normal educational environment, the physically disabled, those with sensory impairment, the mentally retarded, the emotionally disturbed and the delinquent."

By definition then the special educator differs from the instructor even through the latter is specially trained. He differs from the director of a workshop, even one specially qualified for working with handicapped children. He differs from the nurse, the physical therapist, the occupational therapist, and the psychotherapist. All these teach or care for the handicapped under one title or another. They differ from the special educator in that he/she functions outside the normal classroom, outside the workroom, outside the care center.[40]

Someone may ask, "What is then left for the special educator to do?" Precisely all that forms the foundation and basis of a child's or adolescent's life, an irreplaceable role that more normally is held by the mother and father of the family. Some parents are more or less incapable of fulfilling this role in the case of the handicapped child. Sometimes they are separated from the child; sometimes there are no parents or the parents may be in such a physical, mental or moral state that they are not able to fulfill this important role, which involves questions far greater than those habitually raised in the education of a normal child or adolescent, although even there they may require a special competence. That does not mean in any way and we shall state it more carefully further on, that parents, where they exist and are more or less capable of playing their role, must turn over their charge to a special educator. Quite the contrary.

The activity of the special educator covers the totality of the child's life and not only his/her leisure activities. It is in this that he/she differs from the American "recreational worker" who is "specialized in recreation" and who has a professional preparation on the university level, being able to go as far as the "doctorate in recreational work."

One of the roles, and perhaps the essential function, of the special educator, consists in insuring unity in the life of the handicapped child. We have found in the United States where specialization has reached maximum heights that a child, for example motor-impaired and confined in a rehabilitation center, may pass in one day through an impressive number of different hands: those of the doctor, nurse, physical therapist, occupational therapist, teacher, and finally recreational worker, besides submitting to some psychological tests and to an attempt to begin using some "devices" intended to facilitate daily living! No one in that entire group tried to insure the unity of the child's life and stood by as a parental figure in his/her behalf. Certainly, coordination played a role on all these levels: meetings of teams with specialists and the intervention of those responsible for harmonizing the program, for example, with the activities of an educative, psychological or social order. But the child while benefiting from all of these, did not know the process or could not effectively or concretely understand what it was all about.

Each time that we have had the occasion to speak on the special educator and his/her role, and this in the most varied situations (at congresses and programs in institutions dedicated to childhood motor-impairment, mental retardation, emotional disturbances, delinquency or moral abandonment), we have aroused the most active interest and admiration for what has been done in France: "You are fifty years ahead of us in this respect," declared one American. A rare compliment from the other side of the ocean! Moreover, it is exaggerated. Special educators, professionally established as such and duly prepared for their task, hardly existed in France before the end of the last war. But on one point, we have to recognize that France does have some areas to glory in; many schools for special educators actually exist in this country, five in the Paris locality, two at Lyon, the rest at Angers, Bordeaux, Dijon, Lille, Montpellier, Marseille, Nancy, Peynier, Poitiers, Rennes, Strasbourg, Toulouse, Tours, Versailles, etc. Each year these schools receive hundreds of carefully selected students of whom many respond with diffidence to the offers of employment which, paradoxically, are becoming more and more numerous. In fact, specialized educators play such a fundamental role in the lives of exceptional children that their presence is felt everywhere, even when the exercise of their profession is not yet truly protected.

Special educators at times have been caricatured and even vilified. Films such as *Chiens perdus, sans collier* have presented them as boobies, although in Cesbron's novel, the basis for this film, the author manifested an evident sympathy toward them. A book like that of our confrere and friend, Jean Plaquevent, was anachronistic and for a large part unfair. For example, it is inaccurate to portray the special educator, at least today, as one who either failed his/her bid for a B.A. degree or is in search for a possible marriage.[41] We have taught for many years in one school for special educators and for some time less in another. We have had among our students not only very many with bachelor's degrees but also M.A.'s, nurses with state diplomas, and social workers. We have even had married women, mothers of families and religious women among our students. We have met there very intelligent young men and women, well balanced and perfectly capable of engaging in another career. Such professions can, thank God, be the object of deliberate choice and not a last resort made from neurotic motives. However, this last hypothesis always remains possible and methods of screening must be used in order to employ the necessary precautions. Exceptions certainly exist, but they do not make the rule.

It is evident that the formation of the special educator must be demanding (the actual norm is generally three years of training at least, before one receives a permanent diploma, including in proportion and according to various divisions, theory courses, practicum and clinical experience) and that a professional status be permitted which assures satisfactory reimbursement and guarantees the future of those who are engaged in such a profession. The fact that so many young people have already chosen this field and remained faithful to it, in spite of the precarious conditions endured by the pioneers and still a reality for some, is a happy sign of the times. One should not exaggerate this, but it is a proof that modern youth is capable of a generous, enthusiastic and lasting gift of self. This is one of the positive things about our survey, notwithstanding the criticisms we have mentioned.

Special educators, fortunately, are also organized into national and international associations. In certain countries, notably France, one of the most critical problems for them is the attitude of public authorities that utilize their services while pretending to ignore them. This situation, however, they share with others in developing careers. Psychologists, occupational therapists, psychotherapists, or corrective speech therapists, all have been receiving specific training for a long time; yet they still have often been deprived of formal certification. They have even been mentioned in ministerial publications and in France's official press without receiving a state diploma or benefitting by a statute guaranteeing the practice of their profession.

Should one see in this the effect of political strategies or view it as the result of indifference by officials? There have been so many questions to debate in our Chamber of Deputies and so many proposals to draft in our administrative ministries should one feel sorry about this neglect? In any case, the wonderful thing is that the good work is being done all the same and that these professionals, who are becoming more and more numerous, better and better prepared, more and more appreciated, are at work and are eagerly sought after in so many areas.

Moreover, let us recognize that today's special educator is the recipient of the heritage of a century at least of "special" pedagogical tradition. It was at the beginning of the last century but especially toward the middle of this century that interest in the re-education of those with psychic, sensory, and physical impairment was awakened in France, in Europe and very soon thereafter in a large part of the civilized world. It is not the place here to recall what is in the works of Itard, Séguin, Bourneville, Valentin Haüy and of Abbé de L'Eppée, Ovide Decroly, the Brothers of Charity of Gand, of Professor Hanselmann or Alice Descroeudres. Let it be enough for us to recommend the works of these pioneers to our readers. Some of these books are now obsolete because of scientific progress—for example, the education of the deaf-mute which electronic progress has modified—but others remain amazingly relevant. What might have been if the counsels of Séguin or of Bourneville for the education of slow learners had been followed! All of these works witness to a true love and esteem for the handicapped person to whom they are dedicated. We should also try to bring to the surface some of the fundamental principles of the science these pioneers have called by various names, which for lack of something better, we call "special pedagogy of the handicapped," "remedial pedagogy," "orthopedagogy," or, in brief, corrective pedagogy.

Remedial pedagogy ("orthopedagogy") certainly is linked in its evolution and development to the scientific discoveries to which we have alluded. Thus, the psychomatic concept of illness or infirmity, though one had not yet begun to speak of psychosomatic medicine, led to the idea that education was in some measure capable of overcoming handicaps, those physical in origin, or even more, those caused by psychogenic or sociogenic problems. This was the intuition of Séquin and the certitude of Claparède. One has only to recall the discussion at the Congress of Tunis between Claparède and Dupré, champion of "constitutional perversity," when the latter ended his report on such a pessimistic note. Who then today, apart from those behind the times and generally poorly informed, would dare to defend the position of Dupré? It is true that we should not fall into the reverse excess by forgetting the known role that physical constitution and heredity, as well as circumstantial factors of infections or traumatic disease, play in a goodly number of cases.

In any case, we are increasingly optimistic—with an optimism that remains healthy and moderate as to the effectiveness of re-education and other measures taken at the same time to modify the psychosocial condition of the student. If much must still be accomplished in the instruction of the mentally retarded, greater progress has occurred in certain centers for re-education of emotionally disturbed youth, delinquent or not, and in certain homes for problem children, especially in the United States and in the Nordic countries. There remains, of course, much to do here also but the results are such that one ought not to be discouraged or complacent.

Depth, or better, "dynamic" psychology has also contributed to the evolution and the growth of this measured optimism. It has shown in a more intuitive but nonetheless scientifically controlled manner and with unquestionable (if not undisputed) results that certain undesirable pedagogical attitudes, which helped to disturb the equilibrium and exhaust the energy of many a young subject at various levels, could fortunately be counterbalanced by use of such corrective attitudes on the part of cautious educators. It is now admitted that even some pseudo-retarded cases, mistaken for real retardation because of functional symptoms and even some of those characterized as organic, have had these symptoms disappear thanks to such careful pedagogy.

What we have learned in the so-called "new education" has played an important part in this evolution. On the other hand, remedial education has partly originated this movement which has aided normal children as well as the retarded. Everyone is aware of the role played in the beginning of this movement by Froebel, Pestalozzi, Séguin, Decroly, the Brothers of Charity of Gand (real initiators of Montessori methods), and others who first interested themselves in those children who today we consider socially or psychically handicapped and at the same time developed principles which served to liberate so-called normal children from a pedagogy, itself limited, which was basic to many school and social problems.

The concern is to begin with the student where he is—to have faith in his possibilities, and richness, to respect his innate personality and spontaneity, to call forth his active cooperation in his re-education, to blend a positive attitude relying on latent talent with strengths received from struggle and revival, to allow him to reap the rewards which only wait to be harvested—all these are so many fundamental principles in teaching handicapped as well as normal children.

There is the same need to begin with what is at hand and concrete in order to go progressively to the mediate and the abstract. There is the same care to personalize education as well as to lead gradually the child's social need to express himself and to exercise his own initiative and sense of responsibility. One finds there the same climate of joy and even interior certitude on the part of the educator that life must some day triumph over difficulty. We are convinced of these fundamental principles, the only ones possible in education and ones which ought to animate all pedagogy.

Can corrective pedagogy proceed farther? Can it go beyond the role of the special educator such as it is known in France? Can one go so far in educating disturbed persons that it can become a true therapeutic pedagogy? Such a pedagogy would have to be more specifically based on the findings of analytical psychology (without one's becoming a psychoanalyst and ceasing to be an educator). It would utilize the clinical relationship which is established as the framework of all treatment and in a sense every relationship between the teacher and the one to be taught. It would be based on transfer which invariably results from the relationship in the most essential activities of daily life (drinking, eating, sleeping, dressing, games, etc.) precisely because the complexes that bring about conflicts are so closely tied to these activities. Thus, a true healing at the root of the problem, a total restoration of order would be sought. Group dynamics and institutional interaction would also be invaluable aids. The methods of Redl and Bettelheim in the U.S.A., as well as the practice of certain centers in German-language countries, Holland, and Scandinavia, seem to establish experiences debatable but worthy of interest for research and for eventually developing some new approaches. As we see it, efforts in this direction would require for the "healing educator" a training which truly goes beyond that which is given in France and elsewhere in the majority of schools of special education (as formulated by the conference at Amersfoort). At the present time, of these schools only the Institute of Applied Psychopedagogy at Creteil (Seine), the Institute of Healing Pedagogy at Fribourg (Swiss) and Schools of Education at the University of Montreal and Sherbrooke (Canada) supply, from this point of view, an acceptable program. We hope some day to write more on this subject.

*   *   *

In regard to the flowering of these diverse professions, one has to add the principle of teamwork among all the therapists and the educators and especially with the parents. It is noteworthy that in imitation of instructors of "normal" children, the re-education of handicapped young people has become increasingly concerned with working with the families of the children or adolescents; and now there is a very courageous major thrust in this direction. We say courageous for the remarks just made show that the task is not always easy. The parents, where they exist and can be reached, are not necessarily ready to assume the delicate task of re-education.

Therefore, an extremely painstaking work of approach, of education, and even of re-education of families is necessary.

One also has to struggle against deeply rooted prejudices in certain institutions and administrations. According to these quarters, parents of handicapped children are, if not dangerous beings, at least incapable and helpless. Thank God that a change of perspective is taking place and that now one sees parents called upon to take part in meetings, to care for their children, at least during vacations and even each weekend, to visit them frequently, and to be actively associated in the work of re-education for which they are given counseling sessions and informative brochures. In every case possible, parents are encouraged to keep their children at home with them while obtaining help from meetings with re-educators who come to the home or assure the child of visits from appropriate therapists. This supposes that such a visitor lives in relative proximity to the home. In the most successful cases it is the parents themselves who have organized into associations to defend the interests of their children and insure their own information, even their training, while seeking help from specialists.

In the same way, the handicapped themselves are more and more organized into associations. Adult societies for the handicapped are already established and play an important role in the world today. One has only to recall the organizations for the sick and infirm, the associations for paralytics, deaf mutes, blind persons, diabetics, etc. These are not benevolent societies seeking help for the handicapped but groups managed and directed by the disabled themselves. Why not hope that one day all handicapped citizens will organize and control such an activity?

The only risk would be that the world of the disabled persons in question would turn in upon itself and cut itself off from the world of so-called normal or healthy people. We have seen communities of disabled adults living apart from the world and we have regretted this isolation. Convinced of their value to one another, handicapped and healthy must join hands, assured that they share the same world and ought to live and work together. Various welfare and charitable programs to assist the disabled can be of help here. But caution should be taken to avoid, on the one side, a paternalistic attitude, and on the other, a deterioration to dependency.

Without doubt much more could be done in this area. The

improvement and expansion of public services would be welcome. There is a need for new buildings accessible to handicapped people and renovation of older facilities (for example, a system of cottages or at least apartments replacing the barracks of former times and helping to group handicapped youth around special educators in a more humane way).[42] Equally welcome would be a more systematic organization of research. But our purpose here is not to lay out a complete plan for a French or an international setup in the matter of re-education.

We would like to end this positive part of our account by speaking of an important problem, that of rehabilitation—that is, readaptation or reintegration, more words with various interpretations, nuances and adjustments—which is rightly considered to be one of the major problems at the present time.

Indeed, it is not enough to cure or re-educate the "handicapped"; still less must one "adapt" them to the society that should never cease to consider them its members. We have spoken before of the work of the vocational counselor in North America, for example; we have alluded to the existence of societies for the handicapped as well as institutions which cooperate in solving their problems. But these institutions or societies can only act by considering the understanding and active cooperation, let us say interest, in the strict sense of the word, of all people. We are still very far from our goal. Here is an example: In 1956 the French Catholic Aid organized in Paris at the Palais de la Glace with the cooperation of the Catholic Committee of the Sick and Infirm an exposition destined to promote the thesis that states: "Physical disability does not lessen professional ability." Even those organizing this laudable endeavor had to admit that the general public does not yet accept this premise. But it is the general public, both the employer and the person in the street, whom one would have to convert and convince. One must convert the bus driver who we have seen poke fun at the clumsiness, coarse voice, and contortions of a cerebral palsied person, as well as the people on the bus who enjoyed his discomfiture. Now the cerebral palsied youth victim in question was a remarkably intelligent lad who was simply returning from his work; we learned this while chatting with him. This was a surprise to the bus driver and the other riders who quickly changed their attitudes. . . . There are the employees in an office who frown upon a tubercular patient returning from a sanatarium, even though cured, under the pretext that he could communicate the disease to them. There is the by-stander who is astonished at someone with motor impairment or who laughs at a deaf mute. There is the mother who does not dare let her slow-learning son/ daughter go outdoors. There is the crowd who rush to watch and comment on an epileptic seizure. . . . Truly, there is much work to be done.

A world conference now groups international associations that are interested in the rehabilitation of the handicapped, and many international organizations belong to it. This is the Conference of World Organizations Interested in the Handicapped (CWOIH). The International Labor Office in particular has undertaken the task of bringing the question to public notice. There is the World Health Organization. Governments will continue to receive adequate recommendations from it. All that is very good.

But who will set in motion the current of love for this mentally ill person who leaves the psychiatric hospital or for this retarded youth who should not be forced to enter one? Is society leaving a place in its ranks for them? Does this employer accept the risks of hiring a physically disabled man or woman? Does the co-worker overcome his/her fear of being contaminated by his/her neighbor recently dismissed from a sanatarium, and offer a place of semi-liberty? Or does he treat the new employee from the first as the scourge of the neighborhood? Contrary to all of the ridiculous prejudices, scientific studies have proved that the sick or the mentally retarded are not dangerous, that the physically disabled are not less capable, that the cured tubercular patient does not carry germs that are contagious, that the young delinquent can very well correct his/her ways. All this will not be enough to touch hearts. What if such an individual does really constitute a public danger or a threat? The profound value of each human person—even the most dangerous or radically impaired—the conviction that he or she has an inalienable right to be respected and esteemed, the certitude that they merit the sacrifices, even the full and unconditional gift of self— that others may make for them—only a supernatural society animated by God himself and by his unbounded love can truly engrave such sentiments in the hidden recesses of the human heart.

5
The Handicapped
in the Church Today

What then has the Catholic Church[43] done for the handicapped? To give a complete report would be impossible. We will study later the attitude of our Lord himself in regard to the sick and and the handicapped of all kinds. Here it suffices to recall that Christ has entrusted to his Church the task of extending his mission of love and benevolence to the deprived of all times.

The Church is perfect inasmuch as it is Christ himself, the mystical vine (Jn. 15:5), but it is imperfect inasmuch as we are the Church with our sins and our failure to correspond with grace. That is why we constantly have to ask ourselves the questions: "What have we done to answer the call of Christ?" "In what are we faithful to his law" (Jn. 15:12-17) "to the mission that he has intrusted to us?" (Jn. 20:21). "In what way are we unfaithful?" This Christian self-criticism is not disrespectful to venerable Mother Church but, on the contrary, it is an act of deference and a serious obligation on our part. Personal and communal examination of conscience is most certainly a Christian tradition.

Moreover, let Christians set their minds at rest regarding active work on behalf of the handicapped and maladjusted. Long lines of witnesses have professed their esteem and love for the sick, the infirm, the weak and those other individuals thought to be hopeless and often despised. One has only to think of the countless Catholic institutions at the service of the "poor" in the past and the present.

Let them take inventory if possible; let them count, if that is possible, the thousands of religious orders and congregations at the service of all kinds of handicapped, of all those whom "the world" rejects, forgets, or fears—from the deaf-mute blind to the lepers, from the human monstrosities in asylums to the dangerous criminals and to the prostitutes. If more is necessary, let them recall the unflagging charity of a St. Louis, of a St. Vincent de Paul, of a St. John Eudes, of a St. Camillus de Lellis, of a St. John of God, of a Blessed Mother Jovouhey, of an Abbé de I'Epée and the many others. Let them turn also to see in our own time the hundreds of thousands of religious belonging to hospital congregations, to those who conduct facilities for re-education or rehabilitation, as the Brothers of St. Gabriel and their deaf-mutes, the Salesians of Don Bosco and their orphans, and the quiet presence of more and more members of secular institutes, a new proof of the vitality of the Church. Finally, let them not simply forget the militant Christian laity, also members of the Church, witnessing to the love of Jesus Christ in the daily exercise of their duties as special educators or as hospital workers.

All that is known. However, one has to recall it and restate again this primary truth, sometimes strangely absent in the spoken and written word, to know that the Church has been generally a pioneer in all these areas. The Church has always been the guardian of true and efficacious compassion, a tireless inspirer recalling the discouraged to steadfastness, defending as a principle the weak, speaking words of mercy and pardon in season and out, giving back the true meaning to the word "charity," that is, fraternal love.

But here again we would only want to point to the most characteristic initiative of this "Catholic Church" in the recent days of its history, before loyally recognizing the gaps in its service which remain, to a degree, a disappointment to Catholics.

One of the most striking signs of the permanence of the Catholic Church in the service of the handicapped is the maintenance of its institutions in spite of the innumerable difficulties of the present day: material difficulties aggravated by the lack of funds, indifference including hostility or simply the financial inadequacies of public government, difficulties in recruiting members for religious congregations, problems created by modern life, etc. For not only is the continuation of these institutions being upheld as often as possible, but the equipping, remodeling or enlarging of these structures and the establishment of new ones goes on by means of a faith and often a superhuman dedication that wins the admiration of some and arouses the sectarianism of others. It always seems to us as a bit ridiculous, at the same time saddening, to see certain seculars (in the true sense of secular) alarmed that a great many programs for the handicapped are in the hands of "professed believers," as they say. A sad situation which shows so much misunderstanding of the true intention of the Church, as if the sole purpose were to exploit human misery instead of helping to alleviate it or as if defenseless human beings were being forced into its ranks. But wouldn't it be better to smile about it inasmuch as it seems juvenile? And we would even go so far as to rejoice in it, if it is true that such an attitude benefits the handicapped themselves.

Indeed, the number of the needy is so great the field is wide open for a multiplicity of enterprises. Then, let the "seculars" in question create many centers, be it in the spirit of emulation or even in a spirit of competition. For their part, "the clerics," alarmed by this sudden awakening aimed at them, sensing effectively the objective, will also do more. Alas, there will still remain handicapped and maladjusted people to serve. We would wish only that the noblest sentiments accompany or some day supplant the spirit of rivalry so that emulation becomes a stimulus for fruitful action. Would not solidarity and reciprocal esteem be more normal among persons animated by the same ideal of selfless service for the most forsaken and the most abondoned? Would not the fruits from such cooperation be imprinted with a spirit more apt to insure the effectiveness which coordinated efforts would yield?

Moreover, we should joyfully recognize that some national and international organizations have already looked favorably on such a coordination. We are pleased that several Catholic congregations and associations have agreed to modify their objectives, to transform their institutions, even to the point of important changes in their constitutions and regulations to insure greater benefits to the persons in their charge. So we have seen some orphanages, "a catch-all" for many, become "hostels" for children deprived of a "normal" family setting. We have seen medico-professional institutes bring about some sharp distinctions between the disturbed and the retarded, the slightly retarded separated from the profoundly retarded, the delinquent distinguished from children in moral danger, and half-way houses opened alongside rehabilitation centers for adolescents.

Among new foundations we point especially to Catholic schools for educators of the handicapped and maladjusted. Shortly after the last war, two priests, Abbé Courtois and Abbé Barthelémy, opened two of these schools and they were soon followed by the establishment of nine others. Catholic institutes, by educating each year hundreds of men and women including some religious, inspired with an ideal and at the same time qualified, yielded a real network of centers for the formation of special educators.

All of this activity—new institutions, improvements, distribution and coordination of resources—was greatly enhanced by the setting up of national organizations, such as the Union of Hospital and Social Action Religious, National Union of Child Assistants and Educators, the Alumni Association of the Institute of Applied Psycho-Pedagogy and the School of Psycho-Pedagogical Formation in Paris. These parallel the nondenominational organizations as the National Interfederal Union of Private Institutions for Health and Social Service, the National Union of Regional Protective Associations and the National Association of Educators of Handicapped Youth. As a result of their cooperation with these organizations, a large number of religious and lay personnel were not slow in regrouping to insure better effectiveness in their task by a concentration of efforts and a continuous upgrading of their professional qualifications.

In the same way, hospital chaplains were organized; national and regional congresses united priests who stated that never before had they met anyone interested in their special problems; finally, an association of doctors and chaplains was set up to deal with still more specific matters.

It should be recalled that certain professional Catholic groups (U.C.S.S. for nurses and social workers, St. Luke's Association for doctors, etc.), have for a long time had their newsletters and congresses. All this permitted the setting up of true Christian hospital communities as well as the animation of communities heretofore deprived of all supernatural vitality. To be more specific, however, this new vigor in the hospitals and other places for the handicapped was inspired by Catholic Action, which realized that it would be up to the sick and the handicapped themselves to bring such change into being. From this came the birth and development of movements for the sick and the infirm, such as the Catholic Union of the Sick, the fraternities for the sick, branches for the sick and infirm within the big Catholic Action movements such as the J.O.C., and J.O.C.F., the J.A.C.F., the J.I.C.F., etc., and the Catholic Scouts[44] or the movements of CV-AV.[45] Who does not testify to the rechristianization and humanization accomplished by the persevering action of a young Christian worker in the sanatarium, or the witness of a severely handicapped Girl Scout radiating cheer in the midst of her family circle as she waits for the Lord to summon her? Our secular friends should no longer be astonished at this. It is not a question of propaganda but simply of allowing love, justice, and happiness to abound in environments too often deprived of hope and of the most elementary sense of human dignity. We speak of this from experience.

Here again, a coordination of efforts was needed. It came about on the national level thanks to the encouragement given through the express request of the French bishops. A committee for the coordination of social services and movements for the sick and infirm was officially organized.[46] It permitted these Catholic movements to know one another, to exchange information, to work together and to set up common research under the sponsorship of French Catholic Action. Not only associations of the handicapped organized for action or for piety,[47] but also those groups "in the service of the sick" (such as visiting and transportation programs organized under the auspices of Catholic Charities) and the professional associations mentioned before, were invited to work together and to harmonize their services.

In Rome in 1951 at the First World Congress of the Apostolate of the Laity, an effort toward international cooperation was given birth.[48] Inserted into the order of business was the concern of the Church that attention on the world level be given to the sick and the handicapped. In parallel action the existence of Caritas Internationalis, of the Medico-Pedagogical and Psycho-Social Commission of the International Catholic Child Bureau, and the mediation of doctors, nurses, social workers, and pharmacists gave rise to the hope of some day seeing the problems of the world, of the hospitals, and the handicapped, researched and reflected upon in a Christian manner, if not resolved in the same spirit, at the level of the universal Church. Already the "Commission on Health Problems" was giving some attention to this within the Conference of International Catholic Organizations. And a Catholic World Health Conference met in Brussels in July 1958, bringing together doctors, pharmacists, nurses, chaplains and hospital personnel for a first session that offered great promise for the future.

Lastly, one of the crucial points of the Christian presence in the world of the sick, handicapped and maladjusted is their religious formation. "What an open wound in the body of the Church!"—how these words resound in all their sad reality when they are directed to the most abandoned portion of humanity! At the same time there are some efforts to point this out here. (We will return to it in the last part of this book.)

In 1950 at the First International Congress of Religious Education, held in Rome during October of the Holy Year, the problem was raised by this author, a member of the French delegation. He was able to rely on recent research given to him by the general secretariat of the Catholic Committee of the Sick and Infirm. Some weeks later a program was begun in the suburbs of Paris for a group of profoundly retarded. The following year under the auspices of the Advanced Institute of Pastoral Catechesis a chair of Pastoral and Catechetical Psycho-Pathology was founded at the Catholic University of Paris. Lastly, study groups were set up on the French national level to study some of the diverse aspects of a problem both extensive and complex: the catechesis for the disturbed, for delinquents, for deaf-mutes, for the blind, for the sick and infirm adults. This assemblage of study groups had to receive official approval. The national catechetical commission (now called "Religious Instruction") agreed to create within its commission a "sub-commission" charged with studying these diverse problems. Moreover, by October 1959 there was set up, within the framework of the National Center for Religious Instruction, a national service for the handicapped called "special pedagogical catechesis."

It remained then to multiply these pilot programs at the local level by forming and informing small groups. Magazine articles, conferences in France and elsewhere, national congresses of religious instruction, and lastly, national sessions for catechists of mentally retarded children and adolescents mark an effort that is still very modest.

On the international level, contacts were made within the Medico-Pedagogical and Psycho-Social Commission of ICBB[49] which will permit exchanges of studies and common research work beyond our frontiers. Father Otteny at Vienna, Dr. Van Mann at Friburg (Germany), Abbé Paulhus at Sherbrooke (Canada), and Brother Oreste at Bruges, already authorities in their own countries, were some of the first to communicate with this group, and also with Fathers Delceuve and Godin at Brussels.[50] But most of the responses to our international questionnaire made us clearly understand that this problem remains largely untouched. And yet isn't this the work of works for a Christian?

But we come now to the negative side of the balance sheet that we intended to draw up. We shall try to do this with the same accent on objectivity that we hope to have shown in the first part of this chapter.

*   *   *

The deficiency most apparent is without doubt the lack of resources in the face of the pressing needs. In France, for example, there are vast sectors where Catholics have for a long time been almost totally inactive. We are thinking of some types of handicapped mentioned earlier, cerebral palsied and epileptics and also severely retarded adults. One also has to deplore the lack, until recently, of remedial classes in private education even as one must acknowledge the sizable though very inadequate efforts in public education. We know too from experience how difficult, if not impossible, it is to find religion instructors for delinquent boys. Charged recently with the task of researching the possibility of opening centers in Africa, we saw all our appeals, as well as the efforts of interested religious authorities, go unanswered.

Perhaps people respond to such appeals by asserting that there is a lot to do and one has to establish priorities. That is exactly the problem. It is, in fact, a question of knowing if one should begin with the poorest, as the Lord Jesus did in his time, or if one should be concerned with them only after caring for the others. A religious teaching congregation which would change an expensive boarding school for young society girls into an institute for profoundly handicapped children from the poor and lower classes, a prestigious prep school where the teaching brothers would begin to accept spastics to assure them an education, a deluxe hospital that a nursing congregation would transform into a center for epileptics of all ranks of society: these would be obvious witness to the sort of saintly daring reminding one of Saint Vincent de Paul or a Don Bosco and the spirit that animated the founders of religious orders.

"But what about vocations?" some people might retort. We answer: "This is exactly what attracts vocations. How many young girls hesitate to enter a teaching order because they fear they will very likely be asked to serve in the bourgeois milieu they have left? And how many stay away from hospital congregations because they fear they cannot care for the really poor? How can one answer the questions of young members of Catholic lay organizations who fear that in religious life they will not find the spirit of true Catholic service? Certainly all children and all sick people are worthy to be served. But why not be able to say to this young teacher, to that therapist, 'Yes, enter this congregation and you will be able to give your whole life to the service of the real poor, to dedicate yourself to the retarded or the handicapped or the maladjusted, to serve Christ in those who suffer most and are most deprived?' '

Along the same lines, there is a more sensitive and perhaps a more serious problem concerning qualifications and competence. Here, even some existing institutions find themselves in a bind. The workshops of past years where abandoned children were arranged like so many flower pots have had their day. They had some value when they were the only places to put children brought in from the misery of the streets. But the exigencies of today's education and rehabilitation program, as well as the advances in therapy, demand practical and theoretical training that has been acquired under professional circumstances. Nurses certified by the state have replaced the kindly caretakers. Is the special educator and tomorrow the occupational therapist, the speech therapist, the psychotherapist, and even the clinical psychologist going to replace the supervisors or instructors in our religious institutes of rehabilitation? One scarcely sees that even in America . . . and yet! Why must schools for special educators, established for religious, now see their classes filled almost entirely by lay people? Are all those thousands of religious in charge of institutions for the handicapped already qualified? Or did they leave the school after taking just a few courses? Were only a few members of the principal congregations involved? Or was it imagined that one person, after training, would be able to train all the others?

If tomorrow such professional training would be required by the state, we would no doubt see the same classes suddenly filled with sisters but would there still be time to do this? And is this the only plausible argument to make some appreciate this evolution of the situation and still more the ongoing needs of the handicapped people entrusted to us? The Church is not to blame for this situation even if it is the established authority. Indeed, the Holy Father has repeatedly renewed his recommendations and they are explicit. How many times has he reminded us that religious must be as qualified, if not more so, than their lay counterparts? Some congregations, however, are already setting the example.

In what concerns male religious and priests, the same deficiencies are often to be deplored. And here again it seems that the responsibility does not rest entirely on the members themselves. It is not a question simply of blaming the Church authorities. But why have ecclesiastical circles tolerated so long the belief that the duties of chaplains for the sick, the handicapped or maladjusted—such responsible services—should be reserved for priests themselves weak, ill or handicapped? We remember the days when we were listed in the Paris archdioceasan directory as "on leave" when we had charge at Hauterville of two sanatariums with four hundred beds each, not to speak of at least two hundred staff members. Moreover, most of the sick people belonged to our archdiocese. There were groups such as the Scouts, J.O.C., J.O.C.F., adult Catholic Action, a very real and extensive parish! Indeed, one has to realize that a sanatarium of a thousand beds is much more demanding in a certain sense than a parish of a thousand parishioners. Certainly the sick have more spiritual claims than the healthy. There were the needs of the personnel of all their diverse categories from doctors to waitresses, some also being members of Catholic Action groups.

One of our confreres, sent on "leave" for a "rest" to such a position because of respiratory problems, died a few months after his arrival worn out by the demanding service. Another inconvenience of such an arrangement is the inability of some priests to face up to the needs of those in their charge. There is the elderly chaplain bearing responsibility for handicapped young people who is overwhelmed by his "troops" for catechism or unable to understand their mentality. Still another danger is the lack of continuity. We know of a hostel for the sick in the mountains, truly a small parish comprised of about a hundred young girls and children besides resident personnel, which has had at least thirty changes of chaplains in twenty years. Each chaplain, sent there to recover his health, was recalled as soon as he seemed able to resume his former duties. Just as if the service in question had no importance.[51] One can guess the weariness of the sick and the helplessness of those in charge at such a hostel.

This also explains how rare is the case of chaplains who are not only "informed" but "trained" and competent. Perhaps one session of a congress where some of the most conscientious participate gives superficial attention to the problem. The danger of being complacent here is very real. At best a priest's preparation for this work is meager, a hasty study of the literature. Those who acquire real competence are few and they are at the mercy of sudden clerical changes. Yet, how much good could come with a priest thoroughly prepared to work not only with the handicapped of such an institution but also with the specialized personnel with whom dialogue would become possible as well as real cooperation.[52] In particular this training would aid the priest in acquiring an indispensable base for exercising pastoral activity and for giving religious instruction to the handicapped. These two points will end this criticism of our profession, but again, we do not wish it to appear as an indictment.

In recent years many books on pastoral medicine and even pastoral psychiatry have been written. Because of such rapid changes in medical and psychiatric science, these are sometimes questionable and even outdated by the time they appear. They are, however, useful reading for every priest and indispensable for those serving the handicapped and maladjusted. And every priest in pastoral ministry is at times involved with sick people. Isn't it deplorable that so many ill physically or psychically, slightly or seriously—as well as disabled persons in our parishes are so little supported spiritually, so deprived of the sacraments, so seldom visited and sometimes, at least in the cities, so completely disowned? Even in the best of cases the physically and mentally handicapped have special needs which a priest, even though zealous, is not able to understand if he has not had special training. Seminary studies are generally brief, even simplistic about such ministry. One can even be happy when the text or courses do not contain sensational misinformation about the nature of disease, such as one book we saw during our own diaconate year. This created more than one blunder, remedied with difficulty and after serious consequences for the people entrusted to us. Why be astonished that so many priests blunder at the bedside of the sick, or even more so when they meet a psychotic, or a disturbed neurotic person? Why be surprised at the patronizing tone of a sermon addressed to an audience at a "day for the sick,"[53] even when the speaker is well known.

But the case is most grave when a priest is named chaplain for a hospital or of a center for handicapped young people. His ministry in fact introduces him into an enviroment with a special mentality. He is continually faced with delicate problems. He has to meet at times with highly qualified specialists. It is annoying when he sounds and appears as the only one uninformed and "out of place" (maladjusted!) in a milieu where his mission clothes him with a special importance. It is here that a special preparation and not just a brief study, often dangerous because it leaves its beneficiary with the impression that he is sufficiently enlightened, is essential and must be considered a primary requisite of the priest assigned to this chaplaincy.

Unfortunately, in one case as in the other, parish work or chaplaincy, the priest, even admitting that he has the desire and the time, generally has no means available for his training except for the conferences or contacts that we have mentioned before. The fundamental reason is that nothing yet has really been developed in this area.[54] Only a study that is at the same time pastoral, medical, psychological, sociological, and pedagogical could in a definitive manner aid in solving this problem.

In a work of this nature the problems of Catholic Action in hospital environments ought to be treated in particular. Isn't it painfully striking at the congresses of chaplains to see how so many of our confreres are defenseless before a deeply dechristianized milieu and especially how meagerly prepared they are to inspire and to support a militant laity?

Finally, a fundamental aspect of this pastoral work would be a "specialized catechesis," otherwise called a study of how to approach and carry out the Christian education and the religious training of, properly speaking, the socially, physically, and psychically handicapped people in our parishes and institutions.[55]

Here again, as we have already mentioned, the needs are enormous and tremendously varied, and it will be difficult even to begin studies in this area. However, a real unrest is becoming apparent. We only have as proof the enthusiastic welcome given in France to our first attempt. This book was written because of this welcome, the mandate from our superiors and especially the call from those for whom it was written and whom the Lord has preferred, the "handicapped" themselves.

6
The Handicapped
in the Plan of God

We have said that the handicapped are "preferred" by the Lord. It is these words that we now want to explain. This is a difficult task but it seems to us that it is the indispensable basis for all of our work. We would like it to be a real meditation made under God's loving gaze, or better still with the help of his grace so that we might benefit from his inspiration, his concern and his personal love, so as to see the handicapped as he sees them, to welcome them as he welcomes them, to love them as he loves them. Would that the Spirit of love and of light help us to situate handicapped people in God's plan in such a way as to sketch out the "theology" of it![56]

Certainly this theology would require a volume, even several, to tell it all. We make no pretense other than to outline it briefly here. Besides, we have already suggested in our introduction the wide scope of such a task.

As in preceding chapters, we will content ourselves with underlining some of the less appreciated aspects or at least those insufficiently stressed. Moreover, some aspects remain a mystery in the true meaning of the word.

*   *   *

"Master," said the disciples of Jesus concerning the man born blind, "Who has sinned, this man or his parents, since he was born blind?" Jesus answered, "There is no sin either for him or for his parents but it was necessary that the works of God be manifested in him" (Jn. 11:2-3). This alone, this word of the Lord, could be an endless subject for meditation. Indeed, what "light" does it not cast on the problem that involves us?

It is now two thousand years since these words fell from the lips of the Savior. Yet, clearly, this word of God, so well known to all, does not deter numerous Christians from always wishing to ascribe to sin—the sin of the sick or handicapped, the sin of his/her parents, the sin of the world, etc.—every deficiency or handicap they encounter. This reference is made so easily and so thoughtlessly it paralyzes imagination and action!

Is this child retarded? "He is the son of an alcoholic," they will say. Is another child disturbed? "The family is to blame. . . . Oh, if parents would bring up their children better. . . . " Is this young man tubercular? "Oh, if the young were more sensible . . . !" Yes, this is so much second nature that it eases our conscience; it dispenses us from searching out courageously and scientifically the causes of the ailment and the ways to remedy it. This frees us from the necessary effort of "thinking over the problem" and finding its solution before God so that we can the more easily cast the stone at the parents, at society or at the handicapped person herself/himself. And then such an attitude assures a feeling of respectability or at least ethical morality and provides a certain impression of righteous security. We remember a student who always responded to all questions asked in our course in psychopathology, "It is original sin." He used that phrase for the cause of any illness or deficiency. That simplified still more conclusively the question . . . and it appeared beyond argument.[57] But Jesus gives us another explanation: "There is no sin either for him or for his parents. . . . " "There is not any sin."

Yet, how many sick people and even more, how many of their parents, overwhelmed by such "guilt feelings," search ceaselessly into their past or that of their spouses, their ancestry and their relatives: "Who has sinned?" Moreover, the people around them, like the friends of Job, urge them to do it. And so the story goes—as demonstrated at a great international congress—that "Christianity leads parents to believe that they are at fault for the physical or psychical deficiencies of their children." But have they not read the

Gospel? "There is no sin, neither in him nor in his parents. . . . "

Indeed no one would deny that some deficiencies of an infant could be caused, in part at least, by certain irregularities of their parents such as alcoholism, loose living, broken family ties and negligence. But who will say, even here, that the fault lies with the parents? Could there not be some psycho-pathological hereditary causes which have determined to a certain degree the behavior of these unfortunate parents? In addition, we cannot ignore the fact that from a scientific point of view, the experts are much more reserved than they were some years ago as to the number of cases ascribed to "hereditary syphilis" or "hereditary alcoholism." These terms, now considered inadequate and inaccurate, are more and more being abandoned.

As to culpability, properly speaking, moral culpability or "sin," let us say that we have no thought of denying its existence, nor that the effects of this "sin" can touch the person himself/herself, his/her family and even his/her environment. On the contrary, we noted in a short article in a special issue of *Présences* concerning psycho-somatic medicine that in the current perspective of medicine (such as we have touched upon earlier), the notion of "responsibility"[58] even in causing an illness could well become an acceptable or at least debatable position. Indeed, if we admit that the psychological can influence the physical and that the same psychological may in part be submitted to free will, this becomes possible inasmuch as at least the process of somatic change is not entirely unconscious and that is controlled in a certain measure by free will. This would involve a certain responsibility on the part of the person and eventually his guilt. But one sees how dangerous it would be to push such a thesis to its limits. Moreover, according to current science, it is only a weak hypothesis.

Be that as it may, the word of the Lord in the Gospel—and in how many texts in the Old Testament does one see the same attitude of Jesus—invites us not to busy ourselves with systematically seeking out the "culprit" (he or his parents) when we meet a handicapped or retarded person. It is much more important to discover his place in a divine perspective which is positive and expansive: "There is no sin . . . but it is necessary that in this way the works of the Lord be manifested in him." What then are these works?

Christ, the Son of God, shows us immediately one of the works to be made manifest: He cured the man born blind. Let us recall or better still let us reread the entire passage in its exceptional richness—the man cured by the mixture of saliva of the Son of God with the earth of men ... his courageous witness to Jesus in the presence of the Pharisees who seek in vain to make him suppress the truth. ... They accuse him still of being "born entirely in sin," then they put him out. Finally the man meets Jesus again, falls at his feet in an act of faith and adores him.

Let us ponder this deeply in a spirit of meditation and we shall without doubt find a little light on the mystery. Notice first of all that from the start, having cast aside the hypothesis of sin and even the question raised by his apostles, Jesus gave back sight to the blind man.

Because God is life, God is health, God is cure. He loves life and health. He wishes life and good health for mankind. And that is why in the name of the Father, Christ cures and Christ raises to life again. We recalled in our introduction to this work: "The glory of God is man alive" and in the full blossoming of his life. Thus no more morbid grieving, no more masochistic pleasure in suffering, no apathetic resigned escape into illness; nothing of this would be Christian. Let us not seek it either for ourselves or for others. Illness or handicap, mental or physical, under whatever form it appears, is never an end to be sought. Quite the contrary. In itself it is an evil to struggle against. More than anyone else a Christian ought to wish for health, the health of those whom he/she meets, and for their healing. If not, he/she would not be a disciple of the one who raises from the dead or who heals, of the one who has said of himself: "I am the resurrection and the life," and who conquered death.

Of course, it cannot be said that natural life and especially bodily life are the greatest of all goods. If we believe in the value of nature, in the value of the body, we believe also and still more in the infinitely superior value of the supernatural and of the life of grace.[59]

We know that the death of the body is only transitory death after which the body will regain life while the life of the soul continues to subsist. We know that the one and the other, body and soul, raised to a supernatural level by their sharing in the Church of Christ, which is his own mystical body and sanctified by his sacraments, are participants in the divine life. And this divine life, rooted in the natural, infinitely surpasses in value the "natural" without, however, abolishing it, quite the contrary . . .

"For the supernatural is itself part of human nature . . .

And the tree of grace and the tree of nature

Have bound together their two trunks so intimately . . .

That they are both soul and both body."[60]

As we have said at the beginning of this book, despite the morbid grief and victimized souls we find in the religious writings of some over-eloquent authors of dubious success, the Word of God in no way preaches suffering as good for its own sake or to be loved for itself. Illness, handicap, or any kind of deficiency is not to be sought after for itself, nor accepted with passive resignation or submission, and still less as abandonment to death or a flight from life. Quite the contrary. The Word of God raises to life and cures. God wishes man to be healthy, normal and alive.

But, some might say, did not Christ love the sick and the infirm with a love of predilection? Did he not, himself, accept death and suffering? God does not "stop exalting the humble."[61] This is indeed true but it does not involve any contradiction.

Indeed, it is beyond question that Christ reached out with a love of predilection (one has only to recount the Gospel reference) to the sick, to the infirm, and to the handicapped. He freely gave them his time and his strength even in extreme weariness. But he did this to give them health and to "readjust" them to life. Such was the purpose of his "reaching out."

Christ has reached out to the dead: the son of the widow at Naim, Lazarus his friend, but that was to manifest the resurrection and there again it was to lead these people back to life.

Moreover, Christ himself accepted suffering although he was repulsed by it. ("Father, take this cup from me.") Nevertheless, he consented to it not because of the good of suffering in itself, but to do the will of the Father and to be the instrument of our redemption.

He clings then to his Father's will by his love and it is in this sense
that he is a willing sufferer. He took up his cross, died on it to save
us. He did this only to rise from the tomb and to bring back to us a
complete, final victory over death. "Death, where is your victory?"
(Cor. 4:15). "Death was slain when life was willing to die to conquer
it."[62] Is not one able then to say that if Jesus turns to suffering
humanity by preference, if he turns himself to the sick and even the
dead, it is to give them loving health, to restore to them lost life and
those positive values which they desire but lack? He turns to them
not because of what they no longer possess but because of what it is
possible to give them. He does not love in them what they do not
have; that is obvious. He loves them for what they have, for what
they are and in particular for all that his love desires and all that his
power "can" give them because they, more than others, are deficient
in some way.[63]

It is to these needs that he applies his benevolence, his good
will.[64] This is what he expects from his Church. It is this attitude that
he requires from us, from each Christian who approaches handicapped people of all kinds. We have stated this from the beginning.[65]

*   *   *

But now we must examine what God expects from the handicapped themselves. We ask ourselves what place the handicapped
have in the plan of God? By his word, by the same Gospel text, Jesus
answers us: "In order that the works of God be made manifest." But
how can they be manifested?

As in the case of the blind man in the Gospel, it seems that the
works of God are made manifest first by those who come to the aid
of the handicapped person and then by the person himself/herself.
"Evil is in the world like a slave who has to bring up water," said
Claudel.[66] Sickness, infirmity, physical or mental deficiency, the
misery of the socially maladjusted, the orphan, the rootless, or the
delinquent are as so many slaves in the world, so many prods which
are forcing the world to wake up, so many summons for men/women
to the task to be accomplished to finish the work of creation and to
complete universal redemption.

Jesus cured the man born blind—as he has cured the lepers, the fever-ridden, the deaf-mutes and the paralytics, as he brought the dead back to life. He did it miraculously through his omnipotent power as the Son of God. His power continues to manifest the glory of the Father in the world today through other miracles. But all, not only wonder-workers, have to cooperate in this work of healing, of resurrection and of life. This applies in particular to those whose special mission calls them to be present to those who suffer.

From the start the handicapped have this "mission" in the Church: to see that the works of God are made manifest in this way. Said in another way, the action of Christ is manifested in his Church, continuing his living work through members of his body and who, like him and with him, go to the most wretched to give what they lack.

To arouse the Church and humanity whose leaven it is; to inspire love for the Church and humanity animated by the Spirit, sent from the Father in Jesus; to show this Spirit of Love at work making the supernatural effectiveness of his invisible presence shine forth and in this way permit authentic Christians to be witnesses of God's charity, charity by which one has to recognize the Church founded by Christ: all this, it seems to us, is the primary role of the handicapped in the plan conceived by divine wisdom.

One also sees that the handicapped manifest the glory of God by the act of faith they bring forth from others: act of faith "before, during and after." An act of faith "before" any action in order to cause others who approach them to perceive the infinite value of the handicapped, the secretly hidden value in this paralytic or that blind deaf-mute, in this severely retarded person or in that one whose disturbed behavior is repulsive and revolting. An act of faith "during" in order to sustain some often painful and apparently unsuccessful work and to grasp its unseen value, when, humanly speaking, it seems impossible. An act of faith "after" when all efforts will have succeeded or apparently failed so as to return the merit of the cure of God (I treated him, God cured him) when even on the level of pedagogical and medical evaluation, it is unsuccessful on every count . . . to believe that it is worth even the pain. There is always the pain of my giving and of being worn out, of patiently feeding the agonized cancer patient, of patiently educating the dull-witted retardate or the myopathic child or the terminal leukemia victim, or of welcoming back a hundred times the perverse backslider.

It is in this way the handicapped lead us to revise our whole scale of values, to understand, for example, that beauty and physical strength are not everything; that intelligence is only a relative value, that character, even in its altruistic displays, is not an absolute norm, that the essence of a being is something infinitely greater and which goes far beyond, especially when it is elevated to a plane which is fittingly called divine and which makes the human value of the person already priceless.[67]

This profoundly retarded child, this senseless creature, when baptized, has infinitely more value in the eyes of God than some cunning genius, a conscious monster who harangues people on the radio and makes the entire universe shudder. The one is unspeakable light to all that is darkness in the other. And in the end one has to ask oneself which one, the retarded child or the disturbed man or ourselves, which one is in reality the most retarded or the most troubled in behavior. Are we not all terribly retarded, disturbed and deficient in relation to the intelligence and love, the omnipotence, the wisdom and the perfection of God? Are we not all terribly perverse in the face of the loving attention paid us by this God? Are we not terribly handicapped in relation to his plan and to the eternal life of intimacy and profound happiness with him to which he has predestined us?

As always our reflection leads us back to the essentials! Does it not reveal to us the "true riches"? Beyond the contingencies of life, the pseudo-truths, the lying facades, the conventions, all clearly demonstrate how easily we are satisfied with simplistic reasoning. All call us to a realism, brutal perhaps and a bit revolutionary, or rather revolutionizing, but salutary. All makes "manifest the work of God." May this God be praised in his love! Let the handicapped also be thanked for this! Would not such a function in the plan of God suffice to justify their presence, to merit our respect if not our admiration? Indeed, does not their personal worth call forth from us our heartfelt "thank-you"?

In relation to us and to all those from whom they seek aid, arouse love and reawaken faith, they join to this function, we think, another role, which is without doubt in a certain sense primary.

They—the handicapped by themselves and in themselves—manifest the works of God.

We seldom think about this nor do we believe it sufficiently. That these handicapped persons may be "assisted" by us, and that they can permit us to be witnesses to charity, we are willing to admit. But that they most surely by themselves contribute to making the works of God manifest—this is what seems to us a paradox.

However, let us glance again at the blind man of the Gospel. Hardly had he been cured than he immediately began to give witness to Jesus. He had had to suffer for his blindness. His parents experienced abuse and discomfiture (though they did not have his courage); he must have been insulted and even rejected by the local authorities of the town. Then he met Jesus, he recognized him as the Son of God and he adored him: "I believe, Lord."

How many ardent Catholics have in similar fashion emerged from infirmity and illness! We have known of many such cases and even now often see that trials have "converted" them or simply brought them closer interiorly to the Lord. They matured early and were "sanctified," even drawn to authentic holiness, not by trials in themselves, but through the situations that these trials provided and the meeting with the Lord they fostered. This young boy or girl struck down at twenty with tuberculosis or at twelve with paralysis, this weak child or that adult in the prime of life snatched from family and activity. Sometimes, after long months, even years of illness, they have gone from indifference and lukewarmness to become fervent Christians even sometimes responsible for directing Catholic Action groups. What a long list could we not furnish of such activity if we were not restrained by our discretion!

We remember a young girl of twenty terminally ill, dictating a letter to one of her companions at the sanatarium. She had just learned that her friend, also fatally ill, had refused the Sacrament of the Sick: "Me, I demanded it," she said. "I am happy. I feel better. Do what I did." The other girl was at that point discouraged and rebellious, but when she received the letter she was touched by the obviously sincere words of her friend and at the end, she too asked for the sacrament.

We also recall a very helpless lady, paralyzed and atrociously deformed, attacked by illness in the full bloom of youth and literally nailed to her chair for thirty years without being able even to lift a spoon to her mouth. Yet she could smile, she could talk, she could write and she could knit. And these things she did for all these long years. Her words, written or spoken, gave courage to all those from far and near who had been given the grace of having her enter into their lives.

We recall Simone, who died at eighteen, a smile on her lips, saying simply: "I offer my life for the conversion of my father and for Catholic youth." There was Jacqueline, a Girl Scout of the same age comforting her grandmother who came to her bedside: "Do not weep, grandma; death is not sad." And lastly, we think about the little Moslem mentioned by Louis Raillon in *Témoignage des enfants de notre temps*,[68] who at eleven accepts his sufferings for the conversion of his family. And about the many others, known and unknown—one could write an endless anthology.

Someone will ask of those who do not know or who, do not understand the deranged or the severely retarded adults: What sense can their witness have, what value can their adoration assume, if there is so little evidence that any sort of worship can exist? We are here in the presence of mystery; it is useless to deny it. But still, one has to acknowledge and respect this mystery without judging or coming to a conclusion too quickly.

Here again, our experience spreading over many years and the testimony of many special educators permit us to say that when one knows the "backward" child intimately, one is surprised at the sincerity and depth of his/her religious conviction. Later we shall speak more about the delicate consciences of some of the profoundly retarded. We remember being personally touched to the point of tears while hearing their confessions. On leaving the confessional I knelt down to thank God "for having hidden these things from the wise and the prudent and revealed them to the little ones." And what a privilege to prepare these children for baptism or First Communion. Only those who have seen their unbelievable fervor and their unexpected generosity can know how in the midst of disturbing behavior they baffle those around them with their intuition and their manners. Such a wholehearted approach to God is, without doubt, as precious in his sight as the piety of the "good" and intelligent child. Why would not the homage of these children, their way of giving glory to God, be unique, distinctive, exceptional? Why not admit that if they were not here, there would be lacking a way of praising the Lord God and manifesting him, something in the symphony of God's creatures which could be filled by no one else?

Despite the minimal cooperation of, for example, children afflicted with autism or brain damage (is it really minimal?), by what right could I decree that it is not important? This cooperation can have, certainly in the eyes of God, incomparable value and it is for that reason that he keeps them here on earth.

It is then for us to respect the value of their praise, to do everything possible to keep it alive and if possible to foster a fuller exercise of it. We have to watch over this sanctuary lamp, however vacillating may be its flame, and to believe that to insure a reserve of oil each evening and each morning is a great act. Such an action lies on the threshold of the infinite. We think of so many nurses, religious and lay, of evangelical deaconesses and especially a Protestant doctor in Berlin. "It is very rewarding," they agreed in appraising the religious life of the profoundly retarded children whom they cared for, bedridden children in foul-smelling rooms of an asylum. "It is worth the trouble; it is so rewarding." Would that all those who carry on such noble efforts for a lifetime would some day understand that even though their work may now seem all but useless to them.

Without doubt we will be amazed one day when we see the world from God's perspective. Who knows if that child with his large head, who only opens his mouth to eat or to drool, will not have given as much glory to God as the most fervent monk? Who knows if this insane person, restrained and confined, will not have been as pleasing to the heavenly Father as his wisest and most learned doctors? And who knows if this young prostitute, taken ten times in the very act of debauchery and led back to the "reformatory" (without hope of rehabilitation), has not given God as much love and earned as much merit as the purest and most fervent virgin?

On this delicate point we would like to conclude. What justice is there for the handicapped who are called disturbed, deviant or delinquent? Formerly the answer was simple: sinners on one side, the sick on the other. The sinners were either repentant or condemned.

The sick were deserving of pity and care. Today, it can no longer be judged in that fashion.

In fact, one contemporary writer speaks of a "universe sick with guilt." In this way he mixes sickness and sin, and ends with an essay on "morals without sin."[69] Another author writes a book on "defects of children."[70] Though well intentioned, he mixes the ethical with the pathological. Still another, writing in the same vein, prefers to speak of the "child without defects,"[71] which comes back to the same idea and is simpler. Parents and educators no longer know what to make of it all. Must every penal measure be seen as an injustice? Magistrates, judges, directors of reform schools and police officials in high places resent this trend.

In Geneva in 1965 at the first Congress of the United Nations on the prevention of crime and the treatment of delinquents, this same impression emerged from the congress, and the same thing occurred at the meeting of the European Commission that was concerned with pathological and habitual delinquents. If it is true that every delinquent is a conditioned individual and unfree, then every punitive measure becomes an inconceivable lack of honesty on the part of those who pretend to incarnate "justice."

Our houses of "correction," now called centers of "rehabilitation," although a little less disagreeable than formerly, still present— in comparison to normal living—an atmosphere of unjust sanction.

If there are no longer culprits but only sick people, if the inmate is only a victim and not someone responsible for his/her actions, who should be punished? The inevitable restrictions of a hospital stay should at least be imposed, but nothing that is reminiscent, even vaguely, of penitence or of primary restraint. Yet it is a fact that our "delinquents" still have the feeling of being punished. Neither our prisons nor even our rehabilitation centers resemble our institutions for the cure of tuberculosis or for convalescents (although these very institutions on their part sometimes resemble prisons). The public still surrounds the inmates of these centers (even those in half-way houses) with fear and disapproval. Such attitudes are not easily eradicated. What can one say of institutes which were effectively "refuges" of the old style, that is places of welcome where a "lost" young girl could escape the rigors of justice while weeping for her sins, even repenting of them by becoming forever a "Magdalen" for the remissions of her sins? Can any of that spirit remain now that the psychologists and psychiatrists have invaded our observation centers and evaluated delinquency in terms of metabolic drives and electro-encephalograms? Is it still necessary to speak of blame and responsibility? These are serious questions which cannot be treated here.

What appears evident is that moral perversity does exist along-side pathological perversity;[72] at times the two are oddly intermingled. At least theoretically some perversity may only be serious sickness; some is committed by persons who are entirely victims of social conditioning. They are more to be pitied than to be blamed. Some are not at all to blame and ought to be totally excused, if not pitied. Despite their perverse behavior, some of these persons may at the same time be rich in merit in the eyes of God. They may even have authentic sanctity, although the Church could not without difficulties propose them for public veneration.

Still there is no question here of excluding the possibility of moral perversion. Some people are responsible for their mistakes and willing prisoners of their own aberrant actions. For these, then, repentance must be proposed and penitence suggested to them as duty. It is a question for them of "weeping over their mistakes" and really making "reparation." Mercy and pardon, when granted, are in virtue of charity, and not justice owed to them.

Another large group is not entirely culpable nor entirely pathologically perverse. For the most part aren't we all in this group? Exteriorly some actions look the same, whether they are pathological, moral, or relatively conditioned. Of themselves these actions present the same disturbances on the whole, the same dangers for the community. Without doubt this is why up to the present justice has devoted little time to analyzing them and establishing some distinctions as to sanctions and therapy. It is only recently that effective means have been taken for treating juvenile delinquents separately, and also separating pathological or habitual delinquent adults from other inmates. Still there is more than one country in the world that is not ready to accept distinct treatment. Some of the delegates to Geneva in 1955 or 1956 recognized this fact and asked to be permitted first to arouse public awareness of the problem.[73]

Where are the psycho-socially maladjusted and the guilty in the plan of God and in his loving concern? What is certain is that he, indeed, knows them well. Here again his views are not totally different from ours. Where we see the sinner and punish the guilty, he sees the innocent victim, a man of merit and sanctity, the living praise of his glory. Where we are convinced conditioned illness exists (and thus no sin), he knows the secrets of hearts which make us more or less liable. He alone knows where the real handicapped are. He holds them all in his love and all in secret render homage to him.

Because, in the final account, all are known to him through his well beloved Son, he sees them all in the one who suffered first, in him who bore all their sufferings, in him who though just was scorned and though innocent was condemned. Let us remember that in his suffering he has redeemed our sins. Mysteriously sometimes, sickness itself resembles sin in its appearance; sin in its turn sometimes breeds suffering and sickness. There is a strange kinship between suffering and sin because both are evils. There is also a strange union between them which grace seeks to overcome.

All physical and psychical "maladjustments" in effect cause suffering more or less. The mentally retarded one suffers. He only appears to be a "happy imbecile." The perverted suffer deeply in spite of their apparent indifference or their malice. There is no need to point this out in the case of the physically and mentally handicapped. St. Paul asked: "Are they not all 'able' to fill up in their flesh what is lacking in the passion of Christ for the sake of his body which is the church?" (Col. 1:24). All can then participate in the work of redemption. All can enter into the glory of Christ who conquered death and rose again.

To the degree then, small as it may be, that their maladjustment is the result of sin, their own or others, even the suffering which results from it is going to "assist" Christ in the remission of those same sins. Still more, whatever be its cause, suffering can link them to the mystery of the cross of Jesus Christ. With one stroke suffering can make them penetrate the mystery of the triumph over death by the God who is himself life. Finally isn't this a manifestation "par excellence" of the "Work of God" burst forth?

At last the light shines in the darkness and it is through the handicapped. In Christ, conqueror of evil, the first born among the dead, all have already returned to life and are "rehabilitated!"[74] Their triumph is also ours.

Those alone who flee the light, the voluntary blind will understand nothing of this mystery. "I have come," said Jesus," to bring about a distinction; those who did not see see and those who see become blind." God grant that in his plan of love for the handicapped we may not be those who refused to open our eyes. May God grant that enlightened by him and having gazed in that light at those whom he has entrusted to us, we may carry the light to them.

II
Some Possible Solutions

7

Understanding the Handicapped and Their Circumstances

If in education one has to "begin with the person ... and the ways he has been conditioned," whether he be child, adolescent or adult, what approach will be needed if the concern is Christian pedagogy or the religious formation of the handicapped?

To begin with the student is to start with knowledge of the person himself/herself and his/her situation. This orientation is essentially psycho-social, otherwise spoken of as two-dimensional, i.e., the psycho-physiological and the sociological. We can say even more simply that to begin with the person means to start with him/her as he/she is and with his/her milieu, taking these terms broadly. Starting with the "person himself/herself" presupposes that the educator himself/herself does the research utilizing both the information gained and his/her own observations. We have to insist on this research since it is the essential basis and condition for all the rest.

Reading psychology books is excellent, even necessary, if one wishes to take the knowledge of man, woman or child seriously. Unfortunately, educators, who are willing to submit to such serious systematic formation, are still few in number. More numerous are those who think they know "the principles of child psychology"[1] because they have read some popular book on the subject; that is somewhat useful but involves the risk of imparting dangerously inadequate and superficial information. Indeed, in order to approach child psychology and even more the study of the subconscious or various types of behavior, one has to possess a thorough knowledge of general psychology and principally of psycho-physiology. Yet how many educators are content to read a simple treatise on behavior or a "spicy" book on psycho-analysis without bothering to obtain a serious foundation in structural or "classic" elementary psychology?

Consequently and as a beginning, the child is classified in categories: age, character, temperament. In addition, all his/her complexes are probed. Still it must be considered fortunate when the educator, although an amateur in this work, does not utilize some instruments of observation; IQ tests, for example, even projective tests, from which he will draw definite conclusions. In the meantime, he forgets to observe the child!

Despite all this, pedagogy goes its own way: for each mental age experts have determined in advance the proper behavior and has drawn up an education program, a pedagogical "recipe." They decide beforehand what they must do for a child endowed with such and such a temperament. It is so convenient simply to open a drawer and to dispense pedagogy by means of automatic distribution: For this complex, use that system! You can imagine the results. And again, they do not always remember to watch the child.

Even moral pedagogy does not escape this fad: Such a precept at this age, not before; give such direction for this character type; take precaution to avoid emotional frustration; consult this or that expert. There is certainly some value in all this advice. But again, the child is overlooked.

When it's a question of a sick or handicapped person, the medical dossier is consulted. Alone, then in a team, the educators examine it: all aspects of the problem—the progress of the pregnancy, the date of labor, the first cry, the first tooth, the first word, first feeding. The electroencephalogram is used. The IQ test results receive special attention. A pedagogical prescription is discussed at length.

None of these approaches should really be disregarded. But again, who from the first has observed the child in a supportive and serious manner?

Let everyone understand clearly, once more, that we can never recommend enough the study of psychology to an educator, especially if he/she does it seriously and methodically. Never can we praise him/her enough for being willing to adjust his/her teaching methods to encompass what information about age, character, even "complexes" gives him/her, though this last word should be avoided unless it is used prudently and with discretion. (Real psychoanalysts use it less and less.) Never can we praise enough the effort made to think out a moral and religious pedagogy while taking into consideration the data in question, provided that delicate reserve accompanies the research and hasty conclusions are avoided. We cannot repeat too frequently that an educator (catechist or not), provided that he is a qualified specialist, must be able to consult the medical-psychological dossier of a student who is entrusted to him and to discuss it with a team to plan an appropriate pedagogical approach. We cannot insist enough that this pedagogical conduct must concern more or less the religious domain as well as the secular.

But at first hand, or at least at the same time, we have to learn to look at, to listen to, and to observe the child, the adolescent or even the adult. And let us fully understand the meaning of the word "observation." An observer is not someone behind a desk in the act of watching over a patient nor is he/she even a specialist, unseen or not, pencil in hand behind a glass.[2] He is simply one who lives with the child, knows how to observe him, how to hear him, and how to comprehend[3] him. But that is much more difficult than we generally think.

At the end of each year in our meetings with educators and psychologists, we admit our guilt here. We notice once again that we have not known well enough how to "observe" and that by this fact we deprive ourselves from the beginning of the most solid pedagogical foundations—especially when it is a question of the education of the handicapped.

It is the handicapped person—child, adolescent or adult—who more than any other escapes our investigation. Because we are absorbed by the particular difficulties that his/her education presents, we are in such a hurry to act that we forget to look at him/her and to listen to him/her. We do not know how to take the time to see and to understand—to seek to interpret.

That is why we sometimes systematically dedicate an opening session in religious instruction for the handicapped to nothing more than observing the child, allowing him/her freedom of expression, so he/she can be "himself/herself." Numerous means of expression are furnished her/him: finger painting or painting with a large brush on surfaces that the child decides for himself/herself (for which he/she has plenty of paper, even a roll, and if possible, different colors); modeling clay or potter's clay (but in large enough quantities that a child will not exhaust material in five minutes); pictures to look at and to choose, to cut out and to paste freely, various games, and if possible, bodily expression conceived in such a way as to give free rein to the imagination. All this, in a word, allows for choice and fosters initiative and creativity. And all this is done in an atmosphere of joy and confidence, which does not, however, mean total permissiveness. But this freedom is exercised in an pre-determined setting where everything is arranged to facilitate observation of the child, his/her limitations and certain inevitable "frustrations."

It is essential that the educator really know how to observe. Our experience, first of all personal and then the experience of others, has proven how very difficult this is. Some common exercises can help greatly. Repeating them allows for the opportunity to evaluate; they establish prescriptions for improvement. Small details can be important, and in a sense everything warrants notice. Yet, if that is impossible, it is better not to put aside the essentials. At the same time one should not abandon oneself to subjective choices. One-sided choices would not prove anything except what the observer wants to see. As has been noted, final interpretation is sensitive. Here especially one risks greatly subjective judgments projecting themselves; these the group can complete or rectify.

In addition, as we have said, the handicapped person is especially difficult to observe. This can be better understood if we say a few words about his/her psychological makeup.

While it is true that we must avoid unwarranted generalizations, it is no less true that some traits seem typical in the psychology of the handicapped. These traits have been extensively investigated with our students and collaborators for several years and are submitted here tentatively and are subject to a more systematic and scientific confirmation. We have also drawn upon some scholarly studies and numerous other, more popular texts.

Is there then a psychology of the handicapped? This question can be understood in two ways: First, does the handicapped person have a special psychology? Next, are there present some psychological traits that are common to all handicapped persons? Let us try to answer the first of these two questions.

Of course, handicapped persons do not differ radically from other human beings. A handicapped child, whatever his/her handicap, must be first and essentially considered as a child of his/her age, having the same characteristics of that age as well as a temperament like that of others, and lastly, his/her own individual personality. Special traits of the handicapped, where they exist, are only "accidents," only secondary modifications and sometimes passing phases. Handicapped or normal, such a boy or girl is six or thirteen years, has such or such emotional trends and finally has a unique and special personality.[4]

However, there is no doubt that a handicapped person presents special problems. This psychology of the handicapped can be understood and approached from three different angles. For example, let us take the case of a young tubercular patient: 1. From the viewpoint of the influence of the body upon the soul, the problem is to know if a certain toxin can have an immediate influence, or more probably, an indirect influence on his/her psychic life. It is hotly debated whether the toxin in question directly affects the nervous system or glandular equilibrium, especially the sexual glands, and also whether these glands can stimulate the appearance of certain behavior symptoms or even affect mental function. Today, this hypothesis, derived from the study of body chemistry in the last century, is losing ground to the new psychosomatic theories.

The one, however, is not diametrically opposed to the other; two perspectives can be simultaneously valuable. Indeed, it seems hardly debatable that somatic-psychic influences can be produced by malfunctioning of the endocrine glands (for example, in children with excessive or deficient thyroid, early puberty, Addison's disease, etc.). There is nothing here that should trouble a religious person, much less a Christian who believes in the union of the body and soul, in the influence of the body on the soul. It does not mean reducing the whole to an unjustified determinism impossible to measure in any way or wishing to tie such endocrinal secretions to a specific mental symptom.[5] The progress of science, moreover, encourages a moderate view. "One cannot attest that there is a relationship between a particular malfunctioning endocrine gland and a psychopathological case," as Caridroit wrote.[6] We see how ridiculous it would be to reduce all to a "question of glands," as some amateurs in psychophysiology do, or to declare, as one pseudo-medical journal did, that "the capital sins are illness as of the endocrine glands." But this same science is providing us in this perspective with a contribution whose importance we should not disdain.

2. The psychosomatic viewpoint (neither emphasizing nor denying the influence of the body on the psyche but bringing out the influence of the psyche on the body) has enriched the psychology of the handicapped. According to this view, illness is seen as a consequence of the "state of the soul" and at least to some degree conditioned by it, instead of illness being seen as the "cause" of this state of the soul or as conditioning it. Psychological disturbances appear (ontologically if not chronologically) as anterior to physical disturbances such as, for example, a tubercular lesion.

Hypotheses of antecedent affective frustrations, of flight, or of refuge in illness are being proposed and analyzed in some of the current literature. One cannot deny these interesting hypotheses, which help us to grasp, to some degree, the psychology of some sick and handicapped persons. They help to explain the strange correlation between the aggravation, or at times the improvement, of a person's condition. These hypotheses encourage further investigation, even back into someone's early childhood in seeking a partial explanation for their illness as well as their current attitudes.

The analyses of these states and the exact formulation of the theses should be left to specialists. It would be dangerous to become involved without being qualified. It seems preferable to probe less profound levels of the human psyche and to see the things from a perspective which in no way excludes the two previous perspectives. It presents them in a way easier to manage. 3. Thus there is also the viewpoint that we shall call reactional. It involves the "reaction" of the handicapped person to the conditions brought about by the disability or the circumstances that caused it. Using again the example of a tubercular lad: his illness stops him from work or study, limits his circle of companions, establishes him in a new world and by this fact makes him feel isolated, sometimes rejected, distressed about his future; it opens the door to depression and sometimes even to revolt. All this can lead him to suicide or to acceptance of illness on a spiritual level. It can lead to despair or resignation, or sometimes to an insane "mysticism," or on the other hand, to a real loving abandonment to God and his will that is not at all a denial of life.

Moreover, perhaps the somatic-psychic aspect is to be connected with the reactionary aspect. At least this is one of the stronger of the present hypotheses. It fits in well with the organodynamic mode of thought. To tell the truth the psychosomatic drive is equally reactionary in a certain sense. Illness or handicap can be considered as a defense against attack by the organism or against a danger with which the person does not feel otherwise prepared to cope. But it remains to explain why the person chooses such a means rather than a normal or "adjusted" response.[7] Is such a reaction inevitable? Or is it due to insufficient psychic strength? Does it differ with each individual? We return again to the hypothesis stated earlier when we spoke of possible responsibility for the onset or course of an illness.

Taking into consideration these three approaches which correspond to diverse aspects of the one reality (the psychology of the sick and the handicapped), can one not say at least that illness, and in general, disability is a reaction of the healthy part of the person against whatever exteriorly or even interiorly presents a threat? Isn't the psychological makeup of the handicapped individual a reaction, or an integrated part of this reaction, in which the person involves himself totally on the mental as on the physical plane, the one and the other being narrowly and reciprocally bound? This reaction varies then according to the personality of the individual and it bears his mark. In no way should it be mistaken for it. This reaction varies also according to the nature of the threat and the severity of its impact.

Before concluding this reactional aspect of the psychology of the handicapped, we must answer the second question: Is there a psychology common to all the handicapped?

Here again there are three parts to the answer. First of all it is evident that all handicapped people do not have the same psychology for that is precisely what we have just said: Whatever psychological traits may be common to these people are only accidental, secondary, and respect at least to some degree the characteristics of age, sex, temperament and individual personality.

Furthermore, among the great number of handicapped described at the beginning of this work, the causes of disability are very diverse. They differ in kind and in degree of handicap; they also differ according to the damage suffered, which can be either physical, mental or social. Even within these categories the variations will be very perceptible.

Again let us look at examples: A young polio victim will differ in his/her mentality from a cardiac or diabetic person. It is evident that sensory handicaps will act more forcibly than physical handicaps on the person's perceptual ability. The blind or the deaf-mute will differ more psychically from the "normal" person than one who is asthmatic ... unless the latter has a strong psychopathological element in his/her infirmity. But the deaf-mute will differ from the blind man, and one blind person from another according to whether he/she sees nothing (which is rare) or whether he/she has minimal sight. Then he/she is not blind but short-sighted; it is a question of degree. This is still truer for the retarded for whom the IQ will have importance. It is, however, relative and we must remember that mental retardation is not only a question of IQ. A retarded person is not simply an intellectual quotient, nor is he/she wholly retarded, but rather may be comprised of many unharmonious elements. He/she may present some outstanding gifts alongside of dire incapacity; in any case, be more developed in some ways than in others. This is even truer for a disturbed person. For as many behavior difficulties as exist, there are as many possible causes or "psychologies." Finally, it is equally true for the socially maladjusted, whether they be orphans, from broken families, rootless, with or without friends, delinquent or simply in danger of being delinquent, whether or not they have this or that character problem.

Third, it is evident that some causes of maladjustment are related. There are persons who are multi-handicapped. Unfortunately, a paralytic can be an orphan or blind. A deaf-mute can be at the same time retarded. A tubercular person can also have a cardiac affliction and belong to a separated or rootless family. Such cases are more frequent than we imagine.

This is why we can say on the one hand that there is no single psychology of the handicapped. On the contrary, there are among all these infinitely diverse persons as many mentalities, without doubt, as there are handicaps.

On the other hand, despite this affirmation and without denying it, we believe that there are, however, certain traits which are common to all mentally, physically, socially handicapped persons, traits which in a sense constitute "their psychology." Let us say at once that these traits will be found in any particular handicapped person only to a certain degree. Some "handicapped" people will seem to have been absolutely freed from these traits, or at least are on the way to losing them perhaps because of their rehabilitation.

We will outline here some of the important elements of the psychology of the handicapped. First, let us trace the negative elements of the picture by placing ourselves on the affective level. We will recall here a saying of La Palisse: "A maladjusted person is someone for whom something is lacking." At the least, he/she lacks "adjustment."

Is the person physically handicapped paralyzed? Then he/she lacks motor skills, the ability to provide for his/her own needs. Is he/she blind? Then he/she is lacking sight. Is he/she mentally retarded? He/she lacks intelligence. Is he/she an orphan? He/she lacks parents. Is he/she rootless? He/she is without a homeland or country. Finally, has he/she some character disturbance? Humanly speaking, he/she lacks being respectable, even-tempered, chaste. How has this affected him/her on an emotional level? A person is conscious of his/her deficiencies. Moreover, those around him/her play it back to him/her which makes him/her experience it more intensely. More deeply still, at the bottom of all of this, he/she feels a lack not only in "having" but also in "being." Isn't it easy to pass from that feeling to another? Because we lack something, we have the feeling of "not being worth as much" as other persons.[8]

From this lack there results a feeling of "inferiority" (though this may be a poor expression, as it has been used too often and it is liable to be confused with the complex). Let us rather say that the person experiences a feeling of poverty[9] (a feeling of what a person does not have compared with what he should have). He/she passes from a feeling of self-depreciation to a feeling of "no value" or the least value. It is useless to repeat that the feeling of least worth will be aggravated frequently by the attitude of society. We will return to this later.

The consequence of this feeling of having the least and especially of being of the least value are several. For the person himself/herself a feeling of insecurity,[10] the person feels himself/herself less strong, less "capable," then less sure of himself/herself. Face to face with others he/she has the impression of being less worthy of love, then less loved because less esteemed. We speak of a feeling of frustration which concurs with the theory of Fabienne Van Roy[11] concerning the paralyzed, but which holds good for all disabled, while avoiding the statement that it is the principal element of their psychology. Speaking of a feeling of abandonment, we could identify with the interesting classification of Germaine Guex[12] who distinguished among the abandoned some positive lovers and some negative aggressors. But instead of her explanation we prefer the following. There are two kinds of behavior which could result from these basic feelings, whether a behavior of flight or a behavior of search. First the behavior of flight: flight into space, a behavior of retreat from the world (withdrawal), turning back on self, introspection, escape in reverie, into fantasy (to the point of what one could call a mania for lying—mythomania) in an unreal environment that can make up the world of the handicapped, or "flight in time" with displays of infantilism, of settling into the maladjustment. These latter could explain the cases now better known as cessation of intellectual development, of motor responses, of physical growth or of regression in these different areas, and finally of retreat into maladjustment or even death.

There is on the other hand with others (or sometimes with the same persons, through alternating or ambivalent actions) a search for love which can be manifested by a clinging, sticky behavior well known to those who associate with them. Or there may be, on the contrary, an aggressive behavior against the world, against oneself or against both at the same time which can translate into a desire for vengeance toward an unjust and frustrating world or an awkward overcompensation (inferiority then can become a real "complex" as seen in the various works of Adler). Such a person has a will to have himself seen as valuable at any price by the "other" or the community. From thence come the violent and destructive forms of the search for love, the vow to capture attention at any price. This is the manner by which a handicapped person exploits his miserable condition or goes to the point of suicide or crime.

All of this can explain other negative characteristics of the handicapped. He/she can center in on his/her deficiency or illness. In some cases he/she refuses to care for himself/herself or to try to remedy his/her situation. He/she may find solidarity with other handicapped persons who share his/her jealousy and compensating disdain for the goodness and the happiness of the "adjusted."

From the perspective of dynamic psychology, one could also speak of a certain lowering of conscience with the weakening of the ego, a relaxing of self-control coupled with a rigid super-ego and an increase of defense mechanisms. From this there arises immature, even infantile, behavior among many handicapped persons, even adults, and also the phenomenom of affective transfer on the therapist or on any member of his/her group who is able to be a parent figure for the handicapped person and permit him/her the behavior here described.

All this can be aggravated, we must not forget, by deficiencies on the intellectual or scholastic level. In some cases of illness or disability, material or moral abandonment, repeated uprooting or simple displacement, the stages of development (set forth in the laws of Claparede), because exercise of certain functions was lacking, have been missed. There may have been delays and gaps in schooling so that certain skills were not acquired. There are often inconsistencies within the same person: maturity and infantilism, erudition and ignorance, extraordinary skills on certain points and on others almost total helplessness. And what can one say about the deprivation that is caused by poverty of environment, of close confinement, of instability of educational opportunities, and finally of inhibition of a person's means of expression?

From the moral point of view, the handicapped person will all too often appear as someone discouraged or desperate. Sometimes he/she is simply passive and timid, or "resigned," but he/she can also be bitter if not revolutionary, anti-social or withdrawn, "a waif "; a prey to doubt but turned in upon himself/herself and in fear of judgment; given sometimes to self-abuse through frustration; to proseletizing, exhibitionism or prostitution for compensation; losing himself/herself in the fictitious reassurance of alcoholism; or prone to taking delight in violence characterized by masochism or sadism.

From the religious point of view, the dominant negative trait in the psychological picture of the handicapped person could well be the feeling of not deserving even God's love, and then of being rejected or abandoned. This is where faith, hope and love are tested. These people can succumb to despair, revolt or passive resignation, even to pseudo mysticism, disordered into the worst eccentricities. A sentimental sadness could lead him/her to believe that he/she is a chosen victim and thus privileged. On the other hand, an emotional infantilism and the self-centeredness which accompanies it, can also be manifested on the religious level. Gaps in religious instruction can appear as denial of some aspects of dogma. This is the classic story of a young boy shuttled from one preventive shelter to another, from hospital to sanatarium, who had never heard of the Trinity . . . but has seen the catechism chapter on indulgences four times. We will speak of this latter. Religion can also constitute a refuge to which the handicapped person seeks to retreat in his desire to pull himself away from the reality of his ordeal. Religion can appear to him as a beautiful dream, a world apart, a place of escape from the "real" world. It is also in this religious domain that the guilt feelings noted earlier risk being intensified.

But let us end this sad picture and see the other side of the diptych. Thanks be to God who knows how to draw good out of evil, disability can give us some happy surprises. There are positive traits in the psychology of the handicapped.

In the emotional domain, the handicapped will often surprise us with a growing sensitivity that avoids unhealthy sentimentality. We may find extraordinary generosity, a spontaneity in his/her gift of himself/herself and the little he/she has—a precious offering that seems very genuine. His/her esthetic sense will often be refined and his/her maturity, as we have said, can contrast in a striking way with his/her infantilism. Discretion is necessary in dealing with these qualities, so as not to make a handicapped youngster a "victim," a hypersensitive person, or an "old man" or "old woman" before his/her time.

In the intellectual sphere the handicapped (as Claudel noted of the sick) are worthy of note for their capacity for observation, their remarkable memory, the faithfulness of their affections, their keen capacity for abstraction, their vivid imagination as well as artistic gifts developed with unusual vivacity and feeling. Here, too, one has to watch so as not to abuse these "compensations," for fear of leading someone to sheer memorizing, for example, or to a morbid rationalization.

Lastly, in the moral and religious domain, which interests us especially, the handicapped person will often display a very delicate sense of morality and an amazing depth of insight joined with an awareness of the sacred, of mystery and of symbol. His/her generosity can lead him/her to ardent piety, to gift of self in the service of others, even to total sacrifice in the service of God although this is often frustrated by the difficult problem of gaining admission to the priesthood or a religious community.[13] Here, too, even more than in the preceding domains, prudence is called for if one wishes to avoid fostering scruples and obsessions or else the "victim soul attitude" (to which we've referred), illusions in the areas of practical piety, extraordinary favors or special vocations.

But helping the handicapped to be open to all the invisible realities, to their capacity for recollection, contemplation, the fact that for them many trials can be the occasion of a true conversion of heart—these possibilities are difficult to deny. And they appear as so many beams of light in contrast to the depressing picture that we sketched earlier.

What then, in summary, are the "needs of the handicapped person"? The first essential need, it seems, is to be considered someone of "worth," the need to be understood and loved for what one is. It is only possible to respond to a need for security, the most basic need, in the measure that the need to feel "valuable," or better still, "of value," is met. Without this, all security will be precarious.

Loved for what he/she is, the handicapped person needs to be encouraged and approved for his/her efforts, his/her successes. But he/she also needs to be urged to surpass himself/herself, to try again in the face of failure—very simply, to face the obstacle from another side, to climb the mountain and to undertake the ascent in a different way, to make a new start.

On the community level the handicapped person has to see himself/herself useful and occupied. (How idle the life of some "shelters"!) He/she needs to take responsibility for himself/herself, to become more independent of others, and to feel that they depend on him/her. He/she has a basic need to be open to society which has something to give him/her, but he/she also has a need to feel welcomed, admitted and holding his/her place in it.

On the religious level, the handicapped person needs to discover the love of God for him/her, to be aware of the richness of grace, to be profoundly convinced of the victory of good over evil and of life over death. He/she must also understand the call to oblation and the invitation to praise. He/she has to discover the presence and the role of each member, and also his/her own, in the body of Christ that we call the Church.

This is the way we rejoin society once more. Society encompasses human beings from all sides and this applies even for the handicapped. It is true even when society scorns or crushes or simply "alienates" him. He depends on it and society itself depends on him more than it knows. That is why, besides knowing a handicapped person, one also has to know the social milieu in which he lives.

We will, however, insist little on this aspect of the question. Not that we do not recognize its importance, but because we touched some aspects of it in the first part of this work when we treated the handicapped in the world and in the Church today. We will, however, make a few remarks. The two basic environments in which handicapped people, especially handicapped youth, are located are the family and the institution that receives them.

We have said that parents of the handicapped are themselves often "deficient." We do not intend to go back over the controversial theories raised concerning hereditary factors or moral faults which are possible but more rare than one thinks. What we want to say is that no matter how excellent the parents may be, their pedagogy often leaves something to be desired. They are frequently too "harsh" or too "tender." They may demand too much of the child, not recognizing his/her limitations and consequently humiliating him/her. Or they do not expect enough; they "overprotect" him/her, exaggerate his/her limits, and by this attitude they also humiliate him/her.

We do not want to cite the guilt feelings mentioned earlier, but we do wish to add the understandable weariness that sometimes limits parents, the unfulfilled hopes, the domestic tensions, the sacrifices which weigh down the family life and budget, the somber future.

Let us mention the problems the handicapped child presents to the brothers and sisters at home. Will he/she be the "scapegoat" or, on the contrary, the "spoiled" child? In either case the situation will be difficult. Will the family life be saddened, deprived of celebrations and vacations because of him/her? Well he/she always be left behind, a Cinderella or little retarded Peter left at the edge of the garden the day of his/her oldest sister's wedding so that he/she will not make a bad impression on the guests or spoil the prospects of marriage for the younger sister?

These are unquestionably painful problems. At times the solution will be to entrust the handicapped person to an institution which will take him/her in hand. But isn't that a last course? In any event, a stay for a time in a special institution, if the place is duly qualified, may turn out to be favorable, even indispensable, for the good of the person concerned. Consider a young polio victim for whom rehabilitation is necessary; a mentally retarded child who must be awakened to life; or the disturbed child, the family tyrant, whom it would be worthwhile to exclude from the family circle at least for a few months.

For the handicapped person placed in an institution one must make allowances when studying his condition as he reacts to this new social conditioning. A new environment, by its structure and its spirit, can affect the handicapped person in many ways.

Unfortunately, in more than one case, the chief defect of such an environment is its artificial character. It is often too cut off from the world and its realities, and can reach a degree of isolation and unbelievable seclusion. Rehabilitation centers for the disturbed or delinquent, shelters for the mentally retarded, sanatariums high in the mountains can maintain young clients in a real "world apart." In almost all cases, life in an institution remains somewhat less than normal. Look at its architecture and its furniture; look at the absence of mixed company, at least in the case of France (and this is as unusual in the state as well as in the Catholic institutions).[14] There is meager association with the "outside" and little education for living in the world.

In response, a "new world" soon evolves. It has its rules, its vocabulary, its daily happenings. It calls for delicate and laborious initiation to understand the person who lives there. All education which does not take this into consideration is doomed to be ineffective, to be mere verbalism; and this is true especially of all moral and religious education.

Whether it is a question of the basic milieu of the handicapped or the new milieu in a specialized institution, we discover the insufficiency of knowledge gleaned only from sociology books, be they theoretical or practical. Still less can we be satisfied with social research designed in advance according to a fixed plan and actually kept in some medical psycho-social record.

Such records, however, have an importance which we would like to speak about.

We understand the gravity of confidentiality on this subject. We know that professional secrecy must be accorded to records of reports from psychologists and social workers. But we believe that this privacy must be extended as well to educators, especially if they are real professionals.

Privacy extended to the special educator means that such an educator hands over only under the shield of secrecy his/her observations about the child, information that he/she has obtained from conversations with the parents or visits to the family, and the conclusions he/she has reached after observation and reflection. All this must be surrounded with a respect at least equal to that given the reports of the physician, social worker or psychologist.

But this also means that in return an educator must be able to share in the above-mentioned secrecy to the degree that he/she must be able to consult the medical-psycho-social records as do the other members of the team. Moreover, we know that this is being done more and more. How much an educator benefits from these documents in shaping his/her activity! From a negative point of view, how many blunders would have been avoided if he/she had been warned about delicate points, alerted not to making certain gestures, informed about language that would be unwise?

The catechist, if he/she is a special educator or has been taught something about such education, and the priest, provided that he has at least the necessary competence or even desirable special qualifications, should equally be admitted to this shared secrecy.[15] Religious training, indeed more than any other kind of education, presupposes the most complete knowledge of the person. Here more than elsewhere, the educator needs guidance, needs guidance to adjust, to avoid errors, and the blunders are always possible.

But, as we have said, this admittance to professional secrecy presupposes a confidence and presupposes competence. To study a medical record, psychological test results, social details on the family life of a person, or to read a case history or observations from special educators—all this demands serious initiation supported by a solid basic training. For one who does not have such competence, such records could rapidly cause a loss of interest or could be responsible for serious mistakes. His/her teaching abilities would not be improved but rather hindered. The remedy would be worse than the evil, since sometimes a little knowledge can be more dangerous than total ignorance.

If he/she does lack such competence, two solutions are envisaged: either a member of the professional team, sufficiently prudent, can give interested but unqualified religious educators the maximum—and not the minimum—information they can assimilate. Again this would be done in secrecy. This would be the short-term solution.

For the long run a more satisfactory solution should be found and prepared. Everyone would have to know the basic information and explain it to the new members of the team. But here, again, we come back to some problems raised about the qualification of priests and personnel more specially charged with religious training. These lead us to forsee the question of the personnel available.

Before discussing such a topic, we would like to recall a truth as essential as it is forgotten in our day: the behavior of a person, the coordination of age, sex, temperament, or character, the social influences that he experiences, or which he exercises—all that is not enough to determine his personality. Above all, it does not say much about his person.

For us Christians, or more simply, those who believe in spiritual values, the "person" is unique and inexpressible. We say the person is certainly something more than an interesting assembly of his/her characteristics. He/she is neither the product nor the sum of them.

This is very important for us to remember, especially we who are in frequent contact with handicapped persons, we who leaf through the reports and share in staff meetings.

Here, again, the living child will save us, provided that we do not forget him/her, that we keep in touch with him/her, especially that we maintain a profound sense of his/her mystery.

This living child will save us all if we think about him/her, contemplate him/her for a long time and deeply before God, if we see him/her in his light, if we ask God, who himself knows him/her from all eternity and loves him/her, to help us commune from within with his own love and his wisdom.

8
The Setting and the Team: Providing a Climate

In the first part of this book, we considered the importance of the climate in which religious formation takes place and of the personality of the educator appointed to this mission. That is why we now consider the setting and the administrative team.

Problem of setting: the discoveries of modern psychology have sufficiently brought out the importance of affective life in the total development of the person and, consequently, in his education. Without doubt direct educational programs will be exercised with more or less effectiveness to the degree that the climate is more or less favorable, just as a plant will grow and flourish so much better and will benefit from the gardener's care if the climate in which it is planted is more or less favorable to its development. One can even say certain attitudes will or will not be adopted by the child as the climate fosters them or is unfavorable to them. Certainly, some attitudes will be adopted passively, in a certain measure at least, and will have to make place progressively for more spontaneous reactions. But the climate, initially at least, will not have had less importance.[16]

We have also said that this climate ought to be made up essentially of blessed and fraternal charity. We have underlined elsewhere the importance of a setting of beauty and of certain "richness" of environment indispensable for awakening the interest of the child and causing him/her to immerse himself/herself in the lesson. Lastly, we have insisted on the positive spirit, the joy which must animate every educational undertaking, but more especially, special education.

One has indeed to acknowledge that at least at the beginning the "handicapped" are often the least favored from this viewpoint. Speak of the climate of the sacred and think, for example, of the setting in which religious education of our young handicapped often unfolds. It may be the hospital room where one has to catechize while nurses empty urinals or take temperatures, or the chaplain bringing Communion must step aside to avoid being splashed by an orderly mopping the floor. Speak of a climate of fraternal charity and then think of the frenzied individualism which sometimes reigns around a homeless child or the disputes he/she witnesses—household quarrels between parents, bloody brawls in his/her neighborhood, tensions of fierce jealousies within the institution where he/she lives. Speak of a climate of beauty and think of this chapel in the institution cluttered with painted statues and filled with electric lights and artificial flowers. Speak of a "rich" milieu and recall the bare walls of a room in an orthopedic clinic and the paved courts of an institution for deaf-mutes. Or again, speak of an atmosphere of joy and recall the parlors of the orphanage decorated only with a plaque commemorating the founders and benefactors or the portrait of some solemn ecclesiastics. . . .

How can we change these conditions? At one and the same time we must do very little and very much.

A religious, administrator of an institution, told us recently, in speaking of the frightful plaster statues mentioned earlier: "Indeed, we could remove them . . . but then what? They can no longer be resold or even given away (Thank God!) and I cannot bring myself to pulverize them." This is very probably the only solution—and moreover a work of devotion to be accomplished bearing in mind the contribution made to the glory of God and his saints by suppression of veritable caricatures which discourage true piety if they do not provoke scandal. As we have already noted, the reactions of the faithful to modern sacred art should have been accompanied by reactions at least as violent against the bad taste which (in France) is called "Saint Sulpice." There are, moreover, two documents on this subject: a certain encyclical[17] and a directive for the Mass[18]. . . .

Regretfully, they are read only halfway as is the lot of many texts of this kind.

It is necessary then to destroy bad art at times and more rarely to replace it. Such changes will sometimes be complete and decisive, but at times progressive and cautious. One can repaint the walls of this too somber room with a few strokes to make it more joyous, toss into the fire that tasteless color print—even its gilded frame—and replace it by a picture in a simple frame.[19] If the hospital is not too anticlerical, one could ask the orderly to clean the neighboring room while Communion is being given in this one. One could find a calmer time than that of medical care or of visiting hours to hold a catechism lesson. But the real climate of the sacred, and still more that of charity, can only be established or restored from day to day. It is laboriously done and never definitively nor with certainty that such an atmosphere has been created. Indeed, it is not a question, then, of painting a wall or replacing a picture; it is a question of men and women whose hearts must be renewed day after day in their very depths. It is a question of living beings called by the free gift of God's grace who free themselves to refuse or to correspond with it. That is why one passes inevitably from the "setting" to the "team."

*   *   *

We are not going to give another list of the different persons around the handicapped since we have already devoted several pages of this book to such a list, but we shall now ask the question: "Who has charge of the Christian education and the religious training of the handicapped?" After having tried to answer that, we shall see what are the qualities to be desired in those responsible for religious training.

Who has charge of the religious instruction of the handicapped? The only possible answer is the following: "All those far or near who have some relationship with them." We have said that Christian education concerns the total life of man/woman in all his/her doings.

None can be uninterested, at least not those who share the same faith or who have some esteem for spiritual values. From the maid who makes the bed of the sick child and cleans his/her bed table to the department head or the director of the institution who operates it, each one bears some responsibility for this Christian education in the broad sense of the term. Even if they are not involved in the direct religious formation of the child, all those around him/her influence his/her total Christian education. Their witness, even the silent witness of their lives, will have an effect on him/her in one way or another. The handicapped person will reflect in these influences. Psychological mechanisms of identification or opposition will be set in motion. An intuitive grasp of the subconscious itself will lead the handicapped person to take one or the other stance of approval or disapproval, acceptance or refusal. Neutrality is not possible in this regard for neutrality is not neutral. Even taking a position of indecision also exercises influence.

But a more complex problem is that which we call religious formation in the strict sense of the term.

Here responsibilities are shared. We recall presidents of administrative councils distressed, and rightly so, that catechism and the sacramental life of hospitalized handicapped persons in institutions under their charge had not been properly provided, due to neglect by the local administrators or the lack of a priest. For it is a fact that this situation should bind them in conscience. On the other hand, we think of the nursemaids, remarkable women and devoted to their patients but scarcely practicing Catholics, who in a sanatarium for children all but deprived of priestly service, taught catechism to young boys, who never had received instruction because they were unable to read by themselves.

All the same, a still more delicate question is asked: "Who is primarily responsible for the supervision and instruction of religious formation?" We recall that in principle the Church states this formation must be provided principally by the parents, then later by the clergy, religious and lay catechists. Should the parents at this point feel excused from further responsibility? Quite the contrary!

When a child is handicapped, the parents, for reasons already pointed out, are brought to call on specialists because of the particular difficulties that the education or training of their child presents or because the child is sent to an institution away from home and family.

However, let us say that it is always very desirable, if not indispensable, that here again parents consider the all-importance of their role. First of all, it is on them that the responsibility for the possibility and practice of religious instruction for their children rests. When placing a child in an institution, Christian parents have to request catechetical instruction and religious participation for the child. In case of refusal, it is for them to alert the ecclesiastical authorities and courageously take steps by confronting the administration responsible for that institution. Their right and that of their child is sacred. To defend it for the good of their own child and for that of others is a duty. . . . (Alas! too many forget this right and duty and simply "take the atmosphere of the house" as it is.) After the child has entered the institution, the parents must be kept informed on this point as on others. Their solicitude cannot be limited to overwhelming him/her with gifts on First Communion day. . . .

If the child lives in the family, the mother (and equally the father) will have an important role in his/her training. Typically, given the lack of concern for the handicapped child in almost all of our parishes, it is often at the family level and within the home that at least a rudimentary religious education is provided for the child. It would be desirable even in this case that the activities of the parents be followed up by those of special educators and of priests. An interparish catechism class like the one established in Paris in 1956 and at Lyon the following year could assuredly give appreciable aid to these children. But this plan also calls for the support of and cooperation of the parents.[20]

Where the handicapped person is hospitalized, we ought to ask who replaces the parents in this new setting. We have seen that in principle at least this was the role of the special educators. It would be up to them to do this and in accord with the parents where they exist. It would be the educators' responsibility to cooperate with the priest in providing religious training for handicapped youth. It is an integral part of their role.

Let us recall that it is important to distinguish between religious instruction strictly speaking, which requires that one be in close contact with the priest, the chief guardian of doctrine (but not its only dispensor), and the total Christian formation, which is the responsibility of the entire institution, since each staff member, regardless of role, ought to feel this responsibility.

However, it is not only for the priest but initially or in the absence of the chaplain for the special educator as substitute for the parents to care for and to feel principally responsible for the catechical instruction of the handicapped young people assigned to them. We have said "initially" or "in the absence of the chaplain." What do we mean by that?

We mean that where parents would not think of it by themselves, it is the responsibility of the educator to pose the question of the religious education of the person entrusted to him/her. Silence on the parents' part does not equal indifference nor still less, refusal. On the other hand, all "pressure" would be blamable and besides unwise.

Unfortunately, some institutions for the handicapped, theoretically or practically, are deprived of a priest. The special educator is then regarded as having a role like the catechist in a mission land. He/she compensates for the absence of the priest, trying to do his/her best by keeping contact with the priest and from afar, having activities directed by him.

Some substitutions could be envisioned in such a case. The special educator, as we have defined him/her, may not exist in the institutions. Then it would be up to the personnel to assume this office along with the chaplain and take charge of the catechetical formation. Perhaps the special educator is entirely incapable of doing this (we will speak of this aspect further on) either because he/she does not belong to the same religion or thinks he/she really cannot be called a believer. This attitude must certainly be respected so as not to cause scruples. Finally, perhaps catechists must come from outside, but this in principle should not dispense the staff from playing their role. In two instances, however, outside catechists can be partially justified: the first, when in the pretext of neutrality however poorly understood, the institution refuses its personnel the right to participate in the religious formation of the residents; second, when for instance in a rehabilitation center the young delinquents would in principle be opposed to the resident staff. "Religion" would then risk an unpleasant identification with established authority and with disgrace.

The problem of religious formation is not limited, of course, to children and adolescents. It also concerns handicapped adults. And not only does religious instruction in some cases start at zero, it must often fill the gaps and complete a basic formation. The instruction, in more ways than one, must be accompanied by a real spiritual formation, even by an initiation into ascetical life which the handicapped adult often desires.

Here again the clergy are overburdened or unavailable and the lay catechists have to be assiduously prepared and formed. What a wonderful work could be done if more people were willing to involve themselves in responding to the needs and appeals of the handicapped adult.

A word on the subject of religious personnel: the responsibility of religious in institutions for children and adolescents, infirm adults, and the handicapped in general, seems to us to be, indeed, a serious obligation. Isn't it painful to admit that the religious formation in these institutions is often neglected or hindered when the religious who staff them are busy with material tasks, however indispensable, meaningful and important? Isn't it upsetting that these tasks deprive religious of giving eminently relevant witness to their commitment?

Without doubt, in some cases, the fault lies with "totalitarian" chaplains. But don't we also find religious astonishingly indifferent, or so it appears, to these serious questions or else declaring themselves incompetent to handle them? Would that they would recognize their responsibility in this regard and get to work to prepare themselves to face up to them?

*   *   *

Parents, special educators, catechists of the handicapped in parishes or institutions, priests and religious—specialized or not—what can one ask of them? Let them be willing, joyous, zealous, fraternal, and competent.

Let them be joyous so that they show the handicapped child this "positive" mentality, this spirituality of resurrection to which we have referred in this book. Let their face and their tone of voice reflect this deep spirituality. The handicapped child, the adolescent, and the adult may keep only the impression of joy and its radiance in his/her heart after the activity is over. Without wishing to make religious formation a birthday party or entertainment, isn't it natural to have it be truly joyous inasmuch as it brings faith and happiness to humanity?

Let them burn with zeal. We have just mentioned faith. Let them work without strain and without artificiality, without hindering the inner spirit from being manifested even bodily. If they do not know how to express themselves, let them learn "expression" and let them banish the sort of foolish modesty that insists on keeping cool even when one is burning within. Finally, if they do not have this burning zeal, either in deed or work or in depth, let them demand the Spirit of Love from their Father.

This Spirit of Love will summon them also to be fraternal. Here again, it has to be witnessed. Others have to feel that priests and the specialists, whether they be parents, teachers, or simply catechists, love each other. All disputes, if not banished, ought at least to be expressed outside the presence of children and adolescents, especially at the time of preparation sessions or at staff meetings. But it is absolutely essential that these sessions take place regularly and that adequate time be allotted to them at any cost. It is here that the team gets to know each other, to understand each other, to complement each other and consequently to appreciate and love each other and strengthen their common bonds. Here they propose new programs and reflect upon them together before making them part of personal prayer.

It is during these same meetings that formation, which at least in part assures competent educators, can take place. Here again competence is necessary. This competence is twofold: first, parents, educators, catechists of the handicapped have to be formed in a theology of revelation; second, parents, catechists and priests must have a psychological formation and know the fundamental principles of the pedagogy of the handicapped.

Such sessions can furnish this to a certain degree. The meeting on the one hand of priests, who know theology and Scripture but too often lack background in psychology or orthopedagogy, and on the other hand, of special educators who know their profession but too often do not know theology or Scripture, can be extremely profitable for both of them, on the condition that both parties be attentive and open-minded and admit the existence of two aspects of the same reality and the diverse elements of the same problem. It is necessary to insist that priests, especially chaplains in institutions, be better informed in general psychopedagogy and pathology. And all special educators ought to receive a theological formation and catechetical pedagogy.

Volunteers also are too often ignorant of theology, special psychopedagogy and catechetical pedagogy. So they have to receive basic formation through appropriate lectures, through contacts with their co-workers, or by a combination of the two. It is only with this investment that they will be able to acquire relative competence.

In this matter, who then would pretend to be competent? We have said that competence must be at the service of love, as love without competence can only be pseudo-love. It is love finally, love for the handicapped, love wholly understood, that causes one to give him the best. This love to the degree that it animates the "team" will "create the climate."

If only the handicapped person could feel himself/herself loved and be truly loved. Such love would already constitute a religious formation where all other means would fail, even in the case of a very disturbed or severely retarded person. . . . But if such love does not exist, does not show itself, all climate will remain without effect and all catechetics will be in vain. "If I have not love," said St. Paul, "I am only a sounding gong. . . . " But if I have love I will be able to try all things . . . "techniques," for instance, which we will discuss in the next chapter.

9
Utilizing Techniques
of Expression

Many harsh things have been said about techniques. . . . And we understand quite well that one has to speak harshly about such matters. . . .

First, some confuse them with method; others think that techniques alone suffice: they have forgotten the spirit that must animate them.

Techniques are not "participative methods" in themselves. Still less are they participative pedagogy in the real sense of the word. To have a child color a picture is an exercise: that may have nothing to do with participative methods or pedagogy. Let us recall that there is participative pedagogy only in the measure where there is active cooperation and even initiative on the part of the student in the work of his/her own education. One can certainly use techniques passively. The child who copies a picture or cuts out wreaths according to a pattern is scarcely more active than the child who formerly recited his catechism lesson to the parish ladies. Perhaps he/she makes something more attractive but that is not the fundamental question. Unfortunately, some authors who confuse participative pedagogy with techniques believe that it is.

More dangerous still would be utilizing techniques while forgetting the spirit which should animate them. This danger is not unreal. How many educators have we not seen who put activities end to end without ever grasping the link that should bind them? How many children absorbed in making a design or a model have thought nothing about the purpose or the meaning of their work!

Techniques can be an excellent means but they are not the only means! That we should never forget.

*   *   *

But what use are these techniques in religious formation? We have to examine that now. Then we shall see how to use them and which techniques to use.

First, techniques are a means of expression for the handicapped. We have noted before how interesting it is to furnish a person with ways of expressing himself. Such techniques of expression open up a person, reveal him/her to himself/herself and reveal him/her to us while permitting us to know better who and what he/she is. They allow him/her to triumph over feelings of self-depreciation and give him/her a sense of his/her own value in the good sense of the word. Such techniques are, or at least can be, channels or vehicles of sociability facilitating exchanges with others. Finally, they offer him/her the chance of self-affirmation and "cause something" which responds to a fundamental need of any human being, in particular of a child.

Finally, on a loftier and religious plane when the handicapped person has created something, he/she is aware that this is part of himself/herself and he/she can make it return to God. He/she can, as we have said, dedicate it to him.

Here is an example: John, a retarded boy of twelve, has just been presented a short lesson on baptism. We invite him to tell what has struck him the most. (This can be told in child's language: see this paper, paint, clay, etc.) "Will you show what you have found the most beautiful in all that Father has said?" John chose to model in clay a child who had been carried to the baptismal fount. This is evidently elementary and a bit ordinary. But John is proud of his work. He explains the meaning of it. He probably identifies with the newly baptized.[21] Now he takes his little model into his hands. Accompanied by his catechist or perhaps by the priest, he enters the chapel holding in his hand his modest masterpiece; he ascends the altar and places it there. It is a little bit of himself that he holds and returns to God. By this the catechist can aid him to make this gesture as meaningful as possible.

The "technique" in all this is certainly simple but one can grasp, nonetheless, its full significances. It will have provided not only an occasion to observe the child, to verify his knowledge and his accompanying explanation, but also a profound assimilation, a movement of the whole being toward God, which is indeed our essential purpose.

*   *   *

The question is asked: If the purpose is all that counts how useful is the stress on technique? Some would go as far as disdaining it, as considering it dangerous in any case. That is not our opinion.

Without doubt we think that nothing should be exaggerated regarding the "perfection of technique." This would be excessive and at times is carried to extremes: one should not have a person design or paint freely without several years of previous apprenticeship; one should not have him/her use bodily expression without lengthy physical training. There are several dangers here: for example, that of insisting much more on the finished product than on its meaning; that of stifling spontaneity which is invaluable (even aesthetically); that especially of expecting too much from physically and psychically handicapped persons who are unable to do something or only able to do it very slowly. And must we then demand that catechists, of whom we have already asked so much, to now become "technicians" and artists?

But, on the other hand, one should not disdain the importance of methodology, even its absolute necessity. How can a child express himself/herself with a paint brush if we do not first teach him/her to wash the brush with a little water poured on the paper and to avoid mixing the colors by going from one paint pot to the other? Very often retarded people do not realize this. How can this child cut and paste if we have never taught him/her long and patiently to follow the edge of the pattern, at least approximately, with a scissors, or to press so that the glue sticks firmly? What about this young girl who is called on to use bodily expression in some liturgical celebration? Will she not go to God more freely, and in a sense more fully and truly, if previous exercise has prepared her to be totally involved in her gestures?

On the other hand, will the handicapped person not be happier, more accomplished when the expression is less perfect? When he/she is no longer a child, he/she is often conscious of and bored with the imperfection of his/her production and even risks being inhibited thereby.

Lastly, certain technical details are simply indispensable to avoid mishaps with which we must always be concerned—the disorder in group movements which degenerates into hubbub at the most solemn moment, or the fire that starts because the handling of the candles or the vigil lights has been poorly planned ahead of time . . . or, still more common and less dramatic but all the same irritating, the foolish laugh or outcry that so sharply damages appreciation when the slides were poorly arranged for a showing . . . or the poorly designed poster that arouses more disapproval than admiration or interest.

Here is where we see some teachers giving up and limiting themselves to using restricted and poorer means of expression which are judged to be easy and without possible disruptions. They are forever making little sketches with black crayons or pictures that they arrange or cut out from magazines to paste.

It is necessary to supply these teachers with a maximum number of high quality techniques. Practical workshops are organized here and there. Schools for special education have programs of methodology which seem to us totally insufficient on the whole. But it is in the *practicum* that one learns the practical details that we have mentioned: how to organize so that outcomes harmonize without being hemmed in or restricted; where to situate oneself in the room; how to arrange tables and chairs to avoid confusion; how to manage the lighting; how to avoid causes of distraction. One can hardly believe that even intelligent and respected teachers could blunder in these areas and not know how to take the most elementary precautions, omission of which could destroy the whole day.

The use of techniques by teachers or by students requires a simplicity and simplification. We will explain.

A certain simplicity: every person has need of expressing herself/himself, yet he/she fears self-expression and feels embarrassed, paralyzed by a kind of modesty when he/she speaks about himself/ herself. Social restraints, especially the conventions of our society, operate against us here. But there is also in us, whether of social origin or not, some mysterious resistance of which depth psychologists, not without reason, speak. To conquer this resistance, to conquer it in oneself and in others—this is not easy to achieve. Furthermore, it must be done with great delicacy and tact especially if it is a case of a sick person and still more if a disturbed or nervous person. Isn't one of the traits of these last two the existence in the psyche of a sort of barrier which generally can only be eliminated by the subtle skill of a forewarned and prudent psychotherapist?

One has to consider also certain temperaments such as schizothymic[22] for whom this question is more harmful than others as in the case of a syntonic personality. There are also some stages where the person more easily bends back in on himself/herself experiences in a greater degree than at other times. This is the case, for example, with adolescence.

Above all, let us say that real simplicity can only be found at the end of a long and laborious process. In a sense we are not born "simple" but we must become so and that implies real growth. In a word, simplicity is obtained by "simplification" which can be arduous and painful.

Simplification is nothing other than the self-denial and renunciation which form the base of the Gospel. Because it is correlative with poverty of spirit, self-mortification and self-giving, simplification searches for the essential and, at the same time, discards the accessory in favor of what is primary, sees means in relation to their end, accepts the periphery as it relates to the center. This begins with the educator himself/herself. It demands of him/her a psychosomatic unity, a harmony of his/her total self, an obedience of the inferior to the superior in the hierarchy of his/her faculties, beginning with his/her organs and his/her muscles. . . .

In order to give oneself, to express oneself logically, one has to be in possession of oneself. That calls for quite an asceticism. Thank God that he never asks the impossible of us. Nor does he ask all that is possible in one stroke or before there is readiness. . . . Expression itself can be simplifying, and that is why one need not be perfect in the beginning.[23]

Now, what techniques should one use? We think that under the conditions just described all techniques could be valuable. We will enumerate only some of them and comment on how to use them in the area of religious formation of the handicapped. For the "normal" the list in question and their instruction would not be very different. Moreover, for each of these techniques we foresee some use by the teacher and some used by the handicapped person.

From the start we would have liked to set up a hierarchy of values among the different ways of expression or techniques, but this is not at all easy. It is no less true that a level of value is imposed and that the making of little men from wire is not to be put on the same level as music, nor bodily expression compared to the technique of paper tearing.

A classification of ways and means of expression that one in a wide sense can call "technique" follows: *Techniques or modes or means of expression*: 1. verbal; 2. graphic; 3. pictures; 4. modeling; 5. gestures; 6. music; 7. audio-visual; 8. an assemblage of several skills.

Verbal Means

The spoken word is only one way of expression among others. However it remains a preferred means. That is why, while knowing that other means often abandoned, can replace or complete it, we would err greatly and lose very much by neglecting its use.

It is often said that one must weigh and use words sparingly. That is particularly true in religious pedagogy and truer still when it is a question of retarded or handicapped persons. Too many words weary them; some words shock them. So one has to prepare carefully what to say, say it soberly (which does not mean in a terse manner), choose the right word and highlight it by speaking softly, without affectation, repeating without going so far as to bore the listener and not being hesitant or verbose.

That is difficult and requires lengthy previous reflection, a setting of self-confidence and relaxation, and a quiet, attentive atmosphere. Never begin in a hubbub, nor before being in place. Put yourself in the light, but not against the light, and in such a way as to be seen by all eyes.

The tone of voice also carries great importance. It should be pleasing without being juvenile, joyous without giving the impression of slapstick, convincing and at times even enthusiastic, but always it should be set then and there in a calm and "religious" tone.

A good way to establish the proper atmosphere is to precede one's words with a record of beautiful and meditative music. This, however, should not become a "gimmick," and on the other hand, one must know how to move in calmly at the right moment and take his place without disturbing the listeners so as to begin to speak at the precise moment when the melody ends and silence reigns.

It is useful to remember that the choice of words must take into consideration the vocabulary of the listeners and the extent of their knowledge of the subject; inappropriate words, especially those which unleash laughter or disturbance because they are associated with certain situations or ideas in the listeners' milieu, should be avoided. That is why the speaker must have a knowledge of the psychological and social dimensions of his listeners, of their milieu and of their daily life. Finally, remember "to speak is to say something to someone," as our old professor of speech always advised.

Types of verbal expression appreciated by young audiences are commonly the story, tales or anecdotes separate from a speech but which serve to illustrate a point. Books have been written on story telling. It is not our intention to treat the subject here. But we wish to recall that in religious material the story must not be burlesque, nor lose itself in detail and colorful description, nor dissipate the attention to make it more exciting and picturesque at the expense of the central idea.

Under these conditions the story interests us first and it is a very evangelical mode of expression. It might present an account of the life of Jesus or a parable which then could be repeated in formal reading, in a more sacred place and manner.

Reading generally is hard to manage; it easily risks being too long, little adapted, and it wearies listeners quickly. Good readers are rare. However, a reading well done pleases most handicapped people and especially adolescents and adults. Even retarded persons will know how to appreciate reading when the text is beautiful as in music, even though they sometimes do not understand the exact meaning of the words.

Lastly, verbal expressions generally have the advantage of not being used in a one-sided fashion. We mean that a talk, even when it is short and involves story telling, includes the possibility of dialogue. The speaker must be careful here not to lose control of the group. He should not let children answer all at once or shout out pat answers, religious clichés, which generally correspond to one's own ideas or simply to our "fads." Equally, it is important not to be lulled by the impression that all have understood because one or two of the group give intelligent answers. One also must highlight the ideas of those who express themselves more timidly or awkwardly. Sometimes one has to go as far as seeking an answer from their lips if need be, then finally resuming the dialogue while reestablishing calm and if need be a reverential climate in such a way that the listeners derive something clear, coherent and positive.

Even reading can be interrupted for questions. That is a way of holding their attention and avoiding drowsiness.

But above all, dialogue will be of most value in individualized religious education. Small groups—we shall speak of this again—can foster intimate exchange. Obviously they should not end in extorting confidences from persons who have entrusted themselves to us. But neither must we let the opportunity pass for students to express themselves nor fail to answer their real questions. These deep needs will be manifested sometimes in a very clumsy manner. A slow learner lacks words; a spastic puts forth a great effort to articulate them; an inhibited, disturbed or autistic child scarcely uses them; even a child deprived of a normal family setting is sometimes turned in on himself and becomes timid and paralyzed. A receptive, patient attitude is necessary. One has to think that most of the words used have meaning even if for us it remains hidden. Modern psychologists have taught us that "slips of the tongue" and free associations have deep roots in the subconscious and have unusual vibrations. Be very prudent before declaring that what has been said lacks significance. It may for us but not for them.

What works could we not do if we took time to listen to humble little ones? And if our answers were real answers . . . ? But we are so often distracted, filled with ourselves, and so far from others.

Graphic Expression

The written word best expresses the value of the word. Even retarded person who do not read or write prove this. How many times have we not seen profoundly retarded, totally illiterate people tell us: "Write your name for me," then eat the little piece of paper on which our name has been written! Thus they are identifying us and identifying themselves with the written symbol. Don't they demonstrate in their own way the meaning attached to the "written word"? Still others spend hours in recopying or simply tracing in ink or red crayon words written by their teacher. This is not only mechanical. We never know how these persons, unable to write or to read, perceive the value of words.

Written expression can be either private or collective. The personal diary is private. Do not look for one that is all done and complete for each child creates his/her diary and it "creates" him/her. Ask each one a suitable question and suggest gradual, graded activities. One can also make use of some practical written tests in the area of religious formation. But a judicious choice must be made and the directions respected.

There are many means of individual or small group graphic expression; for example, one can have a retreat notebook; one can gather sacred texts into a booklet, a Bible in miniature destined for the person or his/her small group. Finally one can have a personal Mass book, assembling in it simplified and illustrated texts. For a group activity, graphic expression can involve pictures and posters. This is an activity that almost always pleases those who do the work.

The poster, in principle, summarizes an event, illustrates it and announces it for a whole week or month. It is made up of a key sentence that the educational team has looked for, enlarged or even meditated on. This sentence can be from the Gospel but it could be taken from a song or be entirely original and newly fashioned. This sentence must be, as much as possible, an affirmation, and it should have at least a subject and a verb. The more dynamic it is and easy to read, the better it will be. We would readily add that it must be "well balanced."

Sometimes a sentence suffices for a good poster, especially when letters are well made and legible.

Does one have to say that such a poster must be large enough so that it can be easily read from afar? The designs or photos used as illustrations must stand out enough to strike the reader, interest him and attract him from a distance. One should not make a poster without stepping back many times to evaluate it.

The handicapped themselves, especially adolescents but also the very young, are able to work together on the making of such large posters, panels and murals. At the end of the session all will see everyone's work or even take it up again at the beginning of the next session. The poster especially is an important means to support and illustrate a speech, story or dialogue. It will polarize—without excess—and will unify activities.

The poster can also be a simple element for individual work. Some handicapped people will copy it into their notebooks. Others will transpose it according to their taste. One can go closer to the poster and have a little colloquy. Finally, by the way in which it is illustrated, it can serve as a point of departure for painting or sculpture and even for expression in gestures. Also what has been made can be taken for a celebration and used in a liturgy.

Pictorial Means

Let us repeat what we have said in the introduction to this chapter: painting, designing, or carving are only some means to be used. But still these means have to be sufficiently bright and "rich." They should be attractive and permit freedom of expression.

The choice of materials therefore has some importance. They have to be inexpensive and beautiful. To require these two at the same time is less difficult than one might think. The materials have to be cheap so that the handicapped are not stopped in their expression by restrictions on paper or paint. At the same time the paper has to be strong enough, varied in color and attractive, and the paint must be of bright colors, easily spread and of suitable consistency. In addition, have good, strong paint brushes, some sufficiently wide but also others that allow for fine work. As for crayons one knows that they are relatively "poor means" and scarcely allow for any true expression. It is especially for their own peace of mind that educators use them; they are less messy and soiling!

Yet, colored crayons are better than simple black pencil—unless the children, warped by school, absolutely insist on it. Let us banish rulers and erasers, the color books and tracing paper, little squares to fill in—anything that brings into the class canned art or makes expression more artificial.

Teachers of the handicapped especially should know how to

appreciate and to approve what their pupils can do, not automatically and as a general rule, but with gradual praise and some discernment. And let teachers remember that the purpose of this is not the creation of an artistic work but rather the expression of moral or religious feeling, the manifestation of an attitude of soul before a transcendent reality. Symbolism, here more than elsewhere, requires extensive freedom.

That is why artistic expression should be free. To color the Blessed Virgin's dress a beautiful blue or green and to give the Child Jesus rosy cheeks without doubt will not do much for the handicapped, even for those less intellectually endowed. On the other hand, even though to us the silhouette is ugly and misshapen, if it is made by the child himself/herself, it symbolizes the interior feeling of the person himself/herself. This is a higher value from the viewpoint of education for the faith. Flowers can symbolize joy as perhaps a simple display of color or a house can represent for someone intimacy with God.[24]

It is possible to use design for other purposes, for example, as a comprehension check to find out if the person has really understood. But let teachers be careful not to fall back on the rational and the scholastic; let them all in all appreciate the idea and not the way in which it is represented. More valuable might be an investigation of the basic religious attitudes of the person. But one would have to use infinite discretion and very great prudence.[25]

The techniques of decoupage, pasting, paper tearing, coloring, gluing or transparencies are so many variations of the same basic means of expression. There exists a greater danger of losing oneself in the techniques themselves; in principle free expression is there more limited. On the other hand, the handicapped person can more quickly experience the feeling of success and gain a confidence that will help him/her to progress more rapidly. All these little projects can have a charitable or prayerful meaning. The group could decorate a room with garlands or lanterns to welcome someone or to celebrate a birthday; they could make colored glass for a window of the room; or again they could make a carpet of colored sawdust to decorate a place for the repository for Corpus Christi.

Modeling

Let us comment on three-dimensional expression: modeling, making wire characters, weaving straw, making figures from various materials (wood, cardboard, etc.). The advantage of all these means is that they are more concrete, nearer to life and involve bodily expression. What the character in a work of glazed clay or in wire is in the act of doing, the handicapped person makes him/her do and often he/she can do it by himself/herself or he/she will unite himself/herself to the action by gestures. (We are thinking of prayer attitudes and charitable deeds.) Sometimes it is a whole environment that is set in motion and the person will find himself/herself more implicated and involved on the symbolic level or on a crudely realistic level.

Gestures

Much can be said for body language. It is a marvelous means by which a child, an adolescent or even an adult (whether normal or handicapped) develops love for self, for others and for God. Indeed, it implies participation of the entire person, body and soul, and it can be done in groups thus facilitating social relationships. It leads, finally, to religious gestures which are traditional in all cultures and involve both personal prayer and community liturgy.

Bodily expression must above all be authentic and simple. As we have noted, bodily expression should be rooted in daily physical discipline and regular activity which can have great bearing on the general stability of the person and, in the wider sense of the word, can constitute a real asceticism. In any case one ought to avoid caricature and counterfeit, to flee from whatever appears spectacular. There are no actors and no public. All, even those inactive, must consider themselves participating and involved.

Attitudes and gestures thus expressed will be those of daily life: attitudes of mutual fraternal assistance and friendship; prayerful attitudes or liturgical actions, some spontaneous, others inspired by religious tradition. All can be simple and point back to essentials so as to be at the same time eloquent without dramatization and above all without showy display.

All bodily expression can be meaningful and beneficial from a simple walk to elaborate processions, from the movement of the hand which is opened in welcome to authentic dance expressing praise and joy.

Mime will be more difficult especially if it uses biblical or Gospel themes. Extreme prudence must be observed if one wishes to avoid unhealthy buffoonery in the presence of the sacred.

The same holds for puppet shows and shadow shows. We have used them with success in presenting scenes from everyday life and in giving in this way concrete and earthy moral formation. These latter means are besides more audio-visual than gestural and so we will discuss them a little later.

Musical Expression

Apparently the musical approach is less difficult. For a long time it has been a means of instruction and edification. Singing in church or at catechism is a time-honored custom. But now, compared to the recent past, we have a much better choice in the area of the sacred with selections which are authentically religious and at the same time more solidly theological. However, sometimes one will have to compose his own hymns or adapt a particular text. Let teachers be aware that one cannot put just any kind of words to any kind of notes. The handicapped, even the very young, are more sensitive about this kind of error than one would generally believe . . . more sensitive without doubt than teachers themselves.

Songs can be accompanied by musical instruments. It seems the time has come to restore tambourines if well played, even cymbals, fifes and bells. But this should be done with proper respect and dignity.

Also, we are using records more than ever and not only for Gregorian chant and psalms, but also for classical and modern music. Of course, it is a question of choice and discretion. Not every selection can introduce the presentation of religious reality. Some musical selections, even without words, are better suited for the Passion and others for Easter. Some can begin a lesson on penance and others inspire a feeling of joy and peace. There are also some musical selections that are proscribed because of inferior quality. Others have rhythm or tone which corresponds neither to specific age groups nor to handicapped children or adolescents. Recall here that the retarded are particularly sensitive to music, but the records and the record players ought to be of very good quality.

All real music, moreover, must be respected, that is, be performed and listened to in the greatest silence. Let teachers be careful not to abuse the hymns while singing them; they should not blare them out.

Audio-Visual Media

With or without a phonograph or tape recorder, it is possible to make use of movies or slide projections. But we cannot be over cautious about the dangers of A-V media. Many teachers comfort themselves with easy solutions that include movies or slide projections. On some days these same teachers use nothing else.

These are means to use only rarely; never let them become habitual. The screen will instruct more than it will really train. Religious films are especially difficult to use. We would prefer the use of lighter and more entertaining but moral films. In any case puppets are more apt to be intelligently and actively used. Also recommended are the shadow shows (possibly using real persons behind the screen). On the other hand, slides offer several advantages. Generally they have been taken or chosen by the one who projects them. His live and valuable commentary give evidence of his values.

The opaque projector (unfortunately little utilized) is still of great value. Indeed, one can project almost anything with it: post cards, pictures, various objects from the sketches of the teacher to productions of the handicapped. With this machine one can more easily start a session and obtain a contemplative, truly religious atmosphere. Also be careful to keep a sufficiently slow rhythm to allow for assimilation and contemplation and to prepare the machine and the screen well in advance to avoid fumbling, which generally results in some inattention. But the machine will have to be sufficiently powerful to give good projection lest it weary the spectators.

Multi-Media

To be sure, one can bring together these different techniques. This is the aim of a good "technician." Light, sound, gesture, painting and modeling can be coordinated around a text. But all this should not turn into a dramatic production; it should always keep its sacred and authentic character.

The Church gives us the model of this simple and multi-media expression in its liturgy. It is the most harmonious and at the same time the richest mode of expression, but best unified and at the same time the most faithful in simplicity and unity. That is why for us the loftiest and best expression will be the celebration of the liturgy.

*   *   *

On this sensitive point we will end this chapter. We will limit ourselves to a few closing remarks.

A liturgical celebration must be presented neither as a rehearsal nor as a spectacle. It requires total involvement. Consequently, all should share in it and this is not always easy in the case of the handicapped.

Indeed, one will have to rely on the one hand on some persons who understand this poorly and others who are opposed to participation. There will also be the supervisory staff who can be counted on to remain passive because it is not their task or because they believe themselves confined to a certain neutrality. For the handicapped themselves, it is above all a question of direction by the leader or in unusual cases by another person. But there must be no exclusion, punishment or harassment of persons who cannot or will not enter into the action. For personnel—it is more delicate: each time that it is possible they should be invited to participate in the celebration. When that cannot be accomplished, ask them at least to let themselves go unnoticed by being extremely quiet and respectful.

A celebration calls for still more: on the part of the whole team it requires an attitude of deep faith, of calm and solemn seriousness which in no way excludes joy and enthusiasm, but which avoids all agitation and any kind of eccentricity. It is not a question of surprising and conquering the public. It is a question of praying and learning how to do it better.

Consequently, from the start one has to look for authentic liturgical treasures: gestures, furnishings, songs, parts of the Mass and ceremonies. All these riches that preserve meaning and highlight that meaning must be deeply respected. In a word, let symbolism be fully exploited so that its meaning is expressed.

A single gesture or object will sometimes be sufficient for an entire celebration: a profound bow or a large candle or the "Go, the Mass is ended," or the blessing of the priest and the consequent response of the faithful. Little by little all these elements will regain their place in a sort of synthesis toward a still richer and more varied celebration. Never, however, should the liturgy result in rambling which the Church in her wisdom has known well how to avoid.

One of these very meaningful elements, which attracts many children and even adults in an unusual way, is a very solemn reading of the Bible texts. The book is respectfully carried to the podium and sometimes candles are placed on either side of it. One can incense the book as at Mass at the Gospel time. The celebrant reads the text in a loud, clear voice and very slowly. Sometimes the text is simplified without altering its message. On this occasion the priest can present the Bible and have it venerated as he does by kissing it. One can also bow toward the book and place it on the altar. Immediately those assisting the celebrant come forward to venerate it.

Every procession must be carefully planned. It is very difficult for children and even adults who usually don't know how to march. Then there has to be a gradual preparation. They have to learn how to enter the church, to process down the aisle and unaffectedly to moderate their rhythm while advancing toward the altar in a "real" ascent. A teacher or several others could sometimes march into the church and proceed even to the altar as the children and adults watch. Then the children and adults, individually or in groups, will try to do the same. Then all could practice together. Eventually they come to understand a real procession. Such a celebration will always be a joy and like a feast day celebration. It has nothing in common with disorganized, dismal marches of which we all have unpleasant memories.

Finally here are some material details which we think important:

Every liturgical celebration or para-liturgical celebration demands meticulous preparation. Nothing must be left to chance. On this point the Church gives us the model in the rubrics of the Mass and in the administration of the sacraments and in the Holy Week ceremonies. It is necessary even to come beforehand to the place where the ceremony will unfold. Priest and educators must take into consideration what gestures will be used and what special difficulties these might produce.

For good results ample space is needed. An assigned place for each person is generally an arm's length or a bow apart, especially if one requires certain gestures. One should not hesitate to move chairs and hope that ushers will be cooperative.

The church must be inviting, and the room temperature should be neither too warm nor too cold. All children especially, and handicapped people in general, are very sensitive to these conditions. The church should be open and well lighted in advance to avoid interruptions during the celebration to light candles or open closed doors. It takes only a few things to disturb a prayerful attitude especially for those whose attention span is limited.

Lastly, the celebration must include time that is explicitly and concretely given to prayer—time to speak to God—whether done aloud together or in a low voice, or better yet, privately and in silence. This prayer may be either in the middle of the celebration, or better at the end as a conclusion, a summit, a coronation.

*   *   *

"In the beginning was the Word" . . . the Word is the expression of God. God himself is then expression.

The whole world that the Father has created by his Word expresses his goodness, his power, and his beauty. Enlivened by the Spirit it is unity and diversity, as the Holy Trinity is one and three. So though retarded and handicapped as we may be, the man/woman made to the image of God shows his/her face to us.

For the handicapped then to express themselves is to learn to express the divine. It is to complete in them and through them the boundless work of his Incarnate Word.

10
Personalizing the Instruction

As we mentioned in the first part of this book, a Christian education worthy of its name must be personal and communal at the same time. Now it is a question of seeing how to achieve that kind of education under the special conditions imposed by the religious formation of the handicapped.

First, how can we personalize this education?

Without doubt this is the principal stumbling block for many educators: for the teacher who was in charge of eighty boys and girls, aged five to eighteen years, in a sanitarium that we know personally; for the chaplain in an institution to whom children are brought for catechism in groups of one hundred; for the pastor of a parish who conducts a hurried half hour of religious instruction at a neighborhood children's hospital in between a funeral and a Catholic Action meeting; for the kindly catechist who has the sole responsibility for an entire hospital; for the religious, a special educator, who teaches Christian doctrine to a crowd of delinquents and those on the way to delinquency. How will each of these respond when you say that education must be personalized?

And yet, how much value is there in the words of a single speaker to a large group of handicapped children or teenagers in an hour-long speech? Perhaps this good seed, caught in flight by some well-disposed hearts, will germinate and one day bring forth amazing fruits. We certainly would not want to discourage anyone in this. But if some in this large and passive flock will have been awaiting the "good news," how many others will retain nothing from this mass catechism lesson or even will be systematically turned off by such an impersonal approach? Even those who caught some crumbs in this verbal instruction and assimilated them may have gotten only intellectual nourishment and not the sort of experience of the Spirit which can become a part of their life.

"But I turn them on," protests the speaker. "They are very interested and they ask questions." Yes, but how many only imitate the others' reactions? How many really ask questions? And how many keep silent? And even if all ask questions, does that indicate they now have a desire to change their lives?

Are such questions anything more than an intellectual pastime, a little game, a way to break the monotony, a way to make the speaker believe "they are interested" or a kind of aggression, of protest, of criticism against an authoritative indoctrination appearing more like a means of restraint?

All of this does not necessarily bring a person to "conversion"— the change of heart and of life which results in total evangelization and a complete religious formation.

At the end of a few months or several years of such lectures, a handicapped person will perhaps know his catechism, his prayers; he will have acquired something of a religious behavior pattern and some moral principles. But will he have become a Christian possessing faith, hope and charity who loves to pray to God and who really lives a life different from that of others?

Someone has suggested that rather than take sixty children for an hour when one is alone, it would be better to take four groups of fifteen children for fifteen minutes, provided those fifteen minutes are used well and the groups are arranged in a somewhat homogeneous manner. One can at least look into the eyes of ten or fifteen children. With fifty or one hundred, that might be difficult, even impossible, and it makes all the difference in the world.

But such unfortunate situations should be avoided. How? We will propose many solutions going from the most difficult to the most practical. Let us suggest:

1. Increase the number of teachers.
2. Limit the number of students.
3. Use certain techniques and means which imply expression,

choice and involvement of personnel.
4. Increase the opportunities for learning and contact.

*   *   *

Increase the Number of Teachers

This, of course, takes us back to our considerations of "teams." Many priests complain of being alone, and it is a fact—they are alone. Many lay people complain that they are without priests. That, too, is a reality. But there are also many priests who do not know how to find co-workers or when they find them, judge them incompetent. Or they reserve them for thankless tasks: hearing the catechism lesson from memory or some purely supervisory function. And there are some people who, when they do have a priest, always believe him incapable of playing an appropriate role: he is too young or too old; he is too timid or too enterprising; he is so uninformed on medical and pedagogical questions or too conversant with them and does not stay in his own area. Or he relies too much on sanctity and would do better to become a monk, or he is too interested in sports, too much in the know about the latest champion, the latest batting record or the latest film and he would do better to say the Mass more slowly, etc., etc. The result is that religious formation is given by this priest without lay helpers, and by these lay helpers without a priest. The latter case is more frequent in institutions than one would generally imagine. Priests have the tendency of judging themselves incompetent for "these children" and leaving them in the hands of educators who are considered to be specialists. On the other hand, some specialized educators think that catechetical instruction is the task of the priest or some venerable parish ladies who bring kind words "to those poor children." And so the special educators stand aside.

The remedy here is to remember that worthwhile religious formation cannot be assured by a priest alone or by lay people without a priest. The answer for lay people is to strive to cooperate with their chaplains such as they are. For the priest it is to seek out and to take lay workers, such as they are presented him, while striving to assist them to become what they must be. Let me add to all this that a priest should not be slow to entrust lay people of good will with real educational tasks of religious formation, without giving them too much at a time or overwhelming them. And lay people ought to consider this work "their task" and not merely the duty of the priest and the "good sisters" or both together. It ought to pain them that a priest is alone with a large group of children; they should feel themselves clearly and consciously responsible if they have some possibility of helping him or getting help for him. This attitude is even more inadmissable on the part of religious, it seems to us, who would leave the priest without assistance or without seeking to help by recruiting and preparing suitable lay helpers for him.

Religious formation instruction in the form of a sermon or even conceived as a "class" simply has to be regarded as unacceptable. A priest or teacher (lay or religious) all alone in front of a large group of handicapped children, adolescents or adults, is an intolerable sight. We want this to stop at all costs. It is not too high a price to pay for true education in the faith.

With extreme caution and as one solution for this unfortunate condition, one might envision a sort of reduction into smaller groups by asking the handicapped adolescents or adults to assume toward the others part of the role of the religious educator. This is especially possible in institutions that accept both children and adults, as is the case in some homes for the physically disabled. It can be as beneficial for the one as for the other to begin such cooperation even to asking the older children to assist in the instruction of the younger. At the same time these occasional educators have to be taught the importance of their role and the priest must take the time to train them for their service. This continuous preparation requires of a chaplain indefatigable patience, for in these institutions people incessantly come and go. What they receive on these occasions will, however, be helpful to them during their hospitalization (and also for those actually entrusted to them); it will be even more valuable in the future.

Let us say, however, that this half-solution does not constitute a simple and easy formula. Mature, adequately prepared adults remain desirable in any case. If one has some of these young team workers, especially if it is a question of older children, qualified adults will assure the stability which the former could not guarantee, and they will provide the solid foundation which the young people lack.

Various ways exist—and we will name some—to increase the number of educators, in order to avoid the anonymity of large groups and bring about closer contact among children and adolescents.

But how far must one go in increasing the number of workers? We boldly cite some figures which make this appear desirable, notwithstanding all protests.

Some time ago we visited a home in America directed by religious women and supported by Catholic Charities. It was a home for emotionally disturbed young children. We were told that for thirty-four children the staff was made up of thirty-four persons. "But," our readers will protest, "that is America!"[26]

Recently in France, we went to a center operated to give special religious formation to mildly disturbed children while keeping them in the normal communal setting of a parish catechism class. Two teachers were placed in charge of small sections of six children. Each section had a trained and competent catechist assisted by a student teacher from one of the schools of special education. We joined them for the individualized part of the work, and three was not too many to realize sufficiently the possibilities for each child's concentration! In our catechism classes for the retarded, the rule is never to exceed four children to one teacher. Each time we decided to ask that five be taken, the catechist, though excellent, was overwhelmed. The ideal number appears to be three children per catechist or two catechists together for a group of five or six children. For the profoundly retarded we have sometimes succeeded in finding a catechist for every two children.

Of course, such high ratios of teacher to students are understandable for the psychically handicapped (retarded or disturbed). Certainly the number could be a little larger for the physically handicapped. In this case one could have six to eight children per teacher or two educators for a group of ten to twelve children. This would require, however, that the group have some homogeneity of chronological and mental age as well as a similar achievement level.

Obviously, there will have to be sufficient staff if the institution itself enrolls a large number of youths. We know from experience that the question of sufficient catechists will not be easily solved; it will rarely be solved once and for all. This is a problem continuously posed; it is a heavy burden for the priests and lay persons who are chiefly responsible. No one, however, should let himself/herself become so worn out that they ignore the problem or become resigned to it. An equal concern should be to bring these problems to the attention of those responsible for religious formation of the handicapped.

Control the Number of Students

Whether the instructors are numerous or still more if they are few, the question of how many handicapped children and adolescents should be under one instructor presents a continual problem.

Sessions, which are in fact partly individualized, generally involve some communal and group work. The latter proves much more difficult to manage comfortably as the number of young listeners increases. The audience should never exceed twenty to twenty-five, even if they are then redivided into small groups, for activities.

As we have said before, we still have to introduce into institutions the custom of groupings which takes into consideration the age or level of children receiving religious education and the custom of dividing them into small groups as soon as possible.[27] Evidently, this is a problem for the chaplain who if he is overburdened will have the temptation of taking them all at the same time, especially if he knows that his teaching will be reduced and individualized in other respects. We insist that it would be better, if time is lacking, that the priest take each section for a shorter period of time or he should go sometimes to one section and sometimes to another. A few words from the chaplain of from ten to fifteen minutes each session can be sufficient (this can even be too long with profoundly retarded or disturbed children) if it takes place within a complete program and if it is done in the context of personalized religious formation.

Sometimes opposition may be manifested by the management of the institution. Here again someone could fail by oversimplification especially if he does not have a clear idea of what religious formation is. To take a group of one hundred children into a room for an hour-long lecture invites nothing but discipline problems for the central administration. To set up a format utilizing sections which follow each other correctly with a session comprising communal and individualized settings for everyone necessitates a great deal of imagination, of good will and especially work on the part of the team. But the results are also more satisfying.

Within these sections there should be established groups according to the principles that we have mentioned above. This redistribution represents an initial effort which brings rewards, even with respect to atmosphere and self-discipline. It is necessary, in effect, to set up these groups, not by artificially parceling the persons out, but by regrouping them in such a way that each of the sub-sections represents the maximum of homogeneity (without excluding some variety in temperaments). One should take into consideration the laws of sociology and the dynamics of small groups; one should be careful of the personalities of the young people that he/she intends to put together as well as the personalities of the educators he/she imposes on them. Such factors affect all children and adolescents but have considerably more importance when it concerns the young handicapped who defend themselves more or less violently against such pressures. (To react violently often manifests a powerlessness or inability to react properly and calmly.)

This young lad may be too withdrawn to be placed with another boy who is exuberant and hyperactive. The latter will completely crush the first. On the other hand, for these boisterous young girls a teacher, calm enough and at the same time strong enough to demand obedience without arousing their resentment, is needed. This little boy will cooperate better with a woman. Others, on the contrary, who are approaching adolescence, need a man who gives them an ideal of manhood. In some cases we have been able, with remarkable success, to entrust a group of this kind simultaneously to a male and a female teacher. For young adolescent girls deprived of normal family life and thus of their mother, one should provide a young woman. But a priest would do well to stop in from time to time, for they also need a paternal figure, although the priest in question cannot entirely fill the role of a father. If a young teacher is very shy, do not put her in charge of three schizoids. Otherwise they will spend their time in silence looking at each other; with such disturbed children, one needs a firm but gentle hand. Of course, one does the best with what is available. No formula is perfect; no team is ideal.

It is worth a good deal however, not to change team members once they have begun to function. One should avoid the frustrations that departures and changes of teachers provoke. As we have pointed out, handicapped youth have often lived with frustrations from an early age and they have even "relived" them often in the course of their lives. They have experienced departure to an institution, change of personnel and of teams, return to their homes, a new uprooting, visits from parents, then the disappearance of those same parents for months, even years. They attach themselves to their teacher and will react most bitterly at any departure. Without plunging oneself into the problems of such involved attachments, one should not further afflict badly wounded persons.

Finally, it seems desirable that there be articulation among the groups and it will be profitable even in those regrettable cases where more teachers cannot be secured. Groups can indeed be gathered around several tables and the teacher or chaplain pass from table to table assisting individuals or groups one by one. Giving one of the young people responsibility for each group can play an important role. But assignment of small responsibilities is not always useful and can present dangers. It is not advised that we crown the appointed with badges or titles and certainly not transform them into "little wardens."

We have spoken of "tables." This is indeed a good tool and seems very useful, if not indispensable, if one expects work in groups and by individuals to be effective. Basically this is a very simple device: it consists of having tables wide enough so the group of children can spread out their papers, books, magazines, pictures, colors, paints, modeling clay, etc., and work there in the presence of a teacher also seated at the table. If the group is large, two tables can be put together. One has to plan so that chairs are in place, that there is sufficient space between tables so the children can easily exchange places, and that those responsible pass easily from one table to another.

Of course, the presence of these tables does not at all imply that it is at tables and only at tables where individualized group work takes place. Personalized instruction and especially personalized religious formation comprise an array of activities and methods. This is what we have to examine now.

Ways or Methods

It has become a custom to call "table work" these participative catechism sessions for individualized and small group activities. One is tempted to perceive everything from an academic perspective, a temptation that we should be aware of at every moment. This tendency is exhibited by handicapped children and adolescents themselves who will come to the conclusion that this work at tables is only valuable because it is precisely the kind that puts them into a "school" setting. Religious education remains for them a school of a special type where teachers are replaced by catechists and chaplains. The handicapped youth and those responsible for them feel a security in this: a person has his/her chair and is seated. They feel also they are in a pleasant, affectionate atmosphere: one is in a small group, accustomed to the others as in a family with the teacher for whom there is mutual affection. There is, lastly, the awareness of a moment of relative calm for all: they are in their places and busy.

All these factors have value: a free and industrious atmosphere and at the same time an intimate and reflective setting where each one has his task. This atmosphere constitutes one of the most desirable and beneficial for religious education, provided that this climate never becomes schoolish or that group and individualized work is not reduced to mere activity.

That is why we clearly prefer to speak of "individualized work" or "small group activity" rather than of "table work." These two expressions are not synonymous; one could well conceive of an individualization, a personal religious formation of a handicapped person which would not take place in small groups. For example, this could happen when one deals with one handicapped person, included in a group of "normal" students, whom the instructor takes aside before or after the communal session. Even in a small group a person may, or can be, for some time the object of exclusive attention from the teacher who leads him alone into the chapel, to the chalkboard, or some other place while the other members of the group are temporarily entrusted to a nearby teacher, or to the chaplain, or to the principal, if there is one. In the majority of cases it is in the intimacy of the small group and by its instrumentality that individualization, or better yet, the personalization of religious formation is achieved better. That is why we have been lead, practically speaking, to use the terms "individual or personalized sessions" and "small group activities."

What are these individualized or small group activities? As we have said, they are ways of techniques which imply expression, choice, and personal involvement.

We do not think that we have to insist further on what concerns expression since we have already touched on that question several times and especially in the preceding chapter. Let us say more precisely, however, that this "expression" ought to be truly personal, although it will never be easy to achieve. Very young children are often very free, very direct, without reserve even in their expression. Whether it is the effect of adult ridicule or self-control or academic distortion (very few schools as yet foster free expression) or all these reasons taken together, people in growing older become reticent and sometimes refuse to express themselves openly. Other factors discussed in the previous chapter have importance here.

The students then have recourse to copying: their sketches are inspired by those they have done in school, drawn from geometric rule or at least stylized, or traced from pictures of dubious taste; their bodily expression tends to mime or comedy and the like. One has to treat them to "a cure of simplification," to help them lose their biases, their inhibitions. That is not easily done. The least criticism from the catechist, the slightest nuance of depreciation in his/her speech or his/her manner will cause the child, adolescent or adult to hide or tear up his/her design in which he/she had so naively but truly represented himself/herself and to set aside his/her colors or paint brush and not pick them up again. On the contrary, much encouragement, approval and perseverance will slowly put an end to false shyness and its so deadly paralysis. (The first free designs that a person creates when he/she finds himself in a psycho-pedagogical "situation" are often sterotypes. Then little by little the person frees himself/herself and reveals himself/herself.)

Let us add that with mentally handicapped youth especially, but also with the physically and socially deprived, some inhibitions of a pathological nature can be involved. Marked retardation in graphic development can occur with the handicapped and even those hospitalized for a long time. A backwardness that seems like intellectual deficiency or a pseudo-debility of affective origin may manifest itself in primitive and misshapen representations. The informed teacher shouldn't be surprised at them. Let him/her be contented, at least in the beginning, with very elementary even apparently ridiculous expressions without any reproaches. All the while he/she will prudently encourage at least a little bit of improvement. We repeat that excessive compliments are not needed nor are they even always desirable. It is better to give compliments gradually; this will allow the person to feel that he/she is capable of making progress. Avoid any real reprimands.

The religious educator of the handicapped, especially one who is in charge of the retarded, should not give in too easily to the temptation of only supplying children with activities that are already prepared. This warning applies to designs that they will have only to color, letters they have only to trace, papers that they do no more than paste, etc. Obviously, these materials hinder personal creative expression; they limit the sphere of the person to activities that are often passive or at least mechanical and done without understanding the concept. For example, the child who traces around the cloak of St. Joseph with a green or brown crayon is not necessarily assimilating the Gospel lesson corresponding to the picture he/she colors. The one who traces around letters does not necessarily reflect upon their meaning, nor the one who pastes cutouts what they represent. This type of activity is not absolutely proscribed. It can have advantages as we have said before. It can encourage them to begin with a task within their reach and go on to make something more personal and more difficult. It can also ease the relationship between the child and the teacher and serve as a point of departure for an intimate conversation or a reflection in a team. But teachers should be wary of using such materials. They must not be enslaved by them but must go beyond them. How many children have we not seen plunged into tasks of this kind when they did not absolutely understand the purpose but simply made a game of coloring or filling a page!

Let the teacher be equally careful not to be influenced by the moods of the person and by his/her tendency to ask someone to do the task for him/her when effort is demanded. "Draw it for me. I do not know how to draw," the retarded child will say to the teacher. "Write, I do not know how to write that. Copy it for me—this song, this word, this sentence." Let the child try first if we think he/she has a chance of succeeding. (Previous knowledge of his/her motor, intellectual and scholastic skills here proves more than ever indispensable). If he/she is really incapable of performing the task in question, then the teacher should give him/her some other task to work on, but he/she should not do the work for him/her. Perhaps the child is not able to write this text but the educator can guide his/her hand, supply a model for him/her to reproduce or write what the child dictates. Indeed with these children one can in fact read the question, ask for the answer, write it down for them and ask them to copy and recopy it. That requires patience but it is also effective.

Perhaps the child is unable to read these sentences, to recognize them, and put these texts in the right place but the teacher can read them for him/her or decorate them with a design which will enable him/her to recognize them. What is important is that it is the child who chooses them.

We come, therefore, to a second characteristic of individualized activities: the demand for a choice on the part of the student. Indeed we have seen in the first part of this work that choice, freedom of choice, so to speak, was the personalizing element par excellence.

Let the child then, during this part of the religious formation session, "choose." We repeat: this liberty of choice has to be exercised. Moreover, this choice can be exercised in any array of activities or in the midst of activity. It would be ideal if, without yielding too much to the whims of the child, the teacher, at least from time to time, would present an assortment of various activities to him/her, different ways of expression among which the child can select one himself/herself according to his/her "way of approaching God this day." Let him/her then leave his/her paint brushes if he/she prefers to pray in the chapel; let him/her on returning learn a song or play a Gelineau record and accompany it with bodily expression or sacred dance and finish by making a figure in glazed clay. A system of work sessions will sometimes be able to facilitate these activities. Instead of putting these students into set groups, the tables or other set places are designated for various activities such as painting, modeling, bodily expression, song, etc. The students have the opportunity to choose one activity but not with their usual grouping. These activities are each directed by a teacher. In the course of the session the children may change activities. That presents great advantages; it avoids too narrow restriction in the same groups and too much self-interest.

On the other hand, another child may spend all his/her time painting in a corner or designing, with the understanding that painting and designing should be, as much as possible, in the general perspective of ordinary work at least in the totality of religious formation. Finally, allow adolescents to speak intimately and at length with their teacher if on this particular day they experience a healthy need for it; on such occasions let all other concrete activities be suspended.

Of course, we repeat that the educator ought always to be willing to dialogue with the student so as to avoid pure caprice. Above all, the insight of the adult will have to be schooled to see whether it is a question of real need which is expressed or a passing fantasy . . . or idleness.

Even within the proposed activities it is certain in any case that a choice ought to be sought. Whether it be a case of classifying pictures or of pasting, the student will have to discard some and keep others, and he/she should be asked the reason for the choice. But choices will normally be exercised on a fuller and broader scale. There will be prayer that someone will choose to say that he/she has composed himself/herself. There will be the gesture selected for this prayer or a particular body expression with a religious or moral theme. There will be the offerings that one will choose to bring to the altar, the intentions selected or the resolutions made on this occasion.

One sees how such choices will end in "commitment," another characteristic of individualized and personalized sessions. Indeed, it is on such occasions when activities really do involve him/her that the student recognizes his/her responsibilities to God, to others, and to self, and consequently he/she behaves as a person.

A handicapped person will consider himself/herself as invited to such personal commitment from the moment when, during work in small groups or even in the course of a large group, he/she feels himself/herself concerned with the message and personally called by God to give a response. The efforts of the teacher in a individualized or small group format must tend toward making the student sense and respond to this call in a lived, practical way.

If we are not able to achieve this, if the student does not feel concerned, called, changed in some way "converted" and at least turned around some little bit, if he/she has not responded to the divine truth which has been transmitted this day, then we have very probably wasted our time and made an act which simply furnished the brain with knowledge that was sterile and at times even dangerously undigested and toxic.

On the other hand, perhaps we have only revealed a tiny fragment of the truth (Isn't it always a question of a tiny fragment?) inasmuch as that little gleam has really awakened the handicapped child, adolescent or adult to whom we are addressing ourselves. Perhaps we have instilled a feeling of being concerned, and this desire to respond, though only just begun, even hesitant, weak, or clumsy, can be considered a divine call. Then we will not have wasted our time and efforts.

It is by means of a definite "resolution," resolution consciously and voluntarily taken by the student himself/herself and not by the teacher, that the commitment will be concretized at the end of the session. But this resolution can only be valuable and solid when it really constitutes a completion, that is, if it has been prepared and brought to maturity during the whole of the session. If not, it will end up as something very artificial, like the moral in certain "edifying" stories. The child or adolescent will not live it. It can even happen, especially with handicapped youth, that they will react against the process and rapidly turn it into derision, taking malicious pleasure in doing the contrary to what had been suggested to them.

The word "resolution" must sometimes be avoided so as not to lead to confusion with the resolve taken eventually in the confessional. What is involved here is something more fundamental than that which the word resolution sometimes makes us think. It is really an attitude of a change of soul beginning with a conscious awareness of and a meeting with the living and incarnate Truth, the Word of God who is himself a person.

This is, in a word, therefore, the personal response to a person, the reply given in a dialogue which has comprised a demanding appeal and which clamors for a generous acceptance, an active consent, a free willingness, a gift. It is on these conditions and only these conditions that the instructor can make religious formation personal.

But, to repeat this, formation demands that one really know the handicapped student before, during and after each session of religious education which can properly be called "encounters." To do that one will have to:

Increase the Opportunities for Knowledge and Personal Contacts

This is a delicate subject but it is impossible to ignore it without failing seriously in the task we are undertaking here. Indeed, a personal and profound Christian formation appears to us practically impossible if there is not an opportunity for those responsible for religious education to know and to touch personally the children, adolescents or adults entrusted to them. What is so often put into one's hands in an anonymous group, as happens so often with a professor in his/her classroom or a chaplain at a boarding school.

We have mentioned earlier ways for the teacher to know the students, especially when they are handicapped, and the means of directing their formation. We will not repeat here, but we would only insist on the necessity of continually enriching this knowledge by truly personal contacts with them.

The child must speak with the teacher as a son/or daughter to his/her father or mother, especially if this teacher plays a paternal or maternal role in some way. When it is a question of a priest, the same thing is true. We recall an institution where no place was provided for the chaplain to meet with a girl alone. When a child or an adolescent had to address the priest, asking him to bless a medal, as he crossed the recreation court, this really constituted a kind of scandal. Moreover, at times, it was not "proper" for the priest to cross the recreation yard or for a student to speak to him first.

Had the directors in charge of this institution forgotten that the Lord Jesus reprimanded the apostles when they forbade the little children to approach him and that he had special conversations with the Samaritan woman and the woman taken in adultery, as well as with Nicodemus?

We are aware of the difficulties which can sometimes arise regarding the personal relationship of the teacher, religious or lay person, with the child, adolescent or adult. There again, it is not because such difficulties occur that one can solve the problem by refusing to mention it. It is not because young girls in a sanatarium can gossip that it was necessary to forbid the chaplain to receive them. Let them glaze the office window as they did in one institution that we know where they allowed him freedom of action.

Moreover, individual contacts do not necessarily have to take place in a closed room free from public gaze. It is not unusual that in the midst of the hubbub of a room or a playing field very intimate conversations take place. Let evil be to him who thinks evil! After twenty centuries of experience, the Church keeps a confessional room and encourages spiritual direction with a minimum of restrictions. She has never abolished individual instruction.

There are times indeed when the human soul needs to reveal secrets, times when it awaits a word spoken for it alone and addressed only to it. The human spirit of the handicapped person experiences this need more than any other because in a sense a handicapped person is "unique," unparalleled, set apart from others and burdened with his/her own problems. What he/she resents is the difficulty of communication. Only with heart to heart talk, without disturbance, without distractions in his/her surroundings, will he/she become relaxed; he/she will finally let down the barriers, admit his/her anguish, his/her pain and his/her sin. It will not always be in the austere setting of the confessional, rather conventional and pompous, unfitted for a sensitive person, much less for the sick or weary, that this simple confidence or confession occurs. Once again the Church has understood this and gives dispensations prudently and extensively to such persons. Let the teacher, as well as the priest, consider this in his/her attitude. A visit to a child or to an adult when he/she is in an infirmary or isolation will often have more repercussions on his/her spiritual life than ten lessons given to him/her at the same time in his/her group.

Institutions for the handicapped of all kinds, from hospitals to rehabilitation centers, are often very poorly equipped for this kind of personal contact. Everything is communal there, from the dormitory to the dining hall, as well as workrooms or classrooms. In no way is it possible to see someone alone except in the office of the director, or in a doctor's clinic (with questionable privacy and sometimes mixed emotions) or in a lobby where twenty persons come and go at a time.

This picture of modern depersonalization ought to shock a Christian conscience. Is it only the director of an institution and the doctor who need a room reserved for their special conversations? The teacher, religious or lay, must be able to exercise this important part of his/her pedagogical function. Likewise the adult, adolescent, even the child has a right to a place where he/she will be able to express himself/herself and cry if he/she feels like it in the presence of someone who can console him/her without countless eyes looking on. Perhaps some readers will find us sentimental and judge that this is dangerous. We know the dangers but we insist, however, that when elementary precautions are taken, this seems an important means of education and a person's inalienable right.

When it is a question of handicapped youth, it is more true than ever, in spite of the very acute problems it can pose, because the handicapped are sometimes much more simple. When it concerns religious formation this intimacy of soul clothes something sacred. The possibility for the one teaching, especially the priest, to know the profound needs of this soul and to respond to them is a task which one has to accept as received from God. The teacher and all those working with him/her will have to put all their powers to work to allow God to accomplish this task through them and to be keenly aware of the importance of this task, respecting it as a real mission.

Even when these facilities have been provided the teacher let no one think that the task is easy. A child, adolescent or even an adult, especially one who is handicapped, does not "open up" automatically because he/she has been given a sofa or chair and an adult is seated opposite him/her in the semi-darkness. We have known some educators and chaplains who called in children and adolescents for consultation, one by one, in a treatment or rehabilitation center. It is easy to see how this method quickly drew ridicule and the person arbitrarily invited almost automatically put himself/herself on the defensive. The human spirit is not the body, and if the doctor can ask at any time that his/her patient undress (though one would hope that it be done tactfully), the teacher or even the priest does not have the same right to practice a kind of review of conscience. It is for the educator and the priest to be available; it is not for them to demand readiness on the part of students, nor even less to do so through an ordered system.

On the other hand, the educator or priest should not believe too readily that a handicapped person has nothing to say because, in effect, he/she does not tell them anything or at least not much. Frequently, a sick young person who comes to the office, speaks of everything else, accepts a cigarette, after a few minutes blurts out in one sentence what is worrying him/her. Equally frequent is the case of a retarded or disturbed teenager, deprived of a normal family situation, who asks for an interview and remains with mouth opened, frightened, awaiting help. It is especially important not to hurry this young person or give the impression of doing so. Perhaps he or she simply wishes to be with someone for a few minutes, someone who is there "for them." Much more difficult is the problem for the priest or educator who instead of receiving someone, visits the sick. In most cases he has not been expected. Then the sick person has nothing prepared in advance: to be announced a bit in advance can have some advantages. Remember that a sick person, by definition, is in something less than his/her normal condition, except in cases of chronic and habitual illness. Confidences will often come when the visitor has his/her hand on the door to leave. Let him/her understand that he/she has to give up the idea of leaving and seat himself/herself again, without falling into the indiscretion of prolonging the visit indefinitely.

And lastly, let him/her realize that the handicapped are "handicapped" in expression. Does that mean that they have nothing to say? No, rather that they do not know how to say it. One has to have much more patience than boldness, being careful about interruption. The visitor sometimes has to help a little, often knowing how to be silent while remaining present and attentive.

But, as we have mentioned before, the teacher does not play the role of either the confessor or the psychotherapist. On the other hand, the psychotherapist should not play the role of either educator or priest. Each has his/her own role.

It is especially in this way that one responds to the objection which may arise in the mind of the reader in ending this chapter. "That takes time. . . . " That takes time, it is true, and your author has known that for a long time. But in the first place this is not wasted time if one has been employed to listen and to aid personally one of our brothers or sisters, even the "least." To help a retarded child takes as much time as writing a page or two of an article or a book that could reach ten thousand readers. But there is no standard to measure such things. One can be at one and the same time very brief and very intensely present. Or one can waste hours in conversation if he/she only takes into account his/her own needs. Finally, let it be said that the time spent in helping another, especially a handicapped youth, will be considerably lessened if one knows that he/she is not all alone and that he/she is not the only one to play all these roles.

This personal religious formation requires the collaboration of educators, rehabilitators and also the subjects of this education. It is, we repeat, personal; it must be, nonetheless, strictly communitarian.

A remark concerning the parents of handicapped youth: If there is anyone who is in a good position to "individualize" a child's or an adolescent's religious formation, it is his/her father and mother. Is not this, in fact, one of the privileges of family education and one of the reasons that it is irreplaceable?

Education within the family allows each person to have been known, loved, followed step by step in a personal fashion in the setting of a little community of "human size."

When it is a question of handicapped youth this rule remains true: his/her first educators are his/her father and mother. It is their duty to provide a personal religious formation for him/her. It is for them to be on call as much and more so than for other children, to receive his/her confidences, to take them seriously and to aid him/her to solve his/her problems.

Several comments are in order on this subject: First, we have said that parents and above all parents of a handicapped child are not automatically prepared to assume this task, at least not in its totality. It is unquestionably true that religious formation, especially of a handicapped youth, requires a particular competence which exceeds the general and usual competence that every father and mother should possess normally for the education of their children. The personal contact of parents and the individualized formation they can give their children do not exclude other opportunities. Equally, these children can and must have personal relationships with other educators and receive from them individualized religious formation. For the priest, especially, who represents the Church in his mission of teaching, we will have to provide personal contacts with the handicapped child or adolescent even if his/her parents have effectively provided his/her Christian education.

And this leads us to our second comment. Individual religious formation no longer suffices, and the handicapped youth, even though catechized by excellent parents, supported by several special educators, counseled by a priest periodically, must also receive communal religious training. That is why we conclude this chapter that only constitutes one side of the diptych, and what is contained in the next chapter is, in principle at least, a normal and indispensable complement.

11
Building a Community

If it is true that we, and especially the educators among us, are too much inclined to act without observing the people involved and before we have acquired all of the pertinent facts, how much more is this true when it is a question of society as a whole?

Sociological techniques and group dynamics, as are now used in some institutions for handicapped[28] are still little known, are applied in a rather empirical fashion, and are poorly interpreted.

Too often we rely on a psychosociology or psychology of social life, or more precisely social relationships, that are restricted to examining the reactions of particular individuals in a group setting and as a consequence refer only to the study of one person or else are subjected to a mathematical type of inquiry, where the parallels of strengths are traced or the various shifts of attraction and repulsion are noted. Rarely does anyone study the evolution of the composition of the group itself, the betterment or deterioration of interpersonal relationships and the quality of the community. Little attention is paid to the reasons for these changes for better or for worse. This is due perhaps to a concern for wisdom, method and scientific honesty. But it also seems that it is due to the fact that an authentic communitarian psychology is still in its initial stages.

In principle, however, such study should precede or at least accompany all education. Even more it should be associated with all-group pedagogy.

But how, either later or at the same time, can one accomplish such a task: that is, to make a given group of persons become an organized community, and consequently, a living body whose members are unique persons? How should one conceive such an activity and the growth that should stem from it in the perspective and according to the demands of a Christian vision of man and of the world?

We shall not return to the principles of this subject mentioned in the beginning of this book. We will only note here the problems involved in their application and their practice.

*   *   *

Community building is very easy in appearance, and the temptation of not bothering with it is stronger when it is a question of group education than with individual instruction. Obviously, in institutions at least, handicapped people are grouped together, and it would seem by definition that the influence exercised by the educator can be called communal.

In reality, what is present in the beginning is generally not an organized community where real interpersonal relationships have been established, still less is it a Christian community animated by the love of God, even a coming-together of practicing and fervent Catholics; nor is it necessarily "on the way," and "becoming," and thus called to progress in that love.

The Christian educator will have to work to foster such change and he/she must first of all be aware that such a reality is not supplied for him/her at the outset.

Besides, cases of handicapped persons residing with their families or otherwise isolated are frequent. Persons or organizations charged with the care of these adults, adolescents or children, do not always think of assuring them of anything more than an individual religious education. The communal aspect, its importance, even its necessity, does not strike them sufficiently, or else, here again, the difficulties appear to them of such a nature that they do not know how to overcome them. The temptation is strong to be contented with each person taken in hand by a volunteer catechist or by a Christian educator who is more or less qualified and specialized. How many children, instructed in this manner, are one fine day brought to the priest for their confession and Communion, yet have not up to that time had any deep, vital contact with some kind of Christian community!

However, this participation in a Christian communitarian life, as we have said, constitutes for a Catholic who understands the mystery of the Church something as precious and irreplaceable, in a sense, as the arrival at personal commitment that we have spoken of in the preceding chapter.

Undoubtedly, we can say that belonging to the mystical body of Christ can take any form. That is correct. We must affirm, as we did earlier, that God in his love is aware of each person and of his unique and irreplaceable value.

The handicapped person is no less a man or woman created by God; body and soul, mind and heart. Handicapped people go to the abstract through the senses and by means of the concrete for their communitarian education; they need living, material contact with a visible assembly. It is this tangible reality that one has to provide or rather, to help them to provide for themselves, because like all humanity, they have the duty of association and the right to be effectively challenged.

If we consider that this is a human right, then a more complex and difficult problem emerges; it does not suffice that the handicapped person be integrated only into a community of peers, that is, a Christian milieu for handicapped persons. This is, in fact, a partial solution and somewhat simplistic, if the handicapped person is welcomed only into such a "specialized Church," and into a world, Christian or not, of persons with conditions similar to his/her own.

Let us repeat that for a Catholic a communitarian education can only be thought of in reference to the mystery of the Church in its totality. Just as this ecclesial reality constitutes the formation, reason for being and principle, it constitutes also the way and the final purpose. Because he/she (as he/she is saved by and with Christ, of whom the Church is the continuation, the mystical body) is of the Church and saved by it, with and in the Church, a Catholic can and must, infinitely more than any other person, be nurtured in community. At the same time, it is this Church, which gives him/her the means and for whom he/she is meant; he/she supports the Church as a living and active member and is welcomed by it.

The handicapped person does not escape this law that all humanity is called to be saved by, with, and in the Church. Quite the contrary! He/she has his/her own role and it is irreplaceable. Without any doubt, his/her participation is especially precious for the body, and his/her role, as we have already said, is a particularly important one (Col. 1:24). It is necessary, however, that the handicapped person himself/herself and those around him/her understand this fact and be deeply convinced of it—"live it!" Many Christians have what might be conveniently called "human views" on this point. This is a message, a "gospel," which must be ceaselessly repeated to them by our words and our acts, our faith in the value to the Church of our handicapped brothers and sisters.

The Church, inasmuch as it is a praying and acting community, has a role of ecclesial education to fulfill, and it cannot dispense itself from this responsibility. It is upon us, upon each of us in fact, that this task of education depends if this communitarian and ecclesial teaching is to be effectively provided for the handicapped. And it ought always to be a source of suffering for us when a portion of the world of handicapped people is neglected by the Church, by a community (congregation, diocese, etc.), or by an individual member (religious or lay). Without judging the responsibility of people who shirk such work, we ask is it not a kind of desertion in the combat which the kingdom of God wages against the empire of evil? Or a renewal of the apostles' desertion of Jesus in Gethsemane or at his trial before the high priests? Or it is more simply a lack of the spirit of faith and of the Beatitudes?

Christians will always be tempted to abandon the suffering Jesus because he will be in "agony" for a long time, that is, until the end of the world. (And this apparent lack of the spirit of faith can go as far as a more or less conscious eagerness on the part of some Christians to pull others away from the education of the handicapped. "You can do better than that," they say ... or more subtly, "You will serve them better in other ways." What strength of soul is necessary to resist such temptation and remain in this form of service!)

Lastly, it is for the Church that the handicapped person is destined. It is for the Church then to welcome him/her and for him/her in return to give himself/herself to the Church.

We say it is for the Church to welcome him/her. Still it can be assumed that the Church considers him/her a stranger, an alien in the etymological meaning of the term. Would it not be much better to affirm that he/she is and remains, however he/she may appear, one of its members?

But it is a fact that handicap by definition alienates. Unquestionable effort must then be demanded from Christians to make room for the handicapped in the Church, as all men/women must necessarily make an effort to welcome the handicapped into society. Yet, it would seem that in the Church of Christ, in the perspective of a religion of love, in the supernatural vision of the mystical body, such an effort must be, by the grace of God, easier and more spontaneous. In response, we also say, the handicapped person must give himself/herself to the Church? That is not always as easy, as spontaneous as we would think.

The handicapped person, in effect, feels alone and believes he/she is alone. And he/she often is alone, or at least it appears so. As we have seen, this is almost a general rule. A ditch is dug between himself/herself and those around him/her and between himself/herself and the rest of society. It is true that he/she enjoys solidarity with handicapped peers. Yet, he/she must know them and visit them. And this solidarity too often remains founded on very negative motives—participation in the same frustration, the same disapproval, the same failure. Too often it is based in a common defense or a coalition to bring about some legitimate demands. Even when it ends in a very generous and willing desire to assist his/her peers, to triumph with them over similar difficulties, this solidarity remains limited to a narrow world, to this "specialized Church" which we have just mentioned.

It is a welcome to the whole Church, through the totality of the mystical body and of the communion of saints, that we must give to the handicapped. It is a gift to the total Christ without limitations and without exclusions that we must seek for them.

Without doubt, associations for the sick or infirm and the various organizations which group the handicapped of all kinds by categories, can establish here a middle way, a transition community. For many isolated persons, already walled in by their handicap, this welcome implies a first window opening to others, a first call to go out of self, a hand reached out to consider the Church and all humanity. But let those groups and movements take care not to establish themselves in a closed circle or some pious clique. They would then fail in their calling.

Still less would a Christian communal education be achieved if one remained in a restricted milieu, which, whether one wishes it or not, is always somewhat artificial. Such is the case where one experiences meager Christianity in a health or a rehabilitation center, or even in an inter-parish catechism class for the handicapped. There again, let these isolated communities watch to see that they are open to the whole Church.

Let us now suggest various plans for bringing about a gradual solution to these problems.

*   *   *

First, we shall start with isolated handicapped persons and recall that such is the lot of a great many handicapped people, since the number in institutions is really minimal. How can we give this isolated person a feeling of community? It seems to us that two kinds of bonds can be woven or re-established: bonds with the "normal" and bonds with the handicapped.

The isolated handicapped person of whom we have spoken has often more relationships with "normal" people than he/she thinks. The amazing thing is that he/she feels so alone, so "apart" from the world.

The sick, disabled or retarded person has parents, brothers and sisters, neighbors of his/her own age. But they are too often strangers to him/her living at the same time so near and yet so far from him/her, all still fellow members of the human race. Even though they may be at his/her service "for his/her minor wants" they remain strangers to him/her . . . and estranged. Perhaps they are so, precisely because they are so centered around him/her that they relate to him/her "in a one-way sense" and do not expect or claim anything from him/her. There is doubtless a gift but not an exchange of gifts. In any case it is this exchange that we have to establish.

A mentally handicapped child or a crippled teenager who receives everything from relatives but does not give anything remains alone. Make them productive and responsible and let them feel that they are. Nothing should be done around the house that they could have done; it shouldn't be done for them. In their own way they have a need of being "indispensable"; it is much more valuable to them than all our little "services" or "kindnesses."

But the handicapped should also form community with those around them. Someone is going to a movie tonight; why leave Jane out because she cannot walk? Why do we almost never see crippled persons at the entrances of our theaters? Why is it Jane's friends and not her family who take her for a walk? No community will replace her family for her.

Why was it that the day of his oldest sister's wedding, little Peter, of whom we have already spoken, was all alone at the end of the garden, hidden carefully from the guests so as not to disturb the celebration? They say that Peter is mentally handicapped and doubtless they were afraid to show him so as not to spoil the chances of marriage for his younger sister. But in another family, Andrew, a spastic or a mongoloid, will be present everywhere and the older, as well as the younger sister, will marry. Andrew is a part of the community. Peter is not and his handicap becomes a fundamental obstacle to access to the true communitarian life of the Church.

Moreover, there are other societies that will dare to reject the handicapped even if he/she has been accepted and integrated into the family. It is no small problem to get a young handicapped child companions of his/her own age to play with. It will at times be even more difficult to integrate him/her into a school of normal children, even into a catechism class. Furthermore, even if it is always possible and even desirable, who will dare champion it?

However, an effort must be made to avoid systematic segregation. In the United States today every effort is made to facilitate to the greatest degree or to maintain or integrate handicapped children (paralyzed, blind, or slightly retarded) into the normal scholastic milieu. Children and teachers are specially prepared for this.

Sometimes it happens that the handicapped person will be annoying or even bored in the "normal" situation. Various solutions can then be employed. Take, for example, what can occur in the matter of catechetical education of the learning-disabled.[29] What to do when a child does poorly in the parish catechism class? Supposing that it is proven that this child is really mentally deficient, several gradual solutions are envisioned:

If the child is only slightly deficient and does not disturb the other children, keep him/her in the normal setting and inform the priests and other catechists so that they give him/her some special attention without neglecting his/her companions.

If the child cannot be kept with companions of his/her own age because of lesser mental age or behavior problems that easily result in disturbance, then set up a small group of handicapped children (being careful not to label them). Entrust this group to another catechist, not a handicapped person. (Another temptation might be to entrust the children to a very old lady who is a bit irritable or to an inexperienced student teacher). It should be someone who is calm and competent, endowed with a loving disposition, and above all with constancy. Finally, if this child presents such a degree of retardation that his/her case requires a specially qualified catechist, then entrust him/her to special catechism classes, such as now exist in Paris, Lyon, or Reims and should be found everywhere in the world.

Where a class of this kind does not exist, the case will remain, and the child could be placed in the care of someone who would be willing and able to give him/her special catechism lessons. We might say that this is only a last recourse. Even in this case, as well as in others, the child must be kept in real contact with the reality of Christian community.

Let us repeat: it is for the Christian community to open itself. We recall a cathedral just built in Sherbrooke, Canada. A special door with a sloping entrance was arranged by the architect to ease the access of the infirm. God bless this architect and those who saw his plans, inspired them and approved them. But the doors should be open everywhere, special or not, so that those who should never have been set apart may come to our liturgies and celebrations. We made a pilgrimage from Rome with nearly two hundred infirm. Everywhere kindly arms were extended to lift the paralyzed on to the steps of the basilicas. We saw as many paralyzed persons descend into the depths of the catacombs as we saw go up to the Sistine Chapel.

But, unfortunately we saw as well a church at a health spa, where "normal" parishoners recoil, horrified when a tubercular patient coughs during a Mass. We also know a church where a group of epileptics attend services and where parishioners very noticeably wipe off the chairs before sitting down in places where epileptics have dared to sit. They are fearful, without doubt, of catching epilepsy from sitting on the same chairs. Ah, who will give us "well adjusted" Christians?

Youth movements have done much to integrate movements. They would be a special way of opening the handicapped to the meaning of the Church . . . as people of the Church.

Boy and Girl Scouts, as well as Catholic Action movements in France, have been forerunners in this effort for many years. Other movements follow at a slower pace.

Here again, an option is presented: Should we integrate the handicapped into the normal activities or set them apart in special groups? Various plans exist, and other intermediary plans ought to be sought. Above all, we say that here, too, we would like to have those who are talented and dependable accept responsibility for such activity. Chaplains should be specially chosen. And we should not be in a hurry to entrust other activities to those selected, as if these tasks were without real importance.

Finally, where regroupings of the handicapped in their turn constitute a community, the following principles should be of value. They can be applied to all kinds or groups: in an institution, a classroom, a movement, or an agency.

*   *   *

How can we form such a collectivity into an authentic community?

Of course we will not enunciate here principles that would be valuable for any group. We will suppose that these were learned elsewhere and we will only insist on those that are more important specifically for a group of handicapped persons.

First, at all costs we must avoid having handicapped persons group together, shoulder to shoulder, as passive persons of like good will and community. This brings to mind those infirm in a large hospice in the Paris area, deftly "managed" as they say, throughout the year, dragging out their idleness in drab corners or on the cobblestones of another century. There are still worse things: healthy children, and well cared for, at a "receiving center," where, for family or social reasons, they wait for placement. For convenience and to satisfy unreasonable regulations they are treated as if they were sick: required to stay in bed and have temperatures taken morning and evening. There are also all those institutions, which keep mentally defectives for life, where it is said that for those below a specified intelligent quotient, nothing but "custodial care" can be envisioned. Why is it that at a neighboring institution residents of like ability are active, happy and useful?

A severely retarded person comes to our mind; he was taught, not without difficulty, simply to stack empty bottles. He scarcely did anything but that; but he did it well and conscientiously, feeling that it had to be done and was almost jealous of his duties. Starting with this task he was given the assurance of his manhood.

We said before that there is no charity that flourishes on a one-way street. Not that charity should be disinterested and completely giving. But the best charity is giving to others the possibility and the joy of giving themselves and of being able to give. It is that kind of charity that paternalism has forgotten and disdained, paternalism such as that of the headmistress of a boarding school who took her students to decorate a Christmas tree for retarded and dependent children deprived of normal family life. At the beginning of the celebration it was suggested that the students share with the children chocolate milk which was served in abundance. "No," replied the headmistress, "for they are here to give charity and not to receive it." Fortunately, that changed later on.

But we must not believe too readily that we have arrived. Community will not necessarily be realized because groups of handicapped persons prepare vegetables and others assist in domestic tasks. They will not have transformed a collectivity into a community because they have been allotted some wool to knit, or been taught to repair TV sets or mend shoes. All that can be pure and simple exploitation on the part of management or a petty source of pocket money for the sick or disabled. The young delinquent girl who washes the windows of the center is not thereby developing a community sense. She can do it with the same irritation that she experienced two weeks before when she polished the floors of her employer.

In order that community really exist, these people will have to do something together or at least be involved in a common project. That is extremely difficult as long as we remain within the perspectives of hospitalization, shelters, guardianship or welfare. We need only research the root meaning of the word and we will see how paternalism, which is derived from the Latin word for father or nation, can be the enemy of true community. Moreover, we have only to see how furnishings in institutions are treated to understand that the residents have scarcely any sense of maintaining common property.

"We have a family spirit," this gentle directress tells us, but there is no family spirit when a child who knows that his/her own family pays for his/her residence and whose "mother" (some of the directresses are called "mama" to increase the likeness to family living) will say to him/her at the first outburst, "Look, you forget that you are not at home!"

From this we see what a sense of community supposes: the feeling of the handicapped person of being not only one who receives, who is assisted, and who is helped, but also one who gives aid in his/her turn, who is useful, who is co-responsible for the common good. This common good is never a permanent thing and it depends upon everyone, the handicapped as well as others, if this good is to be preserved and to prosper. Excellent programs for this purpose are in use in some institutions for the mentally ill. Why not extend them to other areas?

Finally, true community spirit presupposes unselfishness and generosity. True community is not made, still less is Christian community made, as long as it remains a pure and simple solidarity. Recall what Bergson told us about closed morality. Some current experiences, even the most celebrated remain in the plane of simple, human solidarity. Surely they would not satisfy us.

True community spirit for a Christian means making a total gift of self to the other in the same way as God himself in the Trinity. Circuminsession is not an invention of theologians. It is a marvelous reality which would throw the most brilliant light on our personal lives and on society if we would but contemplate it. Theologians tell us also that circuminsession can be written with a "s" or with a "c," and this which seems a simple curiosity contains a surprising instruction. Each person is destined to go to the other, to throw himself/

herself so to speak into the other, there to give himself/herself to the others in an impulse and in an embrace (circuminsession from *incedere*) and to live in the other, so to speak, to reside there, to give himself/herself interiorly (circuminsession from *insedere*). Such should be the community of Christians. Isn't it this community that Christ himself asked his Father to accomplish among his own? "Father, that they may be one, as we are one" (Jn. 17:22).

Surely such a community will not be realized by simple human means. That is why Christ in his sacerdotal prayer has asked for the Spirit of Love: "Father, let the love with which you have loved me be in them" (Jn. 26). And this is why the Spirit of Love has been given to us: "Even the love of God has been poured into our hearts by the Holy Spirit who has been given us" (Rom. 5:5). We shall make a true Christian community only with the Spirit and indeed it is this very Spirit that animates this community that we call the "Church."

Bergson indeed had this presentiment in terms of his journey toward Christ: an open society, an open morality requires a transcendent principle. He called it the "calling of heroes."[30] Do we wish in our communities of the handicapped that in place of parasitism, individualism, or even simple solidarity, there exist such a sense of the other person, of his/her values and on the part of each one such gift of self that there will no longer be simply a natural offering but an opening out to the supernatural virtue of authentic charity? In that case, the means necessary must be supernatural, that is, divine. These means, one might think, are prayer and the sacraments. But the call of heroes is the call of Christ himself. Moreover, isn't Christ the first, and in a sense, the only sacrament within his Church?[31]

That is why a community will begin with a group of handicapped people only if an awakening, an education in real unselfishness takes place in each person. Even in terms of the entire group, community will happen if this community knows how to sacrifice for a higher transcendent purpose.

We spoke earlier about associations for the sick and disabled and other kinds of handicapped people; insofar as these associations are limited to arousing a feeling of solidarity in order that poor people be united in their misfortune to better defend themselves against adversity, they have not reached the real goal. Without doubt, they have provided a path for the handicapped person. They have, indeed, overcome some of his/her individualism. But these associations have only gone part of the way: a very long road remains before a sense of community and openness to real love can be attained. And longer still is the road which leads to authentic "charity." Let us try then to follow it.

I give myself to another, without doubt, in the setting of such associations. But do I go to him/her so that he/she will come to me? If yes, I am still with him/her in a way that makes me grow in selfishness. Or do I really go to the other because he/she is of value and because I give myself for him/her? If so, I am on the right road.

But even this association that I join and which is my bond with community, do I accept through it the sacrifice of myself and the gift of myself for something greater, for example, for the total group and, better still, for the glory of God?

It is only if I can answer in the affirmative to these questions that I have passed beyond the level of closed morality. I have gone beyond simple human solidarity. I have arrived at the true notion of human community. But I have not reached the level called "supernatural charity." I may still be infinitely far from it.[32]

However, it is at the level of authentic supernatural charity and only at this level that a Christian can situate his/her community ideal. The rest, however, is not stripped of meaning for him/her for it is the natural which is elevated to a supernatural plane.

Even the most perfect human love is not a summit where the Christian has the right to stop. Moreover, is there a summit on this earth for a Christian? True community will be realized only under the new heaven and on the new earth which have been foretold. He/she has, however, the duty to build the new Jerusalem without stain here below. That is why he/she utilizes the means that we have just listed: human means that the Christian has no right to neglect; divine means above all, the very love of God, diffused by his Spirit; the Church of Christ in the sacramental reality, her life of prayer, her theological life, the union in a word to this very act which is God, Trinity, Community, Love. And it is in this way that we have to learn to love.

12
Learning to Love

"In the evening of our life we will be judged on love[33] . . . " said St. John of the Cross, who has left us some pages on love that are undoubtedly some of the most beautiful among the treasures of humanity.

How many things are we not taught in this life? Many, and one of them is how to love. Unfortunately, too often we have instead been taught hate and violence. Contemporary psychology, however, is underscoring for us the importance, if not of love, at least of affectivity.

The value of affectivity, explained so brilliantly by St. Thomas in his treatise on the "Passions," was put to death by the Cartesian guillotine and condemned both yesterday and today by many pseudo-ascetics or pseudo-mystics, who were fearful of love. "The heart has its reasons that reason does not know," wrote Pascal who strangely enough presaged the discoveries of depth psychology. By scorning these reasons and allowing the heart to argue to itself in its dark corner, have we not neglected one of the essential dynamisms for humanity, the one that has the name of "love"? Freed for itself this seedling has given rise to a virgin forest; this subterranean stream has cut out such pockets of water on the mountain sides that they will burst out some day and submerge all. . . .

Some people have even banished the word itself. Have we not lately been counseled to avoid the word in our sermons as too equivocal and troublesome especially for our listeners? At the most we could speak of "spiritual love" or "chaste love." At least we believed we should do this, doubtless a little naively, to avoid all bad thoughts for these good souls.

We cannot help but compare this recommendation with the question one of the "souls" asked us one day. She wanted to know "if it was true that the Bible was on the Index." In putting love on the Index would we not be condemning God himself? For is it not true that "God is love" (cf. Jn. 4:16)?

For that matter, and by way of consequence, have we not restricted and profaned the word "love"? In effect one could not be without the other. "To make love" has become synonymous with bodily relationships in the most restricted and sometimes in the basest meaning of the word, there where, unfortunately, there is at times precisely so little love.

But then, where are John of the Cross, Theresa of Jesus, Catherine of Siena, Ignatius of Loyola, Thomas Aquinas, John the Evangelist and lastly the "Canticle of Canticles"? Will one no longer have the right to speak of "love" in the sense that all of them have written and God has spoken? This love of which John spoke when he said that there where it is, God is, and better still that love is God himself (cf. 1 Jn. 3:23-24, 4:8)—who could conscientiously deny it?

Some may reply that "we play on words." No, but we repeat the word because for a Christian, it, more than any other word, must be used. Yet a Christian must never profane it.

Learning how to love, then, is essential for all Christian and human education. Nothing will be accomplished if that is not done.

We have seen that the handicapped person who is deprived of true love is less "inclined" to love than another person. Indeed love awakens and elicits love—as hate arouses hate and indifference or scorn sterilizes the power to love. From this point of view, sadder than any other is the case of those maladjusted men and women who, for example, are victims of prostitution. These persons who have "made love" without love are often those who do not believe or no longer believe in love. Nothing in this world is more terrible.[34]

How can we give the power of love to the handicapped if not by loving him/her truly first, or better still, giving him/her also the opportunity to love in return?

The whole problem is that the handicapped are too seldom loved, at least really loved. They are deprived of love, at least authentic love. We recall what we have already said: that nothing will be possible, nothing will be done if handicapped people are not loved with a love of esteem and with deep respect; with a love that excludes contemptuous pity and humiliating paternalism; with a love which accepts and desires exchange; with a love that wishes the well-being and the rehabilitation of the one that he/she loves, who would prefer him/her being better in order to admire and to love him/her more and more.

Education for true love for the handicapped begins then with education of the educator himself/herself. It is first of all the educator who must painstakingly learn how to love. Do we always learn to love the handicapped in schools for special educators? Do we learn to love the handicapped in laboratory classes, team meetings, in-service meetings, meetings of professional organizations? Do we learn to love the handicapped not because this one is more amusing or less pitiable or that one is more retrievable, but because the handicapped have a right to our love and because they need to be loved?

Doubtless an instructive psychoanalysis or a similar disentangling process could aid the special educator, the social worker, or the psychologist to evolve toward a better affective maturity and consequently toward authentic giving. But what question does the spreading of such methods pose for us? Certainly, regular checks by supervisors of student teachers or team meetings would give some "insight" that could help the educator or the social worker to understand and to revise some deviate or infantile behavior patterns. However excellent all that may be, it will never give an educator the true love which is a virtue and not merely a degree of psychological maturity. To love truly we have to choose unceasingly between possible egoism and self-giving even to forgetfulness of self. It is here that psychology ends and in a strict sense morality begins. The free option with its risks and the sacrifices that it implies does not derive from attending courses, or from meetings, or from psychological clarifications. It presupposes a response that each one can make only in his/her own heart and in his/her own name. The handicapped person knows those who have responded and he/she loves them.

For love is indeed a way of "knowing." We have said that it is in more than one case the only possible way of entering into contact with certain "handicapped" people. Such is the case of the profoundly retarded or severely disturbed or the seriously mentally ill who seem so impervious to every other action coming from the outside. Affection, or as we prefer, love, will remain our sole means of contact with them or them with us, although some classically speak of their apparent lack of affectivity.

But while we no longer have to be afraid of love because we fear a confusion of terms or over-emotionalism, on the other hand we should not fall into the opposite abuse of setting up all education for the handicapped on a sort of romantic sentimentality. Certain forms of education of the handicapped are based on a distortion of love, prolonged demonstrations of tenderness, even some display of kisses and caresses bordering on the sensual. These have never been the actions of qualified and confident teachers, nor do they mean that love is present in the one who is teaching. On the contrary, such excesses are to be courageously, even strictly proscribed, and handicapped children or teenagers would hardly be deceived by them.

Some directresses of institutions, "fond mamas," cajole the little one who has a fresh lively face, and they display him/her ceaselessly before visitors until another new arrival dethrones him/her . . . like those parents who extol the last born at the expense of the older child. Other educators have sentimental conversations with older children, thrust their troubles upon them or pour out unrestrained tenderness. Others play upon the heartstrings all the way to the breaking point. And from these excesses the male teacher is also not exempt.

*   *   *

Still more dangerous would be transposing this sentimentalism to the supernatural level. For it is at this level that we must place ourselves in the final analysis.

The moral virtue of unselfishness doubtless has its price. But as with all that is of God, charity, the supernatural theological virtue, infinitely transcends it. This virtue is infused. God gave it to us in baptism. In a sense it is the very grace of God, his Spirit of Love diffused in us. It is God in himself in us.

There is nothing more magnificent than the treatise of St.

Francis de Sales on the love of God. Though serious and difficult, it is inexhaustibly rich and amazingly realistic in relation to the discoveries of contemporary psychology. It contains detailed instructions on love in the authentic supernatural meaning of the word.

Supernatural charity is in God, love of God himself and of our neighbor, "two doors," according to Kierkegaard, "which can only be opened or closed at the same time." "The second commandment is like to the first," said Jesus (Mt. 22:59).

But here also, the handicapped need first to discover that God loves them before they are asked to love God. And this is precisely where our responsibility lies. For it is in us that the handicapped person will most often discover the God who loves him/her. It is most often our fault if this love is not revealed to him/her.

That is why those who approach the handicapped must seek love on a much higher level than on the plane of the highest moral virtues. Only the Spirit of God can give it to them. It is a question of a new and continuous Pentecost. But the Spirit can make of each of them apostles or envoys and witnesses of the very love of God.

It is also on this level that the "theological education" of the handicapped will be situated. The divine aspect of this work surpasses all infinity and it also surpasses the educator and all human pedagogy. All the handicapped person can do is to receive grace and to correspond with it, and all the educator can do is to help him/her to do it. Still both the teacher and the pupil have to know how to place themselves within this perspective and again it is the educator who has to do it first.

But one will still have to make good use of the divine gift, putting charity into practice by loving God and his/her neighbor in truth. The educator will be involved as well as the moralist. For basically this is the whole problem that moral education raises.

*   *   *

Without doubt, one of the most serious errors of our time is the confusion of morality and psychology. The moralists lean toward raising psychology to morality. Psychologists, on the other hand, tend toward reducing morality to psychology. And in the end both psychology and morality are frustrated and disfigured.

From here the error goes on to confuse mental hygiene, morality and asceticism, and conversely, psychopathological phenomena and sin.[35]

They call moral perfection the state of affective maturity, recommend a pscyhoanalyst as a spiritual director or conversely they suggest confession as psychotherapy. Even the word "lie" points out the real moral deception, as well as mythomaniacal or "delirious" conduct.

All this makes the problem of moral education of the handicapped particularly delicate and difficult. Most special educators excuse themselves, or aided by priests who are generally little conversant with these questions, they commit some serious errors, or they become the prey of numerous scruples and torments.

How do we judge the responsibility of this epileptic for his outbursts of anger or very violent action? Caught between the doctor who declares that "it is not his/her fault" and the chaplain who is scandalized by such behavior, the special educator asks himself/herself where the truth lies. He/she can easily turn from one excess to the other, going from extreme indulgence to the greatest severity.

Can we approach the egoism in this schizoid or autistic child? Can we condemn masturbation compounded by proselytism, or the cruelties of an adolescent, classified as pathologically perverse? What can we ask of this retarded person? What can we lodge against that disturbed person? In the name of what principle? Just where is morality involved here? What are we to do?

We cannot take up here a detailed examination of these problems. This topic alone would require a whole volume. Above all it would require a profound preliminary study of these questions. But we desire simply, once again, to give some principles with which to start. But each case will certainly demand its own solution.

So it seems that too often we practice in the realm of the "either or else," so harmful on more than one level. This action is "very immoral" or else "very psychopathological." This man is either "culpable" or else he is a "victim." In a word, either he "is responsible" or else he "is not responsible."

Should we not in most cases consider that the person may be a victim and at the same time blameworthy? He/she may be partially determined and relatively responsible. He/she can, therefore, be capable of virtuous deeds and, in some measure, of sin.

Indeed our experience seems to prove that some profoundly mentally handicapped are capable of reaching for the good and checking annoying impulses. A pervert is not all perverse nor is a mentally afflicted person always "entirely mad." It is a duty and an act of respect to appeal to his/her innate abilities and to his/her possibilities for avoiding evil and doing good. Certainly God alone knows to what degree this person is responsible but what we know is that we never have the right to deny him/her all responsibility!

On the other hand, we have to take into account his/her limitations and his/her excuses. These are of many orders: physical, psychic, social and even moral. Extreme severity is as erroneous as indulgence. Both would be injustices.

Here, too, it seems to us that the best way to avoid error is to stress a positive moral pedagogy. To stimulate the handicapped person tirelessly but not without discretion, to help him/her do well and then to act better, rather than reproaching for poorly done tasks and ceaselessly brandishing the horror of sin: this is positive action. Some recent research seems to illustrate that the delinquent child is often the one who identifies himself/herself with what Jung called the "shadow" of his/her father and mother.[36] Often through threats and prohibitions the "shadow" of the educator stands out in profile.

That does not say that we never lay blame on the handicapped for his/her annoying acts and his/her faults. But in more than one case such handling would in effect only accentuate his/her worthlessness, would discourage him/her or crush him/her. On the other hand, to help him/her to see his/her improvement and his/her potential, and to see the happiness that can result from it and which he/she can bring others—this raises his/her self-esteem and encourages him/her to become better.

In all this, moderation is required. Even the appeal to do good, if it is imprudent, can be tiresome. As we have already said it is the same for encouragement wrongly given, compliments made on principle, material rewards lavished in every way. After some time these will not be effective and the person no longer cares. All this is a lack of consideration, if not scorn.

We must be truly sincere. The handicapped child or adult will appreciate simplicity and frankness. Moreover, he/she will gain realism and truth from it. We see some handicapped children who are not aware of their own mistakes because those around them forever excuse or praise them. The moral education involved in "coddling" a child is almost as dangerous as the reverse excess. It lessens his/her value and hardly prepares him/her for life.

For if moral maturity does not correspond with the intellectual or affective maturity—so that someone can be at the same time a retarded person or a pathological pervert and a kind of saint—it is nonetheless true that the educator must work to integrate moral education into the whole context of general rehabilitative or even therapeutic education. We refuse to subscribe to the formula that first it is necessary to give occupational therapy or psychotherapy and then moral or religious education. Both must take place simultaneously for the same person. But this can take place only on condition that moral-religious pedagogy and therapeutic pedagogy are really coordinated and in some manner related.

However, we must keep the distinction: neither morality nor religion should ever become a pedagogical or therapeutic means. We do not have the right to reduce them to this level. Inversely, neither orthopedagogy nor psychotherapy should be turned into morality. We no longer believe that we arrive at religious and moral perfection solely by means of healing pedagogy or by medicine. The goal lies in another direction and is infinitely higher than that.

This danger of confusion is to be feared so much more because the teacher and the therapist will often be the same person. This is in our opinion a good thing which promotes at the same time moral instruction and allows the practice of therapeutic education. The solution does not lie in changing personnel nor in the substitution of roles. There should be a clear distinction even in the heart of the teacher or the therapist of the two orders of value and the two levels to be reached.

However, a change of those responsible certainly has advantages. An eventual change of the setting does also: for example, going to the chapel or into a room specially reserved for religious or moral instruction. But doesn't the student also have to sense that one's moral and Christian life is, in short, life "lived" in a moral and Christian manner and that the educator or the therapist has his/her own moral and religious life as well as his/her professional competence and his/her daily personal cares? Would it not be dangerous for the handicapped person, especially, if religion and morality were taught him/her only by a man wearing a cassock or by a nun, or even by a catechist or by a moralist "specialized" in such functions?

We admit that a rigid division of educational functions, of which we spoke earlier, is too often a facile solution or an escape for men or women who prefer not to have to be religiously involved or who themselves remain somewhat lukewarm in their faith. It seems to us that the real solution still has to lie in a synthesis which upholds diversity and unity.

*   *   *

Starting from here, what can we say concerning the handi-capped in particular about learning to love?

Referring back to what we wrote about their psychology, we can count on particular difficulties (feelings of frustration, temptations of withdrawal, or insatiable demands, etc.) and also special abilities (keen sensitivity, a capacity for complete selflessness). In addition we will have to overcome the physical or moral isolation that the handicapped person encounters in his/her milieu and notably in his/her family, or inversely, the exasperation provoked by the continual impersonal atmosphere in institutions.

Opening to others will have to go beyond the bedroom or the institution in which the handicapped is frequently enclosed. Here many methods can be utilized (lectures, pictures, relationships, ra-dio, television) to open up the handicapped person to today's world and (as we previously mentioned) to the Church.

It is necessary, it seems to us, to remind the handicapped person that charity begins with his/her roomate or his/her father and at the same time to enlarge his/her horizons to include the full dimensions of the universe and of Christianity. If not, we will have sick persons who are charmed by reading about St. Therese but who are pests to their companions, or on the other hand, paralytics, ignorant of the world, who live in "smug" charity in the bosom of a petty, closed world of disability.

Though we try to understand it, we also have to combat the attitude of the handicapped who, frustrated and threatened by life, clings to what is left, claiming that he/she can and ought to possess it just as others do. Again it is desirable to avoid too much encouragement for the somewhat morbid type of renunciation which we have already labeled as "victim soul" attitude, by which a person withdraws from life and rather than giving or opening himself/herself to it, in fact renounces his/her very existence.

Love for God is also developed in this way. That certainly is reason enough to begin with the presentation of revealed truth. The mystery of love which is the Trinity has the power to arouse the most passionate enthusiasm. The mystery of the Incarnate Word has the power to warm the coldest hearts. But we will not awaken the love of God in souls by presenting the Holy Trinity as a triangle or the Incarnate Word as a complicated mathematical problem.

We can't make loving adults sons of God with a few so-called holy pictures or with the anecdotes poured out in certain so-called "pious" books. Let us not impede the religious formation of the handicapped by giving them dry formulas from a catechism to learn by heart. Let us not yield to the temptation either of stifling them with exciting pieties or of building their Christian life on a base of theological novelties or on sentimentality disguised as devotion. How many sick or infirm adults or psychically retarded children have we not seen whose beds were surrounded with a great collection of pilgrimage pictures but who did not know the Gospel and had never heard of the love of God!

If well presented, this message of God's love will be—by all humanity but especially in this case—welcomed with great joy by the weak and frustrated person. He/she learns that he/she is "precious" in the "eyes of God," that his/her God loves him/her better than a mother, with an eternal love, and will never deceive him/her (Is. 49:15:15-16; 54:8; 65:13), that this love of God is always present in his/her life and that he/she is always present to God. In this way we understand that there is in this "revelation" the great and in a way the only true "remedy" for the anguish of disability.

This is not just a pious "consolation"; it is a strength. With the contemplation of God presented in the truth of a love "strong as death," the handicapped person will not only go forth "resigned" and "appeased," but determined to advance and to live better, certain that he/she will be from now on more powerful than suffering and sin. The love of God well understood will no longer separate him/her from the city of people. It can only lead to loving people better.

*   *   *

This love of others entails a very beautiful and normal form of sex, complimentary rather than opposite, that of the other. But we think that human love in its precise sense poses some very special problems for the handicapped.

There are, it seems, some handicapped conditions for which "there are no real problems." And at once we think of the orphans, children deprived of normal family life, the *meztizos* or refugees. In reality the sexual question is particularly delicate for these persons. We take as proof the large number of girls and boys deprived of family, refugees or of mixed race, who are solicited by men or women for prostitution,[37] or of youths, deprived of fathers, and girls, deprived of mothers, tempted by homosexuality; not to mention all the sexual problems that life in an institution brings for children deprived of normal family living and the question that human love poses for those who have never been loved.

But, in another sense, the case of those handicapped by severe physical or psychic disability is more difficult. How do we present sexual love and the prospect of marriage to these persons?

Simplistic solutions are scarcely ever lacking: pure and simple abstinence from conjugal relationships or sterilization. We know what reservations the Church has on this subject. Neither one nor the other resolves the problem in fact. Education in love and sex is something other than a question of intercourse with or without procreation. The love of a man for a woman and a woman for a man presents dimensions other than copulation. Doubtless it is for lack of having had a view of the total question that we sometimes believe it so easy to solve by the principles mentioned above.

Procreation in its turn presents a double problem: that of bringing children into the world and that of raising them. Consider the situation of the husband of a deaf-mute or the children of blind parents, of a seriously retarded father of a family or a mother with severe lifelong motor or psychopathic impairment. Think of the problems of conjugal intimacy, the growing relationship of the couple, the education of children with all the relationships of an affective order and the dynamic interpersonal relationships that these presuppose. Then consider the realities that are involved in such a situation and how they require previous study before the handicapped and his/her educators confront them.

We are painfully surprised when we see how poorly some retarded or epileptic girls and so many disabled youths are prepared, or rather terribly unprepared, to attack these grave questions. Some retarded girls think of a baby only as a doll that they cuddle (fondling themselves a bit through their own child). Some of these youths think simply that to take a wife will permit them to pour out their need to love and to be loved, or even to satisfy their physical instincts while finding a nurse in the bargain. But who has dared to discuss such problems seriously with older girls and boys?

Learning to love is more than that even if it is not only that.

$$* \quad * \quad *$$

Indeed there are other ways of giving and other states of life besides marriage. We spoke of this earlier and will now return to it. Doubtless, there would be a reaction to the attitude of some parents whom we have seen present a handicapped youth and say: "Couldn't you find something for him to do as a lay brother in the monastery? He does good garden work, he can take care of the rabbits and the chickens . . . and he is pious and gentle. He could make a good little monk." It is useless to state that a religious vocation is obviously something very different.

But for handicapped people why isn't the religious life possible? There are blind religious, others deaf and mute, congregations of men and women who are all or partially recruited from the infirm. On the other hand, the psychically deficient and the mentally ill pose more delicate problems that to our knowledge have not been solved up to the present time.

Delicate as well as rather widespread is the admission of orphans and "penitents" into congregations responsible for education and rehabilitation. It seems that this problem has not always taken into consideration given facts of this problem: (a) the question of this kind of vocation and (b) the way that members are recruited. It could well be the object of serious study.

The total gift to God of a handicapped person can be nonetheless a spendid thing. A handicapped condition can also occur, as in marriage, in the midst of religious life. How many missionaries who entered religion to convert distant peoples has not God nailed to a bed for life in the confines of a convent? And how can we express the suffering and value of the mental or chronic illness of a priest or religious? There we touch the heart of the mystery where love finds the tree of the cross.

Finally, celibacy merits being proposed to the handicapped. It constitutes a state of life recognized and honored by the Church. Some have tended to raise it even above marriage, a thought understood with difficulty by the majority of young men and women today. These see it only as a passing state or a last recourse, even a catastrophe. The single girl has had a bad press and the bachelor nearly always elicits gossip.

However, is not the celibate life in itself the most desirable for some handicapped people, for example, the very ill, the severely disabled and the mentally deficient? But celibacy should never be presented as a renunciation of love provided that we understand it, want it and accept it.

For the single person, in professional life especially, the gift of self to others has to have priority if we wish to give meaning to it and make of it "a vocation for loving." But do we praise the grandeur of professional life sufficiently? How many girls today will only consider it as the prelude or means to obtain the desired marriage? Once they have met their prince charming, nothing more is important and their earlier responsibilities are left behind, come what may.

For the handicapped and for many others, a Christian reflection upon professional and social responsibilities, even the most humble, would seem appropriate here. We shall go farther: it is urgently needed. What good and what joy may result from it!

*   *   *

If it is true that the commandment to love contains all the law and the prophets as Jesus said, what we have just written of an apprenticeship of love could be applied to all morality. But morality has also had a bad press, doubtless because we have forgotten that it is the basis of the "art of loving."[38] We have to give morality its profound meaning and thus its real attraction. Then we shall no more be so fearful of the moralists . . . or of "priests."

Some psychotherapists and psychiatrists have indeed great fear of moralists and place themselves as champions of indulgence or neutrality in this area. Let us admit, even though there have been jokes about it, the "benevolent neutrality" of psychoanalysts. But true psychoanalysts are the first to know that morality is good and honorable if only because of the reality principle. One step more is taken when we are not only content to accept morality but to love it. Still we have to see through to the face of God our Father who has given it to us through love for us and in his wish to make us happy. In this way it will be good even if it entails something bitter.

13
Learning to Believe and to Hope

But for all that, it is necessary to believe in the love of God the Father. We have then, basically, a question of learning to believe. This is as true for handicapped people as for others. Again, the faith of the handicapped person is easy and at the same time difficult. Such also is his/her hope and love.

The faith of the handicapped man may seem easy. Isn't a trial often the road to faith? We cite the case of devout sick persons, of pious orphans, of penitents contrite, repentant and edifying. And sometimes we are lulled to sleep on this deceptive certitude that a handicap automatically throws one back into God's arms. Yet, this attitude is so common that one may fear that it indeed is only a refuge. Would not the faith that results risk being fragile and limited?

True, many handicapped people are declared unbelievers and fierce rebels. Rebelliousness, moreover, is less disturbing than the passive indifference we see in some sick or disabled who are completely incapacitated.

In reality, to believe in God is to believe in love ... *"et nos credidimus caritati"* ... and to believe in love is very difficult for a handicapped person. That is why, we repeat, everything has to come back to helping the handicapped discover that God loves them. If a living synthesis of dogma is always necessary, if it is necessary that God be discovered or revealed not as a concept but as a person (or

186

better, three persons), then this is all the more true when it is a question of handicapped people. But it is with them that we run the most risk of being unfaithful.

We know that the religious education of the handicapped is often very fragmented. They have been deprived of regular catechism classes, instructed about this or that by chance contacts with the chaplain of an institution or with a zealous neighbor. Thus, their education is often mostly book learning and limited to some memorized formulas. Notwithstanding such haphazard treatment, they have made their First Communion, sometimes followed by confirmation because "a bishop happened to be passing that way." Or, in an orphanage or rehabilitation center or sanatarium, someone has in a few months supersaturated them with religious instructions and sermons. They remember this painfully, and may even have developed an "allergy" to such spiritual intoxication. The patient has been conditioned against religion and the nausea returns to him even now when religion is being given only in small doses in a sane manner and is conformed to truth.

For him, the priest or religious educator is synonymous with a "wet blanket" or "bore." Perhaps these helpers once intervened at the wrong time by awkwardly putting a finger on his/her wounds saying precisely what should not have been said! Finally, all priests may be a symbol of frustration, of suffering, of mourning, of prohibition, or even of paternalistic authority. In the intuitive perception of those cut off from the world, the priest may be viewed as being on the side of those who have alienated, undervalued and harmed him/her. All that the priest is, as all that he brings, can only reactivate in him/her staunch self-defense, his/her real way of welcoming this priest even if an exterior correctness masks it.

There are many reasons why faith is difficult for the handicapped. These are, therefore, some of the many reasons for us to teach or to re-teach him/her to believe.

*   *   *

Faith is, first of all, a gift from God. Here again all human effort, insofar as it remains human, is radically powerless. The educator and all those in charge of helping handicapped persons to find God should know that first of all they must pray.

But how can the handicapped believe if they are not evangelized? Faith then presupposes evangelization and a catechesis to affirm it. We think that this evangelization can only bring us back to the essentials mentioned before. But these great themes must be presented to the handicapped in a synthetic or at least global fashion. We add here some recommendations of recent note concerning the actual organization of the catechism.[39] For the handicapped, more than for any others, it seems not only desirable but indispensable always to develop all new concepts as a whole or, better still, to present them with that whole. This is true even for material and practical reasons. In a very general way indeed the handicapped, as we have seen, are often entrusted to a succession of catechists. Their formation, even in the most favorable cases, remains almost always fragmentary, and for that reason, disconnected. A person may spend three months in the hospital or at an institution, then he is sent to a sanatarium or to a center. There he receives some instruction, here he gets nothing or else he arrives in the middle of the year's program.

The principle prepares us then always to teach within a context of—or at least to develop all the essentials in—the space of twelve or nine months of a year. But that absolutely does not mean that the student is to swallow everything hastily in one gulp. We repeat that it is to the essentials that one should take first and only later on to the accidentals . . . if there is a later on.

For eight years we taught catechism to young girls in an institution in the vicinity of Paris. Each year we gave the essentials, trying, however, not to repeat too much and to work at some deepening for those children who had followed us faithfully through those years.

The divine mystery, a living reality, should not be cut into little pieces and passed out in slices. Every presentation and each reception of this mystery can only be developed as a function of the whole. Isn't this whole a living God considered in himself and in the dynamism of his saving action in favor of the world he created? Let us add or rather repeat we are helped in this by a cathechesis that is both authentically biblical and liturgical.

Furthermore, we must take into consideration not only the chronological but also the mental age of the pupil, or rather a composite of both. The latter, we should remember, is not a simple affair of "intelligence quotient" but a synthesis of intelligence and maturity that is at times very complex. On this subject we recall that between the degree of verbal, biological and motor development, of affective and social development, there undoubtedly exists real correlation. There are also some very noticeable differences. So obvious is this fact that it always seems to us difficult to say at what age it is appropriate to stress this or that aspect of dogma. But it does seem necessary to arrange a wise sequence in the presentation even of some complex realities, so that after presenting them initially in their entirety, one should clarify successively this or that aspect. Hasn't God himself proceeded in this way when he revealed himself to humanity? And the Church, in turn, in all her tradition seems to have been faithful to this rule. Besides, how could it be otherwise?

What is also advisable with handicapped persons is to anticipate their possible "handicapped" reactions to this or that aspect of dogma. The sight of the cross, for example, could arouse sadistic or masochist reactions in some disturbed persons. The stress put on the dogma of hell or the last judgment could cause anguish for some nervous people; to insist too much on subtle reasoning of sin could disturb the consciences of those suffering from obsessions or scruples. The more positive aspects of dogma will generally not produce such effects. Of course, there is no reason to reject the more negative aspects of the same dogma but only temporarily to leave them in semi-darkness. One must arrange to return to them more openly as soon as the person is psychically strong enough to welcome them soberly and with enough clarity of vision to interpret them as they ought to be interpreted. There, too, all depends on the profound attitude of the one who presents this revealed truth and of his/her loyalty toward the Church and God.

In no case do we have the right to curtail or falsify the truth even on the fallacious pretext of making it more acceptable. God is God, infinitely good and perfect such as he is and not such as our infantile desires would like to fashion him according to our taste.

*   *   *

But the faith is not only a teaching to welcome and assimilate; it is the contemplation of life. It is life itself. We shall still do but little if we content ourselves with teaching, and have not led the handicapped to this contemplation or to this life. It is there that educators, primarily parents, but also substitutes for parents prolong the action of catechism or, so to speak, be prolonged themselves beyond "catechism" into a "catechesis" and a real Christian education.

A bridge, however, should be built to connect this teaching, this contemplation and this life. Truths must be taught in such a way that they not only invite knowing but also respecting and living them. Inversely, contemplation is nourished with these truths, and life will be lived according to the deep imperatives which flow from them. These truths can modify an existence and even revolutionize it.

On this subject, we have said how many handicapped people are often especially well-suited to contemplation, in the broad sense of the word, at least, but also in the strict sense and this is true even with those who have psychic problems.[40] This aptitude must be fostered in that it has authenticity, provided that we take care not to let it fall into a digression which would be pure and simple daydreaming.

We must add that the handicapped are often capable of facing the life of faith in all the severity of its demands. Some of them who are frustrated can be egoists, as we have said, but they also can be extraordinarily generous. We must not then be afraid of presenting Christianity with all its challenges to the handicapped under the pretext of protecting them in their weakness. Taking into account all that we have said previously, the plan of God, his law, his very counsels must be offered to these people. Have we not been amazed to see at what level they enter straightway into the spirit of the Gospel and are moved by its Beatitudes? They jump in with both feet, so to speak.

But there is, nonetheless, the risk of tiring them. The most important thing is that they believe in love and its triumphs, that is to say, in Jesus in his resurrection. This is the fundamental "faith" and the one that handicapped people first have the greatest difficulty in accepting. It is the one that will remain in the somber times and in the midst of a thousand and one difficulties that life holds in store for them. It is also there that the first theological virtue rejoins the second. Charles Péguy wrote, "The faith that I love the best,' says God, 'is hope.' "

*   *   *

How then do we teach the handicapped to hope? We willingly respond: Promise them real good and give them real reasons for hope, but do not embarrass them with false hopes. Here again we shall ask for them and with them that supernatural faculty, this infused virtue of hope that God gives us as between his faith and charity. . . .

It is necessary, as we have said, to "orient" their hope. It is truly good to hope in this God of love so that we may seek him and never leave him. Truly, it is good to hope in his infinite perfection which transcends all that the earth gives us and all that of which we have been deprived; truly, it is good to hope in his life that is stronger than death, in his good triumphing over all evil, in his beauty victorious over all ugliness and all human disgrace.

But beware that this hope is not offered as "a consolation" for the suffering of the handicapped person, a compensation for his/her deprivations, a kind of projection in full for what deficiencies have taken from him/her. "I do not have health; God is infinite strength. I do not have beauty; God is splendor. I don't have a father: God is my Father. No one loves me, but God is my Father. No one loves me, but God does understand me and he loves me." Such a thought process is doubtless not unlawful or inexact. However, it would seem to us not without danger or without risk of reducing the theological virtue of hope to a natural and human level. Actually, it gives to hope a man/woman-centered turn which in reality it does not at all have. Let us not forget that we must hope above all that the reign of God will come, which is first and essentially theocentric and assures all the rest besides.

Therefore, we must give the handicapped real reasons to hope. But let us not coax them with false hopes. Without knowing it, we encourage a feverish sick person that tomorrow his/her fever will be lower by several degrees. We promise a young girl in a foster home that she will go back to her father and mother, or a refugee that he/she will soon return to his/her own country. We tell a paralytic that he/she will walk and a dying man that he will soon leave for the country. But do we dare to say or at least not hide from them our true motive for hope—that Christ is risen?

From this point of view, it is not a question of denying someone's miseries or not trying to remedy them. Entirely to the contrary! But say that sufferings have a meaning and however it may come, the true remedy and true triumph will one day transfigure them. And let us understand that acting in this way is not an opiate to lull people to sleep. It is not an attempt to have them give up the struggle and surrender. On the contrary, it is untiring support in the battle being fought against death and suffering. It is to give them, in the midst of all possible human failures, invincible certitude that the final victory of good over evil is assured.

Certainly the mystery of the resurrection of Christ, the pledge of all our hope as St. Paul said, should not be thrown at the handicapped person in the beginning. It must be situated within the context and at the summit of this revelation which at the beginning of this chapter we learned how to present and also how many precautions are required.

But the motif for hoping must be at least in the hearts of those who approach the handicapped. This is evident from what we wrote in the first pages of this book and even in its title "Pedagogy of Resurrection," the pedagogy of hope, the pedagogy which returns to reveal the end to all suffering: the final triumph of God's love.

14
Initiating the Sacramental Life

God gave us the first fruits of this hope here below: It is the sacrament par excellence, since it is Christ himself and his mystical body: that is, the sacrament of the Eucharist.

The paschal sacrament is the risen Jesus who makes us pass from death to a new existence and from darkness to marvelous light. In the ritual that the Church dedicates to it, the Eucharist is often presented as a remedy. It is the sacrament of faith, a sacrament which communicates and gives charity. It is also a sacrament of unity, the sacrament of hope and the guarantee of our eternity. Then it is infinite richness which cannot be sold to any wealthy person or refused to any poor person. Then can it be denied to the handicapped?

But the Eucharist is first of all the mass and already, how many problems have we not seen arise? The assembly of Christians is, in theory, open to everybody. In actual fact, how many feel rejected and bored there!

Let a retarded person, a bit odd, be brought to the service and someone notices very quickly: "What an idea to bring a child like that here!" A disabled adult drags his leg or uses crutches and he makes noises when entering the pew, or the priest must leave the sanctuary, to give Communion to a paralyzed person . . . and that takes time! Our good parishoners are impatient: "When someone is in that condition, he/she should stay home and not go to church!"

Would that the Eucharist could be for all "these people!"

Pardon our insistence on this subject but it is a scandal. It is a scandal that a Christian community believes that it can be Christian without these persons. It is a scandal that the sacrament of unity cannot unite all of us, even and above all, with those with whom Christ was associated on the cross. A single exclusion because of these false reasons and one has not been faithful to the reality of the Eucharist itself. It is, however, true that in certain churches the approach to the holy table has been denied to "colored" people. O hypocrisy! They have, it seems, their own "churches." Must we have, therefore, special churches for the handicapped?

"Masses for the sick" are often held, as we mentioned, with the result that some devout ladies distribute cups of coffee and milk to the sick of all ages and to old people whom they have brought together. This takes place annually and leaves the whole parish quite tranquil for still another year. The parishioners return home content and pious because all these good people were so difficult to look at. Before them we feel ashamed of being strong and we are threatened in the serenity of our faith!

Certainly we admit that such services represent progress from former times when nothing was done for the sick. But the Christian community cannot consider the problem of the handicapped as already solved.

Even recently at an International Eucharistic Congress in a Christian country, the leaders refused to consider an international participation of the infirm. They contented themselves with a simple morning program which consisted in bringing Holy Communion to the local sick at home. . . . There was no question at all of associating with them at the celebration. Thank God this problem was solved in a more positive way at certain French eucharistic congresses, where among other activities a whole day was reserved for the sick. But here again, these are exceptional displays and not regular and normal participation in the Eucharist of these people who live in a "world apart."

Is it surprising then that so many sick and infirm people only see the Eucharist as the reception of the consecrated host, such as it is practiced according to the ritual for the sick? They do not view the Eucharist as sacrifice, nor do they see it in the perspective of community and of common march of the Church toward its destiny of glory and unity. Communion is for many of them only an act of individual union with Jesus in the host and not "the common union" of the faithful in the risen Christ.

But someone may reply: Isn't it this way also for many Christians, even very fervent ones, whom we don't generally consider "handicapped" (at least not officially)?

Yet it should be easy to understand the great importance of presenting the sacramental order in its entirety to all the faithful, but again, more especially to those who form the special object of this book. For the handicapped, in fact, more than others risk considering Eucharist as a magic rite or at least as "medicine" in the material sense of the word. Moreover, those around them encourage these attitudes. We remember a nurse giving an injection of morphine to a young sick girl to whom we were going to minister. "So that she will not feel anything," she told us as she would have said to the surgeon prior to an operation. We recall also a youth refusing to bring food to a tubercular patient to whom we had just given the sacrament of the sick. "Now, it isn't worth the trouble since the priest has given him extreme unction." We are no longer suprised to see these same sick people making a novena of Communions for some cure and stopping as soon as improvement comes. It is like those who stop taking pills when the desired effect has been obtained.

This fetish of the sacraments is not only found with the sick; it is also typical for the psychically handicapped. More than to others, confession appears to them as a means for becoming spiritually "proper," a necessary precondition for Communion. People around them strengthen this conviction through remarks that are not simply inopportune, because they show evidence of serious errors of judgment: "You said a bad word, you cannot go to Communion like that; go to confession." Or "You have just been to confession and you are angry . . . it was truly not worth the trouble; now all has to be done over."

In orphanages[41] and rehabilitation centers this sort of magic is sometimes extended to all the sacramentals. What uses and abuses are not made with the sign of the cross[42] and holy water?

*   *   *

What is involved then is a question of initiating the handicapped—and often the people around them—to the sacramental order, and this requires a whole catechesis of the sacraments. We must help the handicapped to discover the meaning and the grandeur of baptism as an entry into the mystery of Christ's death and resurrection. It is an entry also into the life of the Church, his mystical body, crucified with him on the cross, buried in the tomb and brought back to life on Easter Day before taking a place with him at the right hand of the Father in heaven (Rom. 5; Gal. 2:19; Eph. 6; Col. 2:12,13,20; 3:1.) The handicapped must be shown the value of the sacrament of confirmation as a more profound entry into the mystery of Christ's suffering and glory by the mark that it imprints and by the spirit of love that Jesus pours out on all of us from the Father through his Church.

We should reveal the fuller sense of the Eucharist to the handicapped by teaching them to be associated in this movement of return to the Creator and Father which has been achieved through the sacrifice and mediation of the triumphant Christ, priest and victim. Penance should be presented not only as the sacrament through which Christ, the redeemer, purifies us but also as the sacrament in which the mystical body of Christ is a beneficiary with us.

We should not hesitate to speak to handicapped people about the sacraments of holy orders and matrimony even if these seem to be denied to them in more than one case. We will show that they were not instituted for the sole benefit of the priest or the married couple, but are received for service to Church and thus for our benefit. We will explain the priesthood as being one with the glorious Christ, the sovereign priest, and the mystery of marriage as great in reference to the gift of Christ dying for his Church, glorifying it with him forever as a resplendent and immaculate spouse (Eph. 5:21:25). Finally, extreme unction should be explained to the handicapped as the "sacrament of the sick" identifying the suffering member with his crucified and redeeming leader and this identification enables him to give better service to the Church to which he belongs.

If the stress is put on the fundamental (but not exceptional) aspects of the sacraments and if each one is linked as a whole to the sacrament which is his mystical body, the Church, and if all is lived around "his holy sacrament," then the danger of "sacramental fetish" will in some measure be avoided. Of course, if all this is to lead to assimilation and thus be lived, it cannot be done in a short time or only in words. Here again we have to see how what we teach has effect long after the time of instruction.

Indeed, what good is there in telling children that they do not go to confession only to prepare to receive Communion and that they will eventually participate in the Eucharist without going to confession if we only provide the occasion for Communion after they have confessed their sins, or only provide the opportunity for confession when they "must" receive Communion? And why draw attention to the grandeur of baptism if we do not give the baptized the consideration that is due them as sons and daughters of God? How can they understand the value of confirmation if we threaten them with a slap while saying: "If you continue I am going to confirm you like this?"[43] How can we restore the meaning of penance if this sacrament is presented to them as a "washing" or as a chance to "empty his bag"? Will they have respect for the sacrament of matrimony if all that they ever hear about it are the taboos or sins? Will they see the grandeur of the sacrament of orders if the priest who comes to them is ridiculous or ridiculed? How will they understand that the sacrament of the sick is a sacrament normally directed toward cure and regaining normal activities in the Christian community if any person who has received it is considered as already dead? Finally, will they grasp the profound unity of the sacramental order in the glorious Christ and in his Church if the sacraments are presented to them as "calming potions" and distributed by a functionary too much in a hurry to close the window?

What is marvelous and dangerous in the catechesis of the sacraments is that theory is here joined to practice. To preach on the Mass is good, but still better is to have them assist at it. An invitation to frequent the sacrament of penance is laudable, but it is still better to provide these penitents with the time and means to confess well.

How many of the faithful are scandalized and hurt by the manner in which some priests, certainly pious, go hastily through the Mass? We dare to tell them this with respect and by respect. The handicapped, according to Claudel, are attentive and more than others notice this kind of failure. One of our tubercular friends, a convert baptized at the age of twenty, has noted the habitual failures of his clergy in this regard.

How many immobilized persons complain equally of not being

able to get anyone to bring them the Holy Eucharist? A bishop recently strictly counseled his priests about their duty here.

How many people who are mentally deficient or simply handicapped in speech, and how many emotionally disturbed persons complain that priests do not take enough time to listen to their confession.[44] A good priest, chaplain in an institution for retarded young girls, heard the confessions of the whole house in a few minutes. "They surely have nothing to say," he declared. Another in similar circumstances, recommended that they come to confession after his Mass, but he celebrated it before dawn and was always in a hurry to leave. Doubtless, he also sincerely believed that for these children a confession had scarcely any meaning since they are "innocent." But he could not know to what degree the "innocent" ones suffered by his actions.

How many handicapped children will take confirmation or baptism seriously if someone tells them one fine day: "The bishop is coming to the parish this week. Have you children been confirmed?" It was a question of retarded children who had never heard about the sacrament, much less that there is a Holy Spirit. In another institution they learned the evening before First Holy Communion that several children had not been baptized. The pastor of the parish came. They caught the children on the run and baptized them swiftly, without any preparation, even immediate, for the reception of this sacrament. Indeed, the preparation for First Communion does not imply that children are also prepared psychologically to receive baptism, not even if this chapter in the catechism had been "studied."

We repeat that the faith of the handicapped depends initially at least and for a great part on the practical faith of those around them. More than anything else they are sensitive to the contradiction between words and deeds.

The sacramental order is the permanent and fundamental structure of the spiritual life for all Christians at the same time that it assures the development of it. The handicapped will find in it the security and the healthy equilibrium that they lack. There, at least, they should not be frustrated. If they are much of the time, it is we who frustrate them by our ignorance and lack of comprehension. When they don't think of taking Jane to the movies, they don't think of taking her to Mass either. In both cases she is on the other side of the fence. Yet, if there is any place where the handicapped ought not to be excluded, it is in this area where every creature is "sacred."

But if the Church is divine, it is human also and we cannot be too scandalized by finding human views and reactions, attitudes which are prevalent as a general rule throughout society. We must only set to work so that this society that claims Christ as its own witnesses each day a little more to the one who preferred the poor.

How painful are the reactions on this subject of some Christians in regard to delinquent boys and girls in our rehabilitation houses, observation centers, or hostels for young workers (formerly called half-way houses). Again on seeing the harshness manifested sometimes toward these young people it would seem that practicing Catholics have forgotten the Gospel. What is worse, the door appears closed to all possible rehabilitation. Have we not seen a small Christian community scandalized when a young girl who previously committed some serious mistakes, as they said, dared to come again to church, or—a worse scandal yet—joined the choir in that church? These so-called Christians believed that past weaknesses of a young girl obliged her to desert the church forever or at least to be silent there. Would the priest have been better advised to send her away or to deprive God of her song?

A similar attitude prevails among administrators who direct centers for young delinquents with great strictness. They believe they have the right to demand that a young girl make her First Communion a "second time" before being allowed to go to the holy table, and this would require a long time of "public penance." Have they forgotten the pages of Scripture where the mercy of God and that of Christ never ceases to be shown? Then where is the joy of the woman who has lost a drahma? In the story of the prodigal son, why is it so many Christians believe themselves obliged to play the role of the older brother?

Chaplains at centers for these young people, as also those who are involved with former prisoners, another class of the handicapped, ceaselessly deplore this caution and severity on the part of so many of the faithful. Pedagogical pessimism and hardness of heart clothe themselves with a studied righteousness and pious excuses. But the reality is that here again, the Word of God is rejected or scorned.

However, how many Christians there are who like the accusers of the woman taken in adultery would—beginning no doubt with the oldest—have to flee if someone suggested that he who has never sinned cast the first stone! How many Christian educators, or those who pretend to be, are earnest about dismissing the "black sheep" but forget the parable of the sheep that was lost and recovered!

In the same way in certain regions, public opinion is so severe toward the young unwed mother that she is influenced to abandon her child in the sense of putting him/her into other hands. Purity of morals is thus better defended, some people assert. Others say that they only wish conveniently to limit in this way the scandal, but they indirectly encourage what they pretend in fact to avoid. Without wishing to take a position in a debate which is not closed and which involves many problems and nuances, we regret that some Christians are able to show so much aversion to pardoning and rehabilitating. Doesn't a woman who after a mistake has the courage to admit it and to accept all the consequences deserve to have the esteem of her brothers and sisters in Jesus Christ? Still more, should not the child born of such a mother be esteemed as much as any other child?[45]

May Jesus Christ in whose genealogy God has willed that only two women are named—both charged with "adventures" that were at least unfortunate—remind us that no sacrifice has more value before God than mercy. Would that Christians who dare to take that holy name not be opposed since the sacraments of his Church are helpful to lost children whom Christ's untiring love is capable of restoring to the true fold.

*   *   *

Two final comments on what concerns the sacramental order and various types of handicap: first, we do not emphasize sufficiently with the sick and the infirm the value of a spiritual desire for the sacraments, above all for the sacrament of the Eucharist. Spiritual communion is too often considered as simple devotion. We are often ignorant of the true grandeur and the astonishing effectiveness of it. How many immobilized, wrongly or rightly deprived of sacramental Communion, would not benefit from this eucharistic desire! We wish that a small pamphlet of solid spirituality could open such perspectives to all. These perspectives, however, should never take people away from the sacrament to the degree that they can really communicate.

Likewise on this subject, we should support the interest of the immobilized in radio or television Masses, reminding them that such programs are specially designed for them. But let us also awaken them by these programs to the liturgical life of the Church, and in the same way remind them from time to time of their invisible presence to all Christian listeners or viewers.

On the other hand, we also recall how much of the sacramental order refers to symbolic modes of expression which are fundamental to all human and divine expression in the history of the world and in the sacred writings. All the sacraments, say the catechism, are signs instituted by Christ to communicate his grace and to sanctify us.

This symbolic knowledge and this language of signs are within the reach of the most humble and the least fortunate. Even severely retarded children seem to grasp intuitively and affectively this symbolic expression. Many among them have seemed particularly skilled in expressing themselves in this way. The famous psychologist Dumas has explained that clearly enough, it seems to us, in his treatise on symbol when he stated that symbol is consistently utilized when the modes of verbal expression are not possible (verbal expressions being, moreover, only more developed and abstract symbols).[46]

Thus the sacramental order not only has power to communicate grace but to constitute an instruction for every person, instruction capable of being understood even by the severely handicapped.

Better yet, it can arouse a response capable of being manifested in a symbolic manner. It is thus, for example, with the ritual of baptism where "significant" gestures are asked of the candidate. It is especially true for the Mass in which the faithful are in some way invited to respond or join with the actions of the priest.

Thus the symbol of the sacraments can become a gold mine at the disposal of the Christian educator and, especially of the catechist. The same holds for all liturgical celebrations that concern the administration of the sacraments or sacramentals or that establish the prayer of the Church in its official and public celebration, a real expression of the Christian community responding to the approaches of God.

15
Master, Teach Us to Pray

As paradoxical as it may seem, it is exactly this liturgical expression that has been found to be the first form of prayer for the handicapped. They do not at all escape the general rule, not even here.

At first sight, however, the liturgical life of the Church is only accessible to the handicapped person with difficulty for all the reasons we have already enumerated. But isn't it true that the handicapped, more than others, have profound need for finding support in this official and public prayer and that they must participate in it in their way?

Too often the handicapped person does not know how to pray or at least he judges himself incapable of it. Physically handicapped, he burns with fever, absorbed by his suffering, turned in on his infirmity. Psychically handicapped, he is deprived in his intellectual evolution: he does not know how to speak or he is disturbed in his emotional life; he feels himself often unskilled and a bit reproached before God. The orphan has never learned on the natural plane to pronounce the name of Father. The delinquent, the refugee, the half-breed feels himself everywhere excluded and a stranger. Then how would he go to this God who nonetheless attracts him? There is nothing like liturgical prayer for the one who does not know how to address God.

It is in fact the prayer of the Church and as such offers total security. We say more: it is the Word of God himself instructing humanity how to speak to him. Indeed, the liturgy is usually arranged with Holy Scripture as the point of departure: it is then the echo of the Holy Spirit giving witness and praise to the Father through the Word Incarnate. Its prayers are the proper expression of the permanent sanctity of the Christian community and the countless bombardment of requests, many times for secular needs; its hymns have been sung by the large following of priests, monks, consecrated virgins and the faithful; its litanies are the tireless appeal that hope casts to the eternal. Better still, it is love "of himself," the Son of God, Jesus risen and immortal in his mystical body securing for himself in a way his own praise and giving in the Spirit of Love all glory to his Father, our Father; it is through him, with him, in him that our prayer ascends to the God of the heavens.

Then all fears can well vanish. I do not know how to pray. This is true. Then, who pretends to know how to talk to God? But God himself puts his word into my mouth. He integrates me into a praying community; better yet, he associates me in the actions of the graces of his own Son.

We remember the joy of some profoundly retarded older girls and children of welfare families who were very competent in Latin as they chanted at Mass in a little village of Savoy where they spent their vacation. We cannot forget these disturbed and delinquent young girls who sang so beautifully the Gelineau Psalms at a Belgian center of rehabilitation. We remain struck by the gravity with which the little slow learners of a special catechism class participated in the liturgical ceremony. We recall the impressive spectacle of about one hundred sick young people joining fervently in the communal celebration at their pilgrimages or summer camps.

But we also recall an afternoon in spring when we went in a car with some severely disabled adults to assist at vespers in the Abbey of Solesmes. The monks welcomed us as brothers, gave us places in church and we were silently united to their chanted prayer. One of the adults later became a contemplative monk. How we wished the participation could be still more frequent and more active! Would this not be an excellent form of integration into the Church of this world for—the handicapped? And for them the most extraordinary form of rehabilitation—one that any Christian worthy of the name would not refuse to any sincere soul and beside which all others have only a limited sense of relative value! Here they have their own function, their role which no other can fill in their place. Here they are the equals of those who sing at their right or at their left. Here their praises of petition are received and considered as precious. Here they achieve in their own way and finally they can live life fully.

For liturgy involves man/woman as he/she is, body and soul together. Do not be too afraid of off-key voices and awkward bodies. Let each one then do very sincerely all he/she can do.

In return, each one thinks of his/her neighbor and takes care to help him/her do his/her best in his/her own tone and his/her own rhythm and to help him/her in any way where that is possible so that the praying assembly becomes truly one community.

The handicapped person in the midst of this group has then to feel sustained and encouraged by the prayers of his/her brothers. We have said it at Mass over and over. But this goes for all liturgy. Let this prayer be beautiful and well done, but don't let concern for perfection exclude anyone who may disrupt the harmony of the group. We are not here to make a work of art but an action of petition and praise. The groans of my brother/sister and the awkward contortions have perhaps and even doubtless more worth than some harmonious song and beautiful gestures in the eyes of God.

Nevertheless, we will have to think also of the one who cannot physically and bodily join in a communal liturgical action. For these we could make greater use of audio-visual methods. These techniques were discussed earlier and, as we recalled, an encyclical was dedicated to the subject.[47] The rosary is recited over the radio each evening in French Canada and it is touching to see so many Christians daily saying Mary's prayer with their bishop. But could they not, there and elsewhere, also have the liturgical prayer of the Church heard and even seen on broadcasts often and more regularly from a monastery or from a devout parish which gives witness of a true community? We think of the broadcast over Eurovision of the Easter ceremonies, beginning with a lively congregation in a Paris church. How many handicapped that very night were able to live the celebration of the resurrection of Christ and from the *tenebrae* on their screens and in themselves finally see the bursting light. But unfortunately how many of our handicapped have not yet seen and never will see television!

It is also necessary—and this is readily apparent—that books be obtained for the handicapped to help them to know the liturgy and to participate in it. Numerous books have appeared during these last years but their quality is uneven and their distribution still limited. We are surprised to see in many parishes however fervent, in some countries from beyond the Atlantic, for example, how the movement of active participation of the faithful is still disregarded. Even more the handicapped in their "world apart" greatly risk not being touched by the liturgical renewal. A serious effort in this direction seems to us a necessary duty.

Here again there is work for special pedagogical action. The small child can already, in a certain measure, be initiated in basics and in a fully human manner of praying. The same is true of psychically and physically handicapped persons. We said in the preceding chapter that many handicapped persons are amazingly sensitive to symbol. We know to what degree liturgical symbols abound. We shouldn't be surprised at the excellent results from all the catechetical experiences celebrated with even profoundly retarded youth to initiate them into the liturgical life starting with basic formation about the gestures and the discovery of essential symbols.

It is a true discovery of prayer in a profound sense that operates at the same time as a corrective for distortions or for lesser forms of devotion which are somewhat infantile and magical. Paradoxically, too, from this initiation to communal prayer, personal and private prayer has flowed forth.

We see well enough how this communal liturgical prayer and the initiation that it allows differs from that accumulation of prayers which filled the schedule of young handicapped people in some houses directed by religious. In response to a questionnaire to religious specialized in rehabilitation of young delinquents, here is what they imposed on their residents: "Each week three quarters of an hour of catechism and Bible history by the chaplain. Three times a week one half hour of religious instruction by the religious in charge of the group and Saturday a conference. Mass is obligatory five days out of seven. The rosary and the Little Office of the Immaculate Conception are recited while the girls work. There is one half hour of spiritual reading and for about an hour they sing hymns."

Such things are scarcely believable. However, these excellent religious were persuaded that they were right. Doubtless they thought that these young girls more than others needed prayers and that the result of this would be an increased piety. On the other hand, did these religious realize in what way, from what milieu, from what living conditions these young girls came? Did they think of the consequences of this inescapable spiritual cramming, so liable to give nausea to many, even the very fervent? This case, it is true, dates from more than twenty years ago but who would dare to say that we would not find the equivalent now?

*   *   *

There remains for us now to see how to handle the problem of the initiation of the handicapped in private prayer, the so-called personal prayer, although liturgical prayer is, or at least ought to be, at the same time communal and personal in the sense that each one must see himself personally involved.

In fact, an excellent way is to start from liturgical prayer in order to invite personal prayer even in a private manner. We have just spoken of liturgical gestures. But why, then, as soon as we are alone do we have the tendency to stiffen, to grow tense or on the contrary to droop? Certainly, we can speak to God in all situations and in any way. It is excellent to teach a sick person that he/she can pray to the Lord tucked in his/her bed, or if paralyzed that he/she can call on him without even opening his/her mouth. But it is desirable insofar as one's gestures reveal the self, to join even very clumsy hands and raise the head to heaven. These gestures also have meaning even when the lips are mute or speech is haltingly impeded. We recall an adolescent, a mongoloid girl, humanly unsightly who prayed admirably, without saying a word but with very simple actions of hands and head. Who would deny that this prayer found favor with God?

As for words, the liturgy supplies us with them. They have the inestimable value of being inspired by God himself for the most part. How many of the faithful say they are too spiritually dry to make their thanksgiving after Communion, who would never even think of opening their Mass book to refer to the precise liturgical texts on

Communion as a basis or at least a starting point for their personal and private thanksgiving? Some handicapped people will not only make use of the prayers of the Mass but will join in reciting prime, vespers, or compline that are found in a great many missals for the faithful. Some others, principally the sick and disabled, could benefit from one of the breviaries or at least one of the shorter versions of which there are now excellent editions with translation into the vernacular. They make a manual of prayer that is infinitely superior to any kind of prayer book.

But it is also good to leave room for simple spontaneous prayer, for conversation with God. It seems important to us to point out to handicapped people with every kind of disability this fundamental form of prayer. Too many Christians, including the handicapped, readily believe that they do not pray when they are not saying formal prayers. They are lost without a prayer book or a rosary.

Indeed, we shall see some very ill people who tell us that they can "no longer pray" because their tongue cannot articulate the "Our Father" and "Hail Mary." Some mentally retarded persons content themselves with reciting formulas generally unintelligible or they remain silent. The disturbed or nervous who are blocked never succeed in pronouncing such and such words nor in getting freed from them. We have to explain to all of these people and sometimes even show them concretely that there are hundreds of ways to speak to God, our Father, even more a thousand and one things we should tell him: all that passes through the head and the heart as to the best and most intimate of friends.

We must show them that they can speak with God by very simply keeping silence and "advising him," like the parishioner of the Curé of Ars, that basically it takes very little to contemplate. "Prayer," a tubercular girl of twelve related one day in a catechism class at the sanatarium, "prayer is a gaze of love fixed on God—to become like to him." And she lived that.

*   *   *

However, it will be very good to open the handicapped to what we would call the great avenues of prayer: praise, thanksgiving, reparation, petition.

We shall begin with the prayer of praise, not that the catechism always begins with that. It is especially important not to fail to reveal this form of prayer. This omission would be a real distortion from what unfortunately many men and women suffer today.

The handicapped person risks suffering from this more than other people. His/her situation in fact causes him/her to feel lesser, deprived of what is due him/her and so to be frustrated and demanding. His/her prayer thus tends to orientate him/her above all toward prayer of petition and even toward egocentric and selfish prayer. It is absolutely necessary to free him/her from this circle, this prison in which such prayer restricts and encloses him/her. The prayer of praise is for him/her in the good sense of the word a wonderful way of liberation; liberation certainly not in the sense in which it would withdraw him/her from reality and he/she would forget to have two feet on the ground, but liberation from himself/herself from his/her miseries, his/her little aches or his/her big torments. Escape to God, for God, to seek only his happiness, his well being in him and his glory, all the while being persuaded that God knows how to busy himself with us during all that time.

Many hesitate to open such a perspective to frustrated souls. They think they have to reserve this for souls "advanced in perfection." Experience tells us that we cannot hold that opinion. We declare that the prayer of praise must be open even to beginners and to retarded persons.

When we learn "the prayers"—and God knows if some are always inclined to begin by teaching first the Our Father, the Hail Mary, the Glory Be—are not each of these prayers, partially at least and the last one entirely, an authentic praise in the most perfect meaning of the word?

We have been startled to see how profoundly retarded people or severely epileptic children were capable of understanding these perspectives of the glorification of our Creator and Father, of entering into this life even of praise which comprises the intimate happiness of God. We are often too timid or perhaps too blinded by our own egoism which makes us afraid to present prayer audaciously and daringly to others.

What joy the handicapped person will have when he/she understands what honor God will give him/her in associating him/her with all the souls and in the name of the entire universe in the most noble action of praise which allows him to enter into the eternal homage that Christ gives to the Father in the Spirit in the most blessed Trinity.

"O Blessed Trinity!" When this is said and repeated, all is in a sense drawn out; there is no other prayer. There are, however, still other ways to pray.

In the same way it is equally useful to open up for the handicapped the prayer of thanksgiving—for those who still think too often of what they are missing and not enough of what has been given to them. To know how to say thank you is always a difficult thing. It is, however, a source of joy when it is done.

Indeed, we think what benefits even in a natural order cannot fail to come to the handicapped from an inventory of what God has generously, daily or continuously granted to them. Aren't there infinitely more things that God gives to us than things he refuses?

We should teach them also to say "thank you" not only for themselves but for and with others for the happiness given to others, even if it is happiness which is denied to them. That, we must know, is difficult but what true joy there still is for the one who can experience it!

We should teach them to say thank you with the Church, with the saints, with Christ himself giving thanks to the Father who saved us from real death and gave us live for all eternity.

As for propitiatory prayer or prayer of reparation, it ought to be in some way the special prayer of those who suffer. In fact, we must present it courageously and exalt it among all categories of the handicapped. Esteem it but don't turn it into sentimentalism! Some pious literature, as we have often said in the course of this book, some preachers, some expressions maintain a certain sadness to the point of masochism and some willing victims risk nervousness rather than holiness, and pride rather than humble generosity.

Presentation of the idea of "making reparation" is very good in itself.[48] But it must be done prudently for the handicapped. A sane theology of redemption will have to underlie it; and a little psychology will not be a luxury if mistakes and a headlong falling into deviation are to be avoided.

It is certain that in this perspective of reparation, every handicapped person will find the key to his/her sufferings and the true reason why this has been asked of him/her or that has been refused to him/her. "I make up in my flesh what is lacking in the passion of Christ for the sake of his body, that is the Church" (Col. 1:24). We recalled these perspectives in speaking of the place of the handicapped in God's plan. The prayer of reparation is integral with the life of the handicapped and with his/her sad, even tragic destiny. If he/she understands it and lives with it, doubtless all will not be solved but what is of more value still, all will be transfigured.

There remains the prayer of intercession, of request; we have put it in last place, not that it is unimportant, unnecessary, or despicable. But in our opinion there are too many who place it in the first place and keep it there.

Of course, the prayer of petition should normally burst from the heart of the handicapped. "Out of the depth I cried to you, O Lord." However, prayer is not always easy for one who suffers; it is often poorly understood by him/her.

That prayer is not always so easy for the one who suffers—this we cannot easily understand unless we ourselves have known adversity at one time or another. Great sorrows, they say, are silent, a muteness which can be prolonged in some cases. And this muteness has value at times in the sight of God. How many handicapped people do we not find for whom prayer in some way stays in the throat? Without dwelling on annoying cases let us think of a sick person who admitted, "I cannot look at a crucifix; the sorrows of Christ, far from making mine less painful, add to my own suffering and it is too heavy." Or the young girl who was violated by her father: what image will she have before her eyes raised in supplication when she pronounces the words, "Our Father"? Moreover, note well that in these cases we must not opt for any hopeless, despairing or overly simplistic solution. The freeing of those muted must take place; the sick who suffer must be able to be associated in the trust of Christ in the midst even of distress. The child violated sexually must one day find a restored image of her father as such.[49] But we do not believe that this comes easily or that it has to be sudden or rapid.

Watch out also that the prayer of petition is not poorly interpreted for the handicapped. Said in another way, the handicapped person should try not to bargain with God or look on him as a vending machine. Isn't this the tendency of too many Christians? They put prayer like money into the machine; they draw out a handful, and if they do not obtain the desired product they ask for a reimbursement from the attendant—in this case from the pastor or chaplain. If they do not get what they pray for, they rebel or they are discouraged. How many handicapped people are there thus wearied, worn out asking God to cure their ills. They had received much encouragement to pray. And when the desired results did not occur, they turned their backs and closed their mouths; above all they closed their hearts which is worse. They have sobered into a real or feigned indifference, always angry. This is much more serious because it stems from what we would call a "misunderstanding."

The prayer of petition is in fact badly understood when considered as a business deal or worse still as an operation of a machine which automatically produces the right result. The merchant from whom we bought the chocolate sells it to us and the vending machine gives it to us even if this chocolate is not good for our health. But our Father in heaven is not a merchant or a machine, he is a father; he knows better than we do what we need and it is in this way he always hears our prayer, giving us not always what we wanted or asked for but what is in reality best for us.

It is important then to dispel the magic that religious infantilism conceals. In this area all of us, especially the handicapped, remain childish for a long time. Rather than have confidence in God, we would like to release our whims and make the paths of infinite wisdom follow those of our fantasy.

In a word, in fact, it is to spiritual maturity that all religious education leads. We cannot hide the fact that immaturity is precisely one of the characteristics of most types of handicap. The sick or disabled, even if they are matured in a certain sense, remain little children for a long time because of their condition. That is true also of the psychically handicapped, of the mentally retarded by definition (although here again a strange maturity can coincide with intellectual retardation), also for the most part, of the disturbed and finally of the many persons deprived of their real parents. Religious pedagogy of the handicapped then must be such that it aids in spiritual and even psychological maturation. This gives us one more chance for us to recall that religious education must be coordinated with all re-education. At least it should not be out of tune in respect to the whole. Let religious formation, in any case, not be the single sector that remains "infantile."

Gradually, courageously then, we will have to give the handicapped person an adult concept of prayer. The magical religious mentality consists in being willing to submit oneself to a divine power. The adult Christian mentality consists, on the contrary, in being willing to put oneself at God's service. Then let prayer, the prayer of petition itself, be presented and lived as God-centered and as consistent, that is, ask that God be known, loved and served. We affirmed it already in discussing the virtue of hope: what we desire above all and in a sense uniquely is that the will of God be accomplished.

The big problem, then, is not so much that of handicapped persons learning prayers. How many "maladjusted" little prayer forms (with limited theological accuracy) are learned and recited in some institutions, such as the latest novena to an unknown saint that this patient has on his/her bedtable, and the songs we have heard sung by young delinquents in the workrooms of that rehabilitation center! The big problem is rather how to teach these patients so they will learn how to pray.

Instead of awakening a sense of prayer, some ways of praying stifle it. Instead of developing piety, they deform it degrading and regressing it toward infantilism which differs essentially from the spirit of childhood where this is well understood.

We must simply return to "Our Father." Isn't he the model of all prayer proposed to his apostles and to us all through Jesus? "Master, teach us to pray," they asked. And Christ taught them the Our Father which remains for us the best of guides in our journey toward God.

We can understand why no one tires of repeating it and adding Hail Mary's and the Glory Be. The Virgin Mary gave the rosary to people to be the simple prayer which appeals to all, ignorant and learned, beginners and saints, adjusted and maladjusted. (But there remains a way of praying the rosary, as well as a way of saying it, which can create an aversion to it forever!) It is a very simple prayer, a school of prayer,[6] and a way perhaps toward the loftiest mystical states in which the mysteries of Christ are contemplated. We might speak also of prayer and of the unusual possibility with some handicapped persons of being initiated into and practicing a "life of prayer" even to an elevated degree of mystical union. But to write of this prudently would require an entire work in itself.

Here spiritual infancy joins the maturity of Christian life. Therese of the Child Jesus knew this well, she on whose feast day we finish this book, she the tubercular patient and thus handicapped. She died at twenty in a cloister and her influence spread throughout the universe. May she obtain from Christ that all his handicapped brothers and sisters on earth be better appreciated, better loved, better served!

And when he will return to bring back to the Father all those who will have risen with him, may this same Jesus welcome them first into his glory, he who has promised that the last shall be first.

Conclusion

Thus ends the writing of this book which has consumed a span of five years. It is then with a kind of exile that we reread the first pages. However, our profound conviction has not changed.

For five years journeys have taken us here and there in Europe, and into the Orient, to America, three times to Africa, from the Arctic Circle and beyond the Equator. Everywhere we have gone in this world we have encountered the same problems and seen the same needs manifested. Then as a conclusion here we would like to present the appeal of all the handicapped in the world to those who will have the patience to read this to the end.

The lepers of Saigon or of Tchad, the physically impaired of the Congo, the mentally retarded of Montreal, Stockholm or Vienna, the children deprived of normal family living, the delinquents of Omaha, Singapore, Hilversum or Rome—all look to us for the same faith and the same love.

The same faith in their infinite value, whether they are yellow, white or black, condemned to die tomorrow or to live for many years a life lessened in the eyes of men/women, poor in strength, intelligence and effectiveness. One same faith in the eternal victory of Christ, their Savior, who too has suffered, who has died and risen.

We desire a like love also for each of them, a love of esteem founded on this faith in their value as human beings, as children of God to whom each person is precious, unique, irreplaceable. An efficacious love which wishes to heal them, to make them integrated or fully adjusted. Finally, a love drawn from its source in God who has spread out his Spirit on us.

For God is Love!

Notes

Part I

1. Here we are also concerned with a further distinction. In the broad sense of the word, one can consider every person whose physical, psychical or social condition calls for some special education or living adjustment as handicapped. In the stricter meaning of the term, however, the handicapped person is one in a condition of maladjustment who finds himself/herself more or less permanently a victim of abnormalities sufficiently severe so that normal conditions or education cannot be used.

2. It must be said that there are some unfortunate, bad adjustments and some good, fortunate maladjustments. In fact, some adjustments are false, as a bent-over posture compensates for an inequality of limbs or the use of a defense mechanism in a psychic conflict. And some pseudo maladjustments are excellent such as the refusal of a person to settle down in a bad set of circumstances.

3. This word pedagogy as one will see farther on is the science and the art of educating the handicapped in a therapeutic as well as pedagogical format.

4. Etymologically "child leading."

5. Cf. the encyclical on the Education of Christian Youth (Pius XI, Dec. 31, 1929), the fourth part: Purpose and Manner of Christian Education.

6. The subject of this work is as vast and varied as it is specific. That may seem risky. Let each one not look here for the full solution for every detail of each problem posed by this or that handicapped person, but seek principles more or less valuable for all. Specialized works will be published completing this one, if not contradicting it.

7. Of course, in taking a census the number of the handicapped of all ages and categories would be higher.

8. "Give him health of soul and body and restore him speedily to your church" (Ritual).

9. Peyrebonne, Micheline, *Leur sale pitié*, Roman, Paris, Amoit-Dumont, 1951; the book deals with inordinate violence and injustice, and provides great insight for special educators.

10. Here let us return again to a film, this one inspired by a play: *The Heiress*. Olivia de Haviland triumphs in the role of the heiress who is loved not for herself but for her inheritance. One day she learns that not only her suitor but even her father does not love her for herself and cannot love her for herself. . . . She becomes a frustrated revolutionary who refuses all love and remains deaf to any appeal, giving scorn for scorn and indifference for indifference.

11. St. Augustine wonderfully analyzed this in a passage of lucidity and unequaled depth. "One could not weary in meditating on it: "You give bread to the hungry; it would be worth more that no one is hungry, that you give to no one. You clothe the naked: if only all were clothed, that there would no longer be such a need! You bury the dead: finally the day will come when no one dies. You settle disputes so that finally there may be eternal peace, the peace of Jerusalem where there is no disagreement! Indeed all these services respond to necessity. Abolish the unfortunate: that will do away with the works of mercy. Will the fire of love then be extinguished? More genuine is the love you bring to a fortunate person whom you cannot obligate to anything; purer will be that love and more open. For if you do a favor for an unfortunate person, perhaps you wish to raise yourself above him and wish him to be below you, who has been the instrument of your kindness. He has found himself in need; you have given part of your resources. Because you have done a favor for him, you seem in some way greater than he, indebted to him. Desire that he be your equal: together submit to him who cannot be indebted to anyone" (*On the First Epistle of St. John*, tract 8, no. 5).

12. Bergson, *Les deux sources de la morale et de la religion*, Alcan, Paris, 1932.

13. Audit, Dr. Jean and Tisseran-Pierrier, Dr. Marie, Paris, Baillière, 1953.

14. Bossuet, *Traité de la connaissance de Dieu et de moi-même*, Ch. IV, par. X.

15. Helen Keller, *Histoire de ma vie, sourde, muette, aveugle*, Paris, Payot, 1950.

16. Paul Foulquié, *L'Eglise et l'Ecole avec l'Encyclique sur l'éducation*. Spes, 1947, p. 225, note C.

17. It is hardly a question of so many fundamental realities, as some catechetical manuals tend to depict it.

18. In this regard let us say that it appears to us unthinkable (while admitting a distinction of roles and competencies) that a Christian educator, whoever he or she may be (we begin with the parents), shift the responsibility of religious instruction entirely into the hands of a priest or a catechist, or the opposite: that a catechist limit himself or herself to didactic teaching. This is even more true when we teach the handicapped or maladjusted.

19. Lest we be misunderstood, we recognize the value a child can have

in meeting people who do not share the faith and in so doing not only recognize the privilege that is his or hers, but also the responsibilities in regard to these other people. But even in this case the basic surroundings, and the family or institution which tries to supply them, must furnish a Christian atmosphere as perfect and complete as possible.

20. Pascal, *Pensées*, Le mystere de Jésus, Brunschwig, p. 576.

21. "Faith also has eyes" (St. Augustine).

22. Definition of Christian education according to the encyclical of Pius XI.

23. *Le surnaturel en nous et la péché*, Blond and Gay, 1932.

24. *Le Sense chrétien de l'homme*, Paris, Montaigne, 1945.

25. Claparède, *L'éducation fonctionelle*, Editions Delachaux et Niestlé, 1946, p. 89.

26. We cannot resist telling this story here. This text by Adolphe Ferriere is a little paradoxical but witty: "One day the devil came on earth and he found to his disgust that there were still men believing in goodness. The people were calm and even-tempered; therefore, they could only feel happy and good. And the devil spoke to the crowd. The crowd adored him and bending down their heads cried out, 'We wished to be saved, what must we do?' 'Found a school,' answered the devil. . . . A child loves nature; pen him up in a closed room. A child loves to play; make him work. He loves to see his own activity serve some purpose; see to it that his activity has no purpose. He likes to move around; have him remain motionless. He likes to manipulate objects; put him in contact with ideas. He likes to use his hands; make him use only mental games. He loves to speak; keep him in strict silence. He would like to reason; have him memorize. He would like to discover science; give him all the answers. He would like to follow fantasy; bend him under the yoke of an adult. He would like to be enthusiastic; find a way to punish it. He would like to act freely; train him to obey passively. The devil laughed up his sleeve and very soon his plan bore fruit."

27. We prefer these terms to those of collective and individual education for passive education is collective without being communal. Collective education, disdainful of the value of person, abounds in the most dangerous individualism.

28. Cf. Cousinet, *Une méthode de travail par groupe*, Paris, Cerf, 1945.

29. Cf. Ferriere, *L'autonomie des écoliers* (a misleading title which has caused comment), Neuchâtel, Paris, Delachaux and Niestlé, 1950.

30. We think of certain "children's republics" whose abuses have been criticized not without reason and which are only caricatures of the system.

31. Toronto did not know how to make the most of its situation and has let docks be set up on the shores of Lake Ontario. Chicago, on the contrary, has one of the most beautiful drives in the world along Lake Michigan.

32. "The true Christian far from renouncing earthly works and lessening his natural faculties, develops them and perfects them while coordinating

them with the spiritual life in a way of ennobling the natural life itself and of bringing more effective help to it, not only in spiritual things but also in material and temporal things as well" (encyclical).

33. Or as they prefer now to say, a developing country.

34. All the remarks cited here are authentic and have been made to the author over the years by those he questioned. For this reason he must let them remain anonymous.

35. Cf. *l'Union*, May 1954, *Présences*, "La Malade Mental," no. 54, 1954.

36. That is, however, inaccurate. A profound study of the mentality of the retarded shows that beneath a placid expression, such a child suffers deeply from his infirmity and from the situations that result from it.

37. Cf. G. Marcel, *Position et Approaches concretes du Mystère ontologique*, Vrin, 1943, or Ch. Brisset, *La médicine psychosomatique en U.R.S.S.: Fondements Théoriques in la Presse Médical*, Dec. 29, 1951.

38. A school of occupational therapy was opened in Paris in 1954 and at the same time another was opened in Nancy. Some will object that we have been doing this kind of therapy for a long time in sanatariums, hospitals and hostels. But do not call "occupational therapy," those little activities given to the sick ... a small rug ... a garden plot.... The counterfeits are as dangerous as they are available. Other schools have been opened since that time and degrees in this field are now officially recognized by the state.

39. *L'Enfance dans le Monde*, no. 2 (new series), February 1953.

40. Still less should he/she be confused with the psychologist or social worker as some insufficiently informed countries and persons have had the tendency to do.

41. Jean Plaquevent, *Misère sans nom*, Seuil, 1955, p. 159.

42. If not "in families," a term which one must use prudently and which can give rise to mistaken ideas.

43. It is not in the framework of this work nor moreover in the expertise of the author to speak, even casually, of the efforts made in favor of the handicapped by other religious groups (Protestant, Jew, Buddhist, Moslem, etc.). He is aware that there exists in the activities of these religious denominations some excellent programs and he has had the opportunity to evaluate some very exceptional ones everywhere in his travels.

44. In France, called *Scouts de France* and *Guides de France*.

45. *Coeurs Vaillants - Ames Vaillants* (Valiant Hearts - Valiant Souls.)

46. Called in short the Catholic Committee for the Sick and Infirm (C.C.M.I.). The Catholic Secretariat of Handicapped Children and Youth, assuming a similar task of information and coordination, later received authorization and support of the Assembly of Cardinals and Archbishops of France (October 1959).

47. Children of Mary, Apostolate of the Sick, Missionaries of the Sick.

48. We regret that the second congress did not pursue this effort.

49. International Catholic Child Bureau.

50. Editors of *Lumen Vitae* review with R. P. Ranwez. We have the pleasure to point out that as a result of this exchange, the International Catechetical Year, established in 1957 at Brussels through the International Center of Studies of Religious Formation, gave a large place in its program to information concerning the catechesis of the handicapped.

51. Indeed, we know that the lack of priests is acute everywhere but isn't the chaplaincy of a sanatorium or a re-education center a service as important, perhaps more so, than the service of a country pastor or dean in some college?

52. Cooperation which would give to each his place and in his own role. We have already spoken of it and will return to it.

53. Parochial or interparochial endeavors always display good will and unquestionable charity, but, except when organized by the sick themselves, they are often a collage of psychological errors. Frequently, they mix the sick of all ages, even the very young and the elderly whose only deficiency is old age. There is also at times a succession of endless ceremonies which display a paternalism more awkward than touching.

54. The major work of Professor Niedermeyer of Vienna, *Pastoral Medizin*, is a valuable contribution to the solution of this problem but it is placed in a different perspective than ours only because it is the work not of a priest but a doctor. We have need here of close cooperation of priests, doctors, and several other specialists. Concerning this, let us cite the remarkable effort of the Priory Saint-Jean at Champrosay, by Draveil (S-et-O) who has published the magazine *Présences* for many years.

55. Since the first editions of this book, the author has published a number of works on these questions of pastoral and specialized catechetics. For example *Pédagogie catechique des enfants arriérés* and *Introduction à la psychopathologie pastorale* (Ed. Fleurus). The first book has been translated into English: *Catechetical Pedagogy of Mentally Deficient Children*. It is available from Lumen Vitae Press, 184 rue Washington, Brussels, Belgium.

56. In the sense of *Théologie des Rèalities Terrestres*, G. Thils, Desclée de Brower, 1945.

57. Of course, it is not a question of denying original sin or its effects, but such a mentality comes from a very simplistic and in reality debatable conception of original sin and its consequences. This sin deprived us of the preternatural privilege of impassibility; but this is relative and we are now in the normal situation of man/woman in which sickness and death are manifested as consequences of our creature status.

58. *Présences*, no. 57, "Le malade en sa totalité," p. 38; "le chrétien devant la médicine psychosomatique."

59. We very much prefer this term to that of "life of the soul" which is dangerously equivocal. An unbaptized man does not in principle have supernatural life. He has, however, a soul. On the other hand, the supernatural life encompasses both body and soul.

60. Charles Péguy, *Eve*.

61. Cf. Lochet, *Fils de l'Eglise*, Paris, 1951, p. 54. "There is a melody

that a musical genius sketches and repeats ten times in the course of a symphony so that in the finale it bursts forth in triumphant strains because the total unity and the first inspiration respond throughout the entire production. This fundamental rhythm of history is the preference given by God to what is lowly over what is great, to what is poor over what is rich, to what is nothing over what seems everything. The divine melody of history finds final expression on the lips of the Virgin Mary: 'He has put down the mighty from their thrones and raised up the lowly. He has filled the hungry with good things and sent the rich away empty' (Lk. 51). From there a series of mysterious reversals, of paradoxical substitutions of those older by those younger, of those great by the small, of the fertile by the barren. It is Jacob preferred to Esau, Joseph triumphant over his brothers, the little shepherd boy David chosen king, Sara, a barren woman, called to be the mother of a child of promise. It is also Mary, the humble virgin, called to be the mother of the Messiah and of a new humanity preferred to all the women of Israel. It is the Church finally, the assembly of nations, poor by divine promise and in temporal power. Nevertheless called, she, the last arrival, preferred to the synagogue and to all the powers of the ages, to be the queen of the eternal kingdom, the mother of the human race to come"(p. 58). "Christ himself first by the utter humiliation of the cross merited a very beautiful resurrection and a glorious ascension. It is this descent to the depth of human misery which won a place for him, a place at the right hand of the Father where he draws all mankind to fill the places left empty by the fallen angels. 'He made himself obedient to death, even to the death of the cross. That is why God has glorified Him and given him a name above all other names' (Phil. 2:8). It is the same law that is active in the Church and draws it, by means of the cross, to triumph."

62. First antiphon of the first vespers of the Exaltation of the Holy Cross.

63. Indeed, it is evident that evil, inasmuch as it is evil, as St. Thomas tells us, cannot constitute an object of love. Love cannot be applied to non-being. Therefore, what we love in the suffering person is what he is and what he can be, his value as a human being and one of the baptized and the good that he lacks which we can procure for him. If we love more the persons in need, it is not their state of being in need that we love. On the contrary, we want that condition to disappear. God does not love non-being. . . . That is unthinkable. And he can not ask us to love it either. What we love in the handicapped is the person; we dislike the maladjustment—and we love the adjustment which we can and must help him to achieve.

64. If one wishes to make the application of this truth on a purely spiritual plane, one will understand why God loves the poor, those who know themselves and make themselves poor before him, that is those who open their hands and recognize their needs. There again, if he loves them, it is because he wishes to make them rich and he is going to make up what is lacking.

65. See Introduction.

66. Claudel, *Le Repos de Septieme Jour,* Act III, edition of the *Pléiade: Théâtre,* Vol. I, p. 778.

67. Cf. the wonderful page from E. Mounier concerning his encephalic child and published in *Esprit,* Dec. 1950, p. 1010. "What sense would all this have if our young one was only a piece of fallen flesh from who knows where, an accident of life, and not this little host who surpasses us all, infinite mystery of love which would dazzle us if we saw him face to face; if each sharp blow was not a new elevation that each time when our heart begins to adapt, to get accustomed to the preceding blow, demands a new expression of love. You hear this poor little voice pleading for all the child martyrs in the world and the hearts of millions of men regretting their lost childhood. They ask us like the poor at the side of the road: 'Tell us, you who have your hands so full of love, that you are willing to give some of it to us.' "

68. Paris-Lyon, National Center of the CV-AV, 1942.

69. Titles of works by Hesnard—censored by the Index, Paris; P.U.F., 1949-54.

70. Title of a book by A. Berge, Paris, Blond and Gay, 1941-53.

71. Title of a book by Gilbert-Robin, Paris, Flammarion, 1953.

72. Henri Ev has very courageously pointed out that in his *Etude sur la perversité,* in the second volume of his *Etudes Psychiatriques,* Paris, Desclée de Brouwer, 1950. We regret only his view on the excess of pessimism in human nature.

73. The Fifth Congress of Social Defense in Stockholm in August, 1958 again noted the progress made in public awareness, concerning psychological factors notably those that concern the category of "young adults" (18-21 years).

74. "You have risen with Christ," says St. Paul (Col. 3:1).

Part II

1. Title of a booklet by Guy Jacquin, Fleurus, 1949.

2. It is not expedient that a student be conscious of being "observed." We recall what a doctor, a neuro-psychiatrist told us one day: A child who had passed through several consultations and observation centers said, "Oh, doctor, you can make me do what you wish: dictation, an arithmetic problem, or an injection, but do not observe me . . . I have had enough of being observed."

3. Etymologically: comprehend = to take with (self).

4. Marie-Colette Angrand (today Madame Willig) noted this in one of the first studies on the psychology of a sick child which appeared in the publication *L'Enfant Malade,* Editions Fleurus, 1946.

5. Cf. on the one hand *La Psychologie des tuberculeux* of Dr. Maurice Porot, Delachaux and Niestlé, 1950, and on the other hand, the remarkable study of a medical team of Barcelona: Irazoquil Villalonga, *Psiquismo y secreciones internas.* See also on this subject the work of Remy Collin, *Les*

hormones, unfortunately out of print . . . and out of fashion.

6. Caridroit, in *Nouveau traité de psychologie* of Dumas, Vol. VII, Book II, p. 93.

7. Actually, illness could well be, in some cases, the most appropriate behavior for the circumstances or the least inadequate.

8. Contrary to what one would imagine and to what some serious authors claim, the mentally retarded do experience this feeling. We have already pointed this out twice and we could give more than one proof.

9. We correctly say a "feeling of poverty" and not "frustration." The feeling of poverty fosters frustration as we shall soon see.

10. Contrary to certain authors we think that the feeling of insecurity is not in this area a cause, but first of all a result.

11. Fabienne Van Roy, *L'Enfant infirme*, Delauchaux, 1954.

12. Germaine Guex, *La nevrose d'abandon*, P.U.F., 1950.

13. Much thought has been given to this problem in recent times. We will speak about it again. But let us point out, for the present, that information about forms of masculine or feminine dedication open to the handicapped can be obtained by writing to Oeuvre des Vocations, 106 rue du Bac, Paris 75007, France, or to one's diocesan Office of Vocations.

14. In some foreign countries, even those that are to some extent Catholic (southern Germany, Austria, Catholic regions of Switzerland, Holland or the United States), most of these institutions for the disturbed, retarded, preventive centers and communities for the young practice a wise mixture of sexes in harmony with the doctrine of the encyclicals.

15. This is different from the Sacrament of Penance which cannot be shared. This makes the position of the priest rather delicate. He will have to learn and to listen. But often he will have to abstain from speaking and the team will have to understand this attitude.

16. The setting also creates, with young people especially but also with adults, associations of sensations and emotions, which continue years later to accompany and color the same notions acquired in a particular atmosphere. Let one only recall a lesson learned or advice received in such and such a situation: sunny or rainy weather, an austere room or a pleasant office, gray walls or colorful tapestry, a room well heated or icy cold; and one will see how color, temperature, even odor and tone of voice have affected in a favorable or unfavorable sense the influence exercised and impression received, and even now in our memory cause these abstract notions or counsels—even strictly moral ones—to be acceptable and agreeable or disagreeable and unacceptable, even ineffective.

17. *Mediator Dei* (Jan. 14 - Feb. 15, 1948).

18. *Directoire pour la Pastorale de la Messe* - paragraph 43.

19. One notices that women have the skill of creating a new climate in a room with a few things, provided that they have good taste. Men more easily let things go barrack fashion. On the other hand, women who are usually less skilled at repairs easily let material things go by the boards:

faulty electrical equipment, doors which close badly, etc. The cooperation of both sexes might produce some happy results.

20. In certain parishes, specialized catechists are assigned to these children. In such cases, the mothers of the children are organized among themselves to provide with the help of a priest, teacher or student the catechical formation of their children . . . and of others. Elsewhere, the diocesan center recruits and forms qualified volunteers.

21. This identification with a baby is not, however, without some risks of infantilism and, consequently, of regression. It has to be controlled and it should not ordinarily be encouraged.

22. For the inexperienced reader, let us state that one ought not to confuse schizothymia and schizophrenia. Schizophrenia is a mental illness, while schizothymia involves a normal person having, according to Kretschmer, a more introvert type of temperament, the syntonic temperament being, on the contrary, more extrovert.

23. Since publication of the French edition of this book, the author has written another book entirely dedicated to the important question started here: *L'Expression, valeur chrètienne*, Fleurus, 1964.

24. Be careful not to take your interpretation for the real intention of the child.

25. One of our study groups actually conducts research on this question.

26. We have found similar arrangements in Sweden.

27. Of course this in no way prevents the sort of interesting and practical arrangement, the so-called vertical system, which apportions children of various ages into groups or small families which form the base for the organization of the home for daily living.

28. We wrote this in 1957. By now, these techniques have more or less been improved.

29. On this subject see the brochure by the same author: *Au catechisme: Que faire pour ceux qui ne peuvent pas suivre*. Editions Fleurus, 1959.

30. Bergson, *Les deux sources de la morale et de la religion*. P.U.F. 1951, p. 31.

31. Graber, *Le Christ dans ses sacrements*, Editions du Vitrail, 1947.

32. In no way do we wish to insinuate that we respond to these diverse plans by a single road and in stages. Closed morality, even turned toward perfection, does not lead to open morality. That is of a different order. It is the same and still more for the passage from the plan of nature to that of grace. It is here a question then of a single route for our mind.

33. *"A la tarde, te examinarian en el amor,"* Maxime 57.

34. It is hell on earth in the strict sense of the term. And if prostitution and all that leads to it, those caricatures of sexuality—pornography, or striptease spectacles, for example—should only be condemned because of it, this would be more than enough motivation to do it.

35. We have stated that books like those of Hesnard, *L'univers morbide*

de la faute or *Morale sans peche*, are a typical illustration of such confusion, as well as more modest but better known books, those of Gilbert Robin or André Berge, cited earlier.

36. According to Jung "the shadow" is a kind of "double" who incarnates the non-being, this other that we ourselves have refused to be.

37. And what do we say when these three factors are combined as in the case of the young Eurasians brought back from Vietnam to France following the recent war?

38. We would not want to say that morality has only one commandment, that of charity. But isn't that the one in which the Lord Jesus summarized all the law and the prophets?

39. An announcement from the Episcopal Commission for Religious Instruction. Cf. *Documentation Catholique*, September 19, 1957, col. 1271, 1272.

40. Cf. the thesis of Abbé Paulhus, *L'éducabilité des déficient mentaux* (Facultés catholiques de Lyon, 1957). We agree with the author on this point among others.

41. We use this word on purpose although we know that it is being replaced with better and more exact terms as children's home or center.

42. We have already said what we thought on the subject of statues. One institute of this kind, not a very large one, contained nearly a hundred. When the poor religious left the institution they did not know what to do with them, so ugly and numerous were these reproductions. These religious, who were too intelligent and too artistic to keep them and too sensitive to destroy them, tried to offer them to country churches. But the rural area had also matured. No one in the city or the country wanted them. Finally the one hundred statues were left in a room where they took up space that could have been better used. Eventually, they will have to be destroyed.

43. Fortunately, this part of the confirmation liturgy has disappeared.

44. For all these persons and even for the physically or socially handicapped, spiritual direction can be of considerable benefit on condition that the director is "faithful" to them, that he knows how to listen and that he possesses the indispensable psychological principles by which to answer their specific needs. How many counselors have bypassed the troubles of the sensitive souls of the handicapped!

45. At the second Vatican Council the Medical, Pedagogical and Psycho-Social Commission of B.I.C.E. introduced, according to the wishes expressed in the meeting at Cologne and at the Congress of Luxembourg (whose theme was "Christian Perspectives on Adoption"), a request calling for immediate changes in Canon 984 of the Code of Canon Law in favor of natural children. The recent decision of Paul VI granting extended powers to bishops in the matter seems a step in this direction.

46. Dumas, *Nouveau traité de psychologie*, Vol. IV, *La symbolization*, p. 293.

47. Encyclical *Miranda Prorsus* of September 8, 1957.

48. Title of a book, *L'idée réparatrice*, by R. P. Plus, Beauchesne, 1917.

49. Moreover we must recall the words of St. Paul according to which "all paternity comes from God" and not God from the notion of human fatherhood, as some psychologists would have us suppose. Even when the earthly father is non-existent or even when he is unworthy, the transcendent fatherhood of God remains in itself intact and must be able to be revealed. What if the word itself is an obstacle, the religious educator will have to help the student to reach beyond words to the transcendent reality in its fullness.